Teamwork and Project Management

Karl A. Smith
University of Minnesota & Purdue University

With chapters by Constance Kampf, Russell Korte, Robert MacNeal, Curt McNamara, Şenay Purzer and Nicholas D. Fila, and Cliff Whitcomb and Leslie Whitcomb; and box features and other contributions by Eric Berkowitz, Shannon Ciston, P. K. Imbrie, Kathryn Jablokow, David Johnson, Shawn Jordan, Billy Koen, Holly Matusovich, Tamara Moore, Matthew Ohland, Randy Pausch, Mary Pilotte, David Radcliffe, Anthony Starfield, Ruth Streveler, and Khairiyah Mohd Yusof.

Fourth Edition

TEAMWORK AND PROJECT MANAGEMENT, FOURTH EDITION

Published by McGraw-Hill Education, 2 Penn Plaza, New York, NY 10121. Copyright © 2014 by McGraw-Hill Education. All rights reserved. Printed in the United States of America. Previous Edition © 2007. No part of this publication may be reproduced or distributed in any form or by any means, or stored in a database or retrieval system, without the prior written consent of McGraw-Hill Education, including, but not limited to, in any network or other electronic storage or transmission, or broadcast for distance learning.

Some ancillaries, including electronic and print components, may not be available to customers outside the United States.

This book is printed on acid-free paper.

2 3 4 5 6 7 8 9 0 DOC/DOC 1 0 9 8 7 6 5 4

ISBN   978-0-07-353490-9
MHID   0-07-353490-0

Senior Vice President, Products & Markets: *Kurt L. Strand*
Vice President & Editor-in-Chief: *Marty Lange*
Vice President, Content Production & Technology Services: *Kimberly Meriwether David*
Managing Director: *Thomas Timp*
Executive Brand Manager: *Raghu Srinivasan*
Executive Brand Manager: *Bill Stenquist*
Marketing Manager: *Curt Reynolds*
Development Editor: *Lorraine Buczek/Samantha Donisi-Hamm*
Director, Content Production: *Terri Schiesl*
Project Manager: *Judi David*
Buyer: *Sandy Ludovissy*
Cover Image: *Royalty-Free/CORBIS*
Compositor: *Aptara®, Inc.*
Typeface: *10/12 Palatino*
Printer: *R. R. Donnelley Crawfordsville*

All credits appearing on page or at the end of the book are considered to be an extension of the copyright page.

Library of Congress Cataloging-in-Publication Data

Smith, Karl A. (Karl Aldrich), 1947–
     Teamwork and project management / Karl A. Smith, University of Minnesota and Purdue University. — Fourth edition.
          pages cm
     Includes bibliographical references and index.
     ISBN-13: 978-0-07-353490-9 (alk. paper)
     ISBN-10: (invalid) 0-07-353490-9 (alk. paper) 1. Engineering management. 2. Teams in the workplace. 3. Project management. I. II. Title. III. Title: Team work and project management.

TA190.S63   2013
658.4′04—dc23   2013015636

The Internet addresses listed in the text were accurate at the time of publication. The inclusion of a website does not indicate an endorsement by the authors or McGraw-Hill Education, and McGraw-Hill Education does not guarantee the accuracy of the information presented at these sites.

www.mhhe.com

Contents

Preface

In the early 1990s I designed and started teaching a project management course for third- and fourth-year civil engineering students at the University of Minnesota. I had been teaching an engineering systems course that was problem driven and made use of project teams and used a similar approach in the project management course. I also started teaching project management and teamwork courses for graduate students in professional master's programs, especially at the University of Minnesota's Technological Leadership Institute, and for participants in short courses for government agencies, such as the Minnesota Department of Transportation (Mn/DOT), and private companies.

When McGraw-Hill invited me in 1997 to write a book on project management and teamwork for their BEST series, I thought, What a terrific idea! Real world engineering problems require teamwork to be solved. Involving first-year engineering students in teamwork and project management as soon as possible would help them prepare for engineering practice. I immediately embraced the idea and started working on a book for them.

Along with colleagues and undergraduate student teaching assistants I had taught an introductory engineering course for first-year students at the University of Minnesota for more than 20 years. It evolved into a course titled How to Model It: Building Models to Solve Engineering Problems, which I have taught with colleagues and undergraduate student teaching assistants. We also wrote a book to accompany the course—*How to Model It: Problem Solving for the Computer Age* (Starfield, Smith, and Bleloch, 1990, 1994). Since the course made extensive use of project teams, I knew that a book on project management and teamwork was needed. Teamwork and projects are at the heart of the approach I use in teaching students at all levels, including participants in faculty development workshops. I've learned that it isn't easy for students to work effectively in project teams or for faculty to organize and manage them, but the potential for extraordinary work from teams makes it worth the effort. Also, projects and teamwork are a central part of engineering work in the world outside the classroom.

The book went through two iterations prior to the Fourth Edition. Though the first edition of *Project Management and Teamwork* was designed for first-year students, we found that other students used it, especially those in senior-level capstone design courses. So the second edition, retitled *Teamwork and Project Management*, was redesigned to be accessible to first-year students but also to be applicable for upper-division students who hadn't had an opportunity to focus on teamwork and project management skills in earlier courses and programs and for students in graduate and professional programs. The third edition was primarily an update to the second and included some collaboration with P. K. Imbrie. The nearby box feature summarizes P. K.'s connection to the third edition.

A number of years ago I attended a workshop on cooperative learning given by Prof. Smith (yes the same Prof. Smith that is the principal author of this book). At that time, I strongly believed "the lecture" was the quintessential way to promote student learning and I saw no value (from a learning perspective) in using student teams. After his workshop I came to realize the most important thing we do as a faculty member is help students learn how to learn—or, another way of saying it, we need to prepare them for the idea of lifelong learning. What I discovered is through a traditional lecture class, we teach them (our students) how to be stenographers and to memorize whatever it is we teach. However, in the active, cooperative classroom, students actually have to learn how to learn, because they have to learn how to communicate their ideas to other individuals while they're in a team environment.

So you might be asking yourself, what does this have to do with "teaming"? What I have found is whether you are in the classroom, working on homework, or completing a term-long project, moving from being individualistic learners to partner learners and moving from a textbook, faculty-centered learning style to "my peers and everybody else can be equal contributors in this" can provide a phenomenal learning experience. However, it requires you to learn how to be an effective team member. To be an effective member of a team (or an informal learning group) one must learn how to work interdependently, specify goals, develop a sense of cohesiveness, and communicate (and, if you are on a formal team, one needs clearly defined roles and rules of accountability, or norms). The teaming chapters of this book will help you understand what we have found to be important and will hopefully make your teaming experience more enjoyable.

P. K. Imbrie

Since the engineering method involves progressive refinement, that is, taking what we know at the present (labeled state of the art, sota$_{2013}$) and identifying opportunities for improvement, the changes in this edition continue to reflect a focused emphasis on preparing engineering students for professional practice. In the spirit of advancing the state of the art, I've made major changes to several chapters and have updated the entire book.

The Fourth Edition represents a major redesign and includes an expanded number of collaborators. There are new chapters by Constance Kampf, Russell Korte, Robert MacNeal, Curt McNamara, Şenay Purzer and Nicholas D. Fila, and Cliff Whitcomb and Leslie Whitcomb; and box features and other contributions by Eric Berkowitz, Shannon Ciston, P. K. Imbrie, Kathryn Jablokow, David Johnson, Shawn Jordan, Billy Koen, Holly Matusovich, Tamara Moore, Matthew Ohland, Randy Pausch, Mary Pilotte, David Radcliffe, Anthony Starfield, Ruth Streveler, and Khairiyah Mohd Yusof. I am confident that these new chapters and larger collection of contributions by other authors have strengthened the book considerably.

Chapter 1, which is an introduction and overview, was extensively revised to reflect the changing landscape of teamwork and project management. Chapter 2 is new and provides a framework for project management based on the clarity of the goal as well as the clarity of the process. The framing is based on March's (1991) work on exploration versus exploitation and also draws on Wysocki's (2012) *Effective Project Management: Traditional, Agile, Extreme*. Chapters 3 and 4, the teamwork chapters, were updated and expanded. Chapters 5, 6, 7 and 8 are new and contributed by Cliff Whitcomb and Leslie Whitcomb, Russell Korte, Şenay Purzer and Nicholas Fila, and Robert MacNeal, respectively. Each of these chapters represents cutting-edge ideas in teamwork and project management. Chapters 9, 10 and 11, on project management basics, were updated. Chapter 12, on project monitoring and evaluation, was updated to include team functioning and detailed material on team and project charters. Chapter 12, on communication and documentation, was extensively revised by Constance Kampf. Chapters 14 and 16 were updated to include some of the latest technology, as well as speculations on the future of teamwork and project management. Chapter 15, contributed by Curt McNamara, provides an introduction to complex adaptive systems in the teamwork and project management arena. I continue to provide my own Reflections, have added the many new features by others, and encourage you to reflect on your experience and learning and add your stories to dialogues you engage in.

Overall, my goals for readers of *Teamwork and Project Management* are the following:

- To improve your understand of the dynamics of team development and interpersonal problem solving.
- To identify strategies for accelerating the development of true team effectiveness.
- To help you frame the project and team and identify and use an appropriate project management approach.
- To understand the critical dimensions of project scope, time, and cost management.
- To understand critical technical competencies in project management.
- To explore a variety of "best practices" including anticipating, preventing, and overcoming barriers to project success.

As you engage with this book, be sure to continually reflect on what you're learning and how you can apply what you are learning to the projects and teams you work on each day, in classes, on the job, and in social, professional, and community organizations. An important key to success in projects and teams is to routinely work at a "meta level." That means you are simultaneously thinking about the task and how well the team is working. Talk with others about how the projects and teams you're involved with are going, share successes and insights, and work together to identify and solve team problems. The personal story in the accompanying box about "Engineering Problem Solving" describes some of the questions I've grappled with and how I got interested in this project. I encourage you to develop your own stories as you work your way through this book.

One of the messages of the story in the "Engineering Problem Solving" box is the importance of checking a variety of resources to help formulate and solve the problems you encounter. Another message is that, although engineers spend some of their time working alone, engineering is not individual, isolated work. Collaborative problem solving and teamwork are central to engineering. Engineers must learn to solve problems by themselves, of course, but they must also learn to work collaboratively to effectively solve the other 95 percent of the problems they will face as professional engineers. There may be a tendency to think that this 95 percent—this asking questions and searching other sources for the solution—is either trivial or else unrelated

Engineering Problem Solving

I have been involved in engineering, as a student and as a professional, for over 40 years. Frequently I have grappled with the questions, What is the engineering method? Is it applied science? Is it design? As a professor I have struggled with the question, What should my students learn and how should they learn it? These concerns prompted me to address the question, What is the nature of engineering expertise and how can it be developed effectively (Smith, 1988, 2011)?

A study conducted by one of my colleagues (Johnson, 1982) provides valuable insight into the activities of engineers. My colleague was hired to collect protocol from engineering experts while they solved difficult problems. Working with a team of professors, he developed a set of difficult and interesting problems, which he took to chief engineers in large companies. In case after case the following scenario was repeated.

The engineer would read the problem and say, "This is an interesting problem."

My colleague would ask, "How would you solve it?"

The engineer would say, "I'd check with the engineers on the floor to see if any of them had solved it."

In response, my colleague would say, "Suppose that didn't work."

"I'd assign the problem to one of my engineers to check the literature to see if a solution was available in the literature."

"Suppose that didn't work," retorted my colleague.

"Well, then I'd call my friends in other companies to see if any of them had solved it."

Again my colleague would say, "Suppose that didn't work."

"Then I'd call some vendors to see if any of them had a solution."

My colleague, growing impatient at not hearing a solution, would say, "Suppose that didn't work."

At some stage in this interchange, the engineer would say, "Well, gee, I guess I'd have to solve it myself."

To which my colleague would reply, "What percentage of the problems you encounter fall into this category?"

Engineer after engineer replied, "About five percent"!

to engineering. However, working with others to formulate and solve problems and accomplish joint tasks is critical to success in engineering.

Acknowledgments

Many people deserve credit for their guidance in this project. Former students with whom I've taught and worked on project management for many years provided enormous insight into the process of what will work for students and were a source of constant support and encouragement. My heartfelt thanks to my many mentors, and especially to David and Roger Johnson, Billy Koen, and Tony Starfield for generously sharing their insights and enthusiasm and permitting me to stand on the shoulders of these giants. Billy Koen has been an inspiration to me since we first met in the early 80s. His wonderful ideas show up in several places in the book. Anthony M. Starfield, co-creator of the first-year course, How to Model It, and co-author of the book by the same title encouraged me to use the questioning format of the *How to Model It* book to engage the reader. David and Roger Johnson (whose cooperative learning model provides the theoretical basis for this book) generously provided their great ideas and steadfast support.

I thank the hundreds of students who learned from and with me in project management courses for their patience, perseverance, wonderful suggestions and ideas, and interest and enthusiasm in project management and teamwork.

The team at McGraw-Hill, beginning with the initial editors, Holly Stark and Eric Munson, and Byron Gottfried, Consulting Editor, provided guidance throughout. Editors for the second edition, Kelly Lowery and John Griffin, encouraged extensive redesign and the title change from *Project Management and Teamwork* to *Teamwork and Project Management*. Bill Stenquist, editor for the Third edition and new Fourth edition, has been both delightful to work with and demanding. His support for my vision for the future of the book made it possible to increase the length and include six new chapters.

A special note of thanks to my daughters, Riawa Thomas-Smith and Sharla Stremski, who helped with the editing and graphics; and to my wonderful wife, Lila M. Arduser Smith, for her patience and unwavering support.

Acknowledgments

Chapter 5. Clifford Whitcomb (Naval Postgraduate School) and Leslie Whitcomb (Intentional Exchanges)

Chapter 6. Russell Korte (Colorado State University-Fort Collins)

Chapter 7. Şenay Purzer and Nicholas D. Fila (Purdue University)

Chapter 8. Robert MacNeal (Founder of Working Company)

Chapter 13. Connie Kampf (Business & Social Sciences, Aarhus University)

Chapter 15. Curt McNamara (Minneapolis College of Art and Design, Logic PD)

References

Johnson, P. E. 1982. Personal communication.

March, James G. 1991. Exploration and exploitation in organizational learning. *Organization Science* 2 (1), 71–87.

Project Management Institute. 2008. *A guide to the project management body of knowledge,* 4th ed. (PMBOK). Upper Darby, PA: Project Management Institute (http://www.pmi.org).

Smith, Karl A. 1988. The nature and development of engineering expertise. *European Journal of Engineering Education* 13 (3), 317–330.

Smith, Karl A. 2011. Preparing students for an interdependent world: Role of cooperation and social interdependence theory. In James Cooper and Pamela Robinson, eds., *Small group learning in higher education: Research and practice.* Stillwater, OK: New Forums Press.

Starfield, Anthony M., Karl A. Smith, and Andrew L. Bleloch. 1990. *How to model it: Problem solving for the computer age.* New York: McGraw-Hill.

Starfield, Anthony M., Karl A. Smith, and Andrew L. Bleloch. 1994. *How to model it: Problem solving for the computer age.* Edina, MN: Interaction Book (updated and sofware added).

Wysocki, Robert K. 2012. *Effective project management: Traditional, agile, extreme,* 6th ed. New York: Wiley.

Comments and Suggestions

Please send your comments and suggestions to me at ksmith@umn.edu.

CHAPTER 1

Teamwork and Project Management in Engineering and Related Disciplines

Teamwork and Project Management is designed to help you prepare for professional practice in the global economy. Teamwork is receiving increased emphasis from employers, leaders in engineering education, and researchers. The world has gotten smaller and our sense of interdependence has greatly increased; the importance of professional responsibility and ethics has magnified (although engineering ethics has always been central to engineering); and projects (and project-type organizations) are becoming much more common. All these changes, as well as further changes that are likely to occur, highlight the importance of learning, practicing, and continually refining the skills, concepts, principles, and heuristics in this book.

More and more the broader community is calling for engineering graduates who have not only the traditionally expected technical skills and widely sought-after problem-solving orientation, but also the set of six "professional" skills from the ABET list (Shuman, Besterfield-Sacre, and McGourty, 2005). These skills include communication, teamwork, and understanding ethics and professionalism, which Shuman et al. label "process skills," and engineering within a global and societal context, lifelong learning, and a knowledge of contemporary issues, which they designate as "awareness skills."

Thomas Friedman wrote in 2000 that "the world is ten years old." Friedman's central notion was *globalization*, that is, "the inexorable integration of markets, nation-states, and technologies to a degree never witnessed before—in a way that is enabling individuals, corporations, and nation-states to reach around the world farther, faster, deeper, and cheaper than ever before, and in a way that is enabling the world to reach into individuals, corporations, and nation-states farther, faster, deeper, and cheaper than ever before" (p. 9). Four years later Friedman claimed that "the world is flat." He addressed the graduating class at Washington University in St. Louis on May 21, 2004, with the following assertion: "The job world you are entering is an increasingly flat world. That's right. I know that this great scientific university taught you that the world was round. I am here to tell you that the world is flat, or at least in the process of being flattened. That is actually the title of my next book, *The World Is Flat: A Brief History of the 21st Century*. By that I mean the competitive playing field is being leveled. You are entering a world where more people have PCs. More people have Internet connections and the bandwidth to communicate. More people have good educations, and more people have the enabling softwares, like Google, Microsoft Net Meeting, or Instant Messaging, to gain knowledge, to innovate, and to spread new ideas."

Friedman argued that in this increasingly flat world, collaboration and connectivity as well as adaptability and a creative imagination are essential attributes. We're increasing the emphasis on collaboration and connectivity (networking) and creativity and innovation in this edition of *Teamwork and Project Management*.

Friedman (2005) described 10 flatteners, the first three of which provide a platform for collaboration:

1. November 9, 1989: The Berlin wall came down and six months later Microsoft Windows came up.
2. August 9, 1995: Netscape went public.
3. Work Flow Software, such as that supporting around-the-clock design work (sometimes referred to as work that follows the sun).

Interestingly, these first three "flatteners" occurred within the life span of even the youngest engineering college student and they created the need for expanded skill and knowledge sets. Friedman argues that we need to "horizontalize" ourselves, that is, we need to learn how to connect and collaborate with others. Tim Brown (2009), CEO at IDEO, the product design firm, states that IDEO recruits T-shaped people—people with both disciplinary thinking (vertical) strengths and design thinking (horizontal) strengths.

Friedman's latest book (Friedman and Mandelbaum, 2011), *That Used to Be Us: How America Fell Behind the World It Invented and How We Can Come Back*, notes that "Today's major challenges are different." The authors argue that globalization, the IT revolution, deficits and debt, and energy demand and climate change are occuring incrementally, that is, they are creeping up on us. Their formula for addressing the challenges involves focusing on five pillars that together constitute the country's strengths:

1. Providing public education for more and more Americans.
2. Building and continual modernizing of our infrastructure.
3. Keeping America's doors open to immigration.
4. Government support for research and development.
5. Implementation of necessary regulations on private economic activity.

All of these pillars involve projects and teamwork and several of them, numbers 2 and 5 especially, require the involvement and commitment of engineers.

As I was reading Friedman and Mandelbaum's new book, I was reminded of Jane Jacobs' classic work, *The Death and Life of Great American Cities*, and especially how she helped reshape our thinking about urban planning. Jacobs' latest book, *Dark Age Ahead* (2004) argues that North American civilization is showing signs of decline due to the collapse of "five pillars of our culture that we depend on to stand firm," which can be summarized as family and community, education, science, representational government and taxes, and corporate and professional accountability. Note the similarity among the "pillars" and concerns about their demise.

In *A Whole New Mind: Moving from the Information Age to the Conceptual Age,* Dan Pink (2005) makes a compelling case for moving from the knowledge age to the conceptual age. In the conceptual age it is creators and empathizers who will have the most influence! According to Pink the drivers of this change are affluence, technology, and globalization. Note the similarities and differences to Friedman's flatteners.

This is the world in which you'll be working. It is very different from the world I started working in as an engineer in 1969, but it is the world I try to cope with every semester especially with graduate students in two professional masters programs in which I teach, Management of Technology and Infrastructure Systems Management and Engineering. The engineering graduates in these one-day-per-week, two-year programs are working full-time and most of the participants work globally. Their extensive international interaction and collaboration as well as their international travel (both physical and virtual) are indicative of the lives of many if not most engineers in the future.

The essence of the globalization economy (according to Surowiecki, 1997) is this notion: "Innovation replaces tradition. The present—or perhaps the future—replaces the past." Surowiecki's view is shared by the authors of the 2005 National Academy of Engineering report *Assessing the Capacity of the U.S. Engineering Research Enterprise,* who wrote in their introduction, "American success has been based on the creativity, ingenuity, and courage of innovators, and innovation will continue to be critical to American success in the twenty-first century" (p. 7).

Surowiecki argues in a subsequent work, *The Wisdom of Crowds* (2004), that "under the right circumstances, groups are remarkably intelligent, and are often smarter than the smartest people in them." David Perkins (2002) makes similar claims in *King Arthur's Round Table: How Collaborative Conversations Create Smart Organizations.* Perkins' (2002) central question is "What is organizational intelligence, why is it so hard to come by, and how can we get more of it?" (p. 14). His general reply is: "How smart an organization or community is reflects the kind of conversations that people have with one another, taking conversation in a broad sense to include all sorts of interactions" (p. 14). Surowiecki's and Perkins' ideas and recommendations are elaborated upon in this chapter.

The principal goal of this book is to provide you, the reader, guidance on how to engage in intelligent teamwork in engineering contexts that emphasize design and innovation. As we start this journey together, I offer you the following suggestions that will help you get the most from this book. The essence of the suggestions is reflected in the words *activity, reflection,* and *collaboration.* First, I encourage you to engage in the *activities,* especially the exercises, in the book, as they will help you connect with the material and its real-world applications. Second, periodically throughout the book I'll ask you to stop and *reflect.* Take advantage of the opportunity. The goal is to give you a chance to describe to yourself what you already know and to get you to think. Then when you read on about the topic, you'll have a basis for comparing and contrasting. Finally, I encourage you to *collaborate* with others. Working together is the norm in projects. Working together to learn the material in this book will make it easier, and very likely you'll remember it longer.

Ruth Streveler's reflection on a sports metaphor for learning (in the nearby box) will help many readers maximize their benefit from the book.

A Sports Metaphor

Karl and I have worked together for many years on a variety of projects. During the past few years we co-designed and have been co-teaching a course, Content, Assessment and Pedagogy: An Integrated Engineering Design Approach. The course is project based and the participants redesign a course that they are teaching or plan to teach in the future. We use a variety of resources, and for the past few years have been using the book, *Making Learning Whole: How Seven Principles of Teaching Can Transform Education*, in which Harvard psychologist David Perkins uses baseball as a metaphor for explaining exemplary instructional methods. Perkins' seven principles summarized below are relevant and applicable well beyond designing a course. I offer them to you as heuristics for preparing for teamwork and project management.

1. **Play the whole game.** When learning the kind of complex task often involved in project management, it is important to find a way to see the "big picture," the larger context of what you are learning. Because the complexity of the real situation may be overwhelming, Perkins suggests creating a "junior game" which simplifies the situation while maintaining all the elements of the real task. Junior games should be constructed to approximate practice, without getting bogged down with all the details. An example of a junior game in a business context would be creating and running a small business for a short period of time. Even if the business is selling lemonade at a school's sports events, you will still have the experience of learning about market research, customer service, bookkeeping, etc.

2. **Make the game worth playing.** Motivation plays an important role in learning. Find ways to link what you are learning to things that motivate you. Allow your curiosity to flourish. Switch your perspective. Instead of viewing an assignment as being "given" to you, think about how you can use it to learn something that interests you.

3. **Work on the hard parts.** Find ways to deliberately practice aspects of a learning task that are difficult for you. Don't avoid the hard parts—embrace them! Bumps in the road of learning are opportunities to excel! Remember that composers created études that provided creative and beautiful ways for musicians to practice difficult scales. How can you construct your own études? Find inventive ways to practice difficult elements in your learning.

4. **Play out of town.** Applying knowledge in a new setting, called *transfer*, is notoriously difficult to accomplish. You can help yourself transfer what you have learned by thinking of examples of how the target knowledge is used in different domains. Perkins calls this "low road transfer." "High road transfer," which is more robust, is promoted when you strengthen your conceptual understanding of what you are learning and then reflect on how this fundamental knowledge might be used in different ways.

5. **Uncover the hidden game.** When learning in a new area, find ways to discover the "unwritten rules" of that domain. Tap into the tacit knowledge of experts in the field by asking them to talk you through their approach to a problem. Seeing their approach will give you insights into how you can tackle similar problems.

6. **Learn from the team.** Think about how you can *learn from* your teammates. When approaching a project with your team, employ strategies that encourage you to socially construct knowledge through true collaboration, rather than simply dividing to conquer.

7. **Learn the game of learning.** Become aware of the strategies you use to understand, retain, and apply new material. Learning about how you learn (called metacognition) will help you learn more efficiently and effectively.

I hope you will find these seven principles useful. May they help you attain your learning goals!

Ruth Streveler

4

My goal for this first chapter is to create a context for teamwork and project management in engineering. Let's start by exploring the nature of engineering. But before you read ahead for various answers to the question "What is engineering?" please complete the following reflection.

 REFLECTION What is engineering? What does it mean to learn to engineer in school? What is your experience with engineering? Did you learn about engineering in high school? Do you have a brother or sister, mother or father, or other family relative or friend who is an engineer? Take a minute to reflect on where you learned about engineering and what your impressions of engineering are.
What did you come up with?

What Is Engineering?

Because there are few high school courses in engineering, most first-year students have not had much exposure to engineering. Yet we are surrounded by engineering accomplishments; they are so ubiquitous that we don't notice most of them. One of the foremost thinkers and writers on engineering, mechanical engineering professor Billy Koen, is noted for asking four probing questions of his audiences (Koen, 1984, 2002). The first is this:

1. Can you name one thing in the room in which you are sitting (excluding yourself, of course) that was not developed, produced, or delivered by an engineer?

Koen finds that the question is usually greeted with bewildered silence. I have posed Koen's questions to hundreds of first-year students, and they come up with some great suggestions: the air (but how does it get into the room?), dirt (trapped in people's shoes), electromagnetic radiation (but the lights generate much more than the background). Almost everything that we encounter was developed, produced, or delivered by engineers.

Here is Koen's second question:

2. Can you name a profession that is affecting your life more incisively than engineering?

Again, students name several professions but on reflection note that if it were not for engineering, politicians would have a difficult time spreading their ideas; doctors, without their tools, would be severely limited in what they could do; lawyers wouldn't have much to read; and so forth. Things such as telephones, computers, airplanes, and skyscrapers—which have enormous effects on our lives—are all products of engineering.

Koen's third question is this:

3. Since engineering is evidently very important, can you now define the engineering method for solving a problem?

Many students respond with a puzzled look, as if being asked an unfair question. They note that they have a ready response to the question "What is the scientific method?" Students list things like "applied science," "problem solving," and "trial and error," but very few (over the 20 or so years that I've been asking this question) say "design." Fortunately, the portion answering "design" is increasing.

If you were to ask practicing engineers what the engineering method is, they would likely respond "Engineering is design!" A group of national engineering leaders has said:

> Design in a major sense is the essence of engineering; it begins with the identification of a need and ends with a product or system in the hands of a user. It is primarily concerned with synthesis rather than the analysis which is central to engineering science. Design, above all else, distinguishes engineering from science. (Hancock, 1986)

Distinguished engineers such as von Kármán and Wulf support this claim:

> A scientist discovers that which exists. An engineer creates that which never was.
>
> —Theodore von Kármán (1881–1963)

> The engineering method is design under constraints.
>
> —Wm. Wulf, past president, U.S. National Academy of Engineering

Koen (1971, 2003) argued that "The engineering method is the use of heuristics to cause the best change in a poorly understood situation within the available resources." He updated his definition at a presentation in 2011 (Koen, 2011). He argued that "The engineering method (design) is the use of state-of-the-art heuristics to create the best change in an uncertain situation within the available resources."

We'll explore the concept of engineering design next, and save Koen's fourth and final question for the end of the chapter. But first, let's explore the history of the term *engineer* and elaborate on engineering as a profession.

The term *engineer* is derived from the French term *ingénieur*. Vitruvius, author of *De Architecture*, written in about 20 B.C.E., wrote in the introduction that master builders were ingenious, or possessed *ingenium*. From the eleventh century, master builders were called *ingeniator* (in Latin), which through the French, *ingénieur*, became the English *engineer* (Auyang, 2004). Recapturing some of the ingeniousness of engineering is one of our goals in this edition.

Referring to engineers as "master builders" reminds me of another French connection, *bricoleur*. A *bricoleur* is a handyman or handywoman who uses the tools available to complete a task (Kincheloe and Berry, 2004). Using the tools available to complete a task is a central idea in this book, and engineer as *bricoleur* captures it very well.

A distinguishing feature of engineering is that it is a profession (Davis, 1998). Graduates of accredited engineering programs are expected to abide by the Codes of Ethics of Engineers for their respective professional organization. The Codes of Ethics consist of two parts, Fundamental Principles and Fundamental Canons. Here are these elements from the American Society of Civil Engineers (ASCE) (www.asce.org):

Fundamental Principles: Engineers uphold and advance the integrity, honor, and dignity of the engineering profession by:
1. Using their knowledge and skill for the enhancement of human welfare and the environment;
2. Being honest and impartial and serving with fidelity the public, their employers, and clients;
3. Striving to increase the competence and prestige of the engineering profession; and
4. Supporting the professional and technical societies of their disciplines.

Fundamental Canons:
1. Engineers shall hold paramount the safety, health, and welfare of the public and shall strive to comply with the principles of sustainable development in the performance of their professional duties.
2. Engineers shall perform services only in areas of their competence.
3. Engineers shall issue public statements only in an objective and truthful manner.
4. Engineers shall act in professional matters for each employer or client as faithful agents or trustees, and shall avoid conflicts of interest.
5. Engineers shall build their professional reputation on the merit of their services and shall not compete unfairly with others.
6. Engineers shall act in such a manner as to uphold and enhance the honor, integrity, and dignity of the engineering profession.
7. Engineers shall continue their professional development throughout their careers, and shall provide opportunities for the professional development of those engineers under their supervision.

In 1996 the ASCE added "sustainable development" to its Fundamental Canons, and in 2004 the *Civil Engineering Body of Knowledge for the 21st Century* added four outcomes to the eleven ABET outcomes:

1. An ability to apply knowledge in a specialized area related to civil engineering.
2. An understanding of the elements of project management, construction, and asset management.
3. An understanding of business and public policy and administration fundamentals.
4. An understanding of the role of the leader and leadership principles and attitudes.

Please notice that three of the four additional outcomes involve "soft skills" or what are increasingly being referred to as professional skills (Shuman, Besterfied-Sacre, and McGourty, 2005).

The Fundamental Canons have a long history, and can be traced in part to the Code of Hammurabi (ca 1700 B.C.E.):

> If a builder builds a house for a man and does not make its construction sturdy and the house collapses and causes the death of the owner of the house, then that builder shall be put to death. If it destroys property, he shall restore whatever is destroyed, and because he did not make the house sturdy he shall rebuild the house that collapsed at his own expense. If a builder builds a house for a man and does not make its construction meet the requirements and a wall falls, then that builder shall strengthen the wall at his own expense.

The reflection by David Radcliffe (in the nearby box) on the death of engineer Roger Boisjoly articulates how difficult it can be to uphold these principles.

The Courage to Engineer

Roger Boisjoly, a mechanical engineer who worked at Morton Thiokol, passed away in January 2012, although news of his death did not reach the mainstream media immediately. Why is this significant? Roger Boisjoly exemplified the moral courage that it takes to be an engineer. Based on his technical expertise and supporting evidence, he became concerned that the seals on solid booster rockets, made by Morton Thiokol, and which power the space shuttle on take-off, might fail in very cold weather. He strenuously warned his management and that of NASA of the possible consequences if the Challenger was launched in the very cold conditions that prevailed on the morning of January 28, 1986. His warning was not heeded, and we all know what happened.

But rather than being seen as a hero who tried to sound the alarm, Boisjoly was ostracized and suffered significantly as a result of being a true professional. An article in the *New York Times* has outlined some of the pressure he endured (for this, see Martin, 2012).

Engineering is not just applied mathematics and science; it is a deeply value-laden enterprise that involves choices that have real consequences for people and the planet. Decisions we make as engineers about what we choose to work on and how we choose to do things have an unavoidable moral and ethical dimension. I recommend you explore this case of an engineer who had the moral courage to stick by his professional opinion and hang the personal or social consequences; see the Online Ethics Center for Engineering and Research: http://www.onlineethics.org/cms/7123.aspx.

In a famous minority opinion to the official report on the Challenger disaster, Appendix F, Nobel Prize–winning physicist Richard Feynman concluded with the following statement: "For a successful technology, reality must take precedence over public relations, for nature cannot be fooled." Even if we have a perfect set of calculations, if these do not model the actuality of nature, then there could be dire consequences. To engineer is to have the courage to make critical judgment calls.

Even if we are not called upon to display the moral courage shown by Roger Boisjoly in raising the alarm about the Challenger, we all have a role to play. In his *New York Times* article, Douglas Martin (2012) recalls that Boisjoly "was sustained by a single gesture of support. Sally Ride, the first American woman in space, hugged him after his appearance before the commission. 'She was the only one,' he said in a whisper to a *Newsday* reporter in 1988. 'The only one.'"

Food for thought and cause for deep reflection on what it takes to engineer.

David Radcliffe

An article by Sheppard, Colby, Macatangay, and Sullivan (2005) exploring the question, "What is engineering practice?" opens with the following statement: "Professions, such as engineering, medicine, teaching, nursing, law, and the clergy share a common set of tenets; namely to:

1. provide worthwhile service in the pursuit of important human and social ends;
2. possess fundamental knowledge and skill (especially an academic knowledge base and research);
3. develop the capacity to engage in complex forms of professional practice;
4. make judgments under conditions of uncertainty;
5. learn from experience; and
6. create and participate in a responsible and effective professional community."

David Billington (1985) summarizes one of the challenges of professional practice as follows: "Engineers are always confronted with two ideals, efficiency and economy, and the world's best computer could not tell them how to reconcile the two. There is never 'one best way.' Like doctors or politicians or poets, *engineers face a vast array of choices every time they begin work, and every design is subject to criticism and compromise.*"

James Adams (1991) argues that engineering school does not necessarily prepare people for professional practice (and may even deter some):

> Engineering: In School and Out—Engineering schools recognize the overlap in industry between engineering and science, and they design their curricula accordingly. Engineering education is strongly theoretical and geared toward math and science. This is partly because of the natural interests of people who are attracted to a professorial life and who set the curriculum. It is also because engineers can learn the more applied portions of their field on the job, while they are unlikely to learn math and science on the job. But because the activities of the engineering student have little relation to the activities of many practicing engineers, it is likely that engineering education discourages some students who would make excellent engineers and encourages other who will not. *The mentality to do well in engineering schools emphasizes the ability to work problem sets and get right answers. In engineering, there are never right answers and [there are] few problem sets.*

Engineering Design

If design is the essence of engineering, the next question is, What is design? What comes to mind when you consider the term *design*? Do you think of product design (such as automobiles), architectural design, set and costume design (as in theater), or interface design (as in computer)? Take a moment to collect your thoughts on design.

ABET, the group that accredits engineering programs, defined engineering design as "the process of devising a system, component or process to meet a desired need" (ABET, 2000).

Researchers who carefully observe the engineering design process are increasingly noting that it is quite different from the formal process typically described in textbooks. For example, Eugene Ferguson (1992, p. 32) writes:

> Those who observe the process of engineering design find that it is not a totally formal affair, and that drawings and specifications come into existence as a result of a social process. The various members of a design group can be expected to have divergent views of the most desirable ways to accomplish the design they are working on. As Louis Bucciarelli (1994), an engineering professor who has observed engineering designers at work, points out, informal negotiations, discussions, laughter, gossip, and banter among members of a design group often have a leavening effect on its outcome.

Recent work on engineering design indicates that design is a more social process than we once thought. Larry Leifer (1997) of the Stanford Center for Design Research claims that engineering design is "a social process that identifies a need, defines a problem, and specifies a plan that enables others to manufacture the solutions." Leifer's research shows that design is fundamentally a social activity. He describes practices such as "negotiating understanding," "conserving ambiguity," "tailoring engineering communications for recipients," and "manipulating mundane representations."

The state of the art definition of engineering design is from a 2005 article, "Engineering Design Thinking, Teaching, and Learning" (Dym, Agogino, Eris, Frey, and Leifer, 2005): "*Engineering design* is a systematic, intelligent process in which designers generate, evaluate, and specify concepts for devices, systems, or processes whose form and function achieve clients' objectives or users' needs while satisfying a specified set of constraints." The authors say good designers have the ability to:

- tolerate ambiguity that shows up in viewing design as inquiry or as an iterative loop of divergent-convergent thinking;
- maintain sight of the big picture by including systems thinking and systems design;
- handle uncertainty;
- make decisions;
- think as part of a team in a social process; and
- think and communicate in the several languages of design.

The role of failure in engineering design must be considered, despite the popular saying from Gene Kranz, flight director in Mission Control for the Apollo 13 moon launch, "Failure is not an option." Rumor has it that many engineering students embrace Kranz's statement and are afraid to fail, raising the concern that they are therefore uneasy about pushing themselves or their designs to the limit. Failure is an important part of engineering; in fact, engineers such as Henry Petroski argue that "Failure is always an option." Petroski (2003) wrote in a *New York Times* op-ed piece, "The design of any device, machine or system is fraught with failure. Indeed, the way engineers achieve success in their designs is by imagining how they might fail." Petroski also devoted a book (2003) to this topic, *Small Things Considered: Why There Is No Perfect Design.*

Engineers are not alone in accepting (and learning from) failure. Consider these quotes from three innovators and entrepreneurs:

> The fastest way to succeed is to double your failure rate. (Thomas Watson, IBM)
>
> Fail often to succeed sooner. (Tom Kelley, IDEO)
>
> You must learn to fail intelligently. Failing is one of the greatest arts in the world. One fails toward success. (Thomas Edison)

Another way to conceptualize the role of failure is to consider the heuristic: use feedback to stabilize design (Koen, 2002). Sometimes the feedback comes from failure, but more commonly it comes from modeling, testing, prototyping, and other less catastrophic forms of failure.

If design is the heart of engineering and design is a social process, then it follows that teamwork and project management are essential to engineering. Many problems with engineering result from poor team dynamics and inadequate project management.

> *Design team failure is usually due to failed team dynamics.*
>
> LARRY LEIFER
> Director, Stanford Center for Design Research

A lot has been written about engineering and engineering design. Adams (1991), Hapgood (1992), and Ferguson (1992), for example, can give students considerable insight into engineering. I devoted two *Journal of Engineering Education* Academic Bookshelf columns to these topics. You can find summaries of several of the books on my website, www.ce.umn.edu/~smith. Follow the Teamwork and Project Management link. One of the most interesting insights into engineering design was presented in an *ABC News Nightline* show documenting the design process at the product design firm IDEO ("The Deep Dive," July 13, 1999). David Kelly, head of IDEO, challenged the viewer: "Look around—the only things not designed by humans are in nature." Five steps are key to IDEO's expertise in innovative design:

1. Understand the market/client/technology/constraints.
2. Observe real people in real situations.
3. Visualize new-to-the-world concepts and ultimate customers.
4. Evaluate and refine prototypes.
5. Implement new concepts for commercialization.

I hope you have an opportunity to view the IDEO Deep Dive on DVD on YouTube. Students I've shown it to exclaim, "I want to work at a place like that!" It is possible, however, if the engineering and business leaders are right, that many of us will be working in places where design is emphasized. Bruce Nussbaum wrote in *BusinessWeek*, March 8, 2005, that "'Design thinking' can create rewarding experiences for consumers—the key to earnings growth and an edge that outsourcing can't beat." Nussbaum cites Roger Martin, dean of the Rotman School of Management at the University of Toronto, who is reshaping the entire MBA program around the principle that "businesspeople will have to become more 'masters of heuristics' than 'managers of algorithms,'" and that "design skills and business skills are converging." Martin's 2009 book, *The Design of Business: Why Design Thinking Is the Next Competitive Advantage*, provides elaboration on this idea. He writes, "Design thinking focuses on accelerating the pace at which knowledge advances from *mystery* (an unexplainable problem) to *heuristic* (a rule of thumb that guides us toward a solution) to *algorithm* (a replicable success formula)." I'll elaborate further on Martin's ideas in Chapter 2.

Until recently the predominant design approach used in engineering was "cradle to grave" and most things were designed to be thrown away. The concept of "away" was described in an interesting way as the "toilet assumption" by Bennis and Slater (1968) in their book *The Temporary Society.* The engineering design paradigm is slowly changing from "cradle to grave" to "cradle to cradle." The idea of "cradle to cradle" was developed and championed by the international collaboration of Michael Braungart, a German chemist, and William McDonough, a U.S. architect (McDonough and Braungart, 2002).

Increasingly, design is conducted by globally distributed teams, and Shawn Jordan's reflection in the nearby box provides insights into his research and experience.

In today's fast-paced and innovation-driven world, the nature of the design problems facing industry often requires the use of cross-disciplinary teams in order to maximize innovation. Assembling face-to-face teams to solve the wide variety of design problems that exist is costly, time-consuming, and sometimes impossible, leaving companies with no choice but to call upon virtual cross-disciplinary engineering design teams to quickly and cost-effectively solve design problems. These teams are crucial to competitiveness in the future, but virtual team members need a stronger set of skills in order for virtual teams to be successful.

As part of my dissertation work, I spent 6 months embedded in a multi-national engineering design and manufacturing company to answer the question, *what factors contribute to the success of virtual cross-disciplinary engineering design teams in industry?* Three case studies were constructed on three distinctly different pre-existing virtual cross-disciplinary engineering design teams. One team was designing a process for working virtually, the second was redesigning an existing product to reduce cost, and the third was working as a part of a customer-led virtual team to design a brand new product. Team members completed questionnaires, participated in interviews, and went through observations of their virtual work experiences.

The results of this study showed that factors that contribute to the success of virtual cross-disciplinary engineering design teams fall into three major categories: the *context* in which teams work, the *method* by which teams do their work, and the *media* by which teams communicate. The specific factors are shown in Figure 1.1.

My study also found that virtual teams need (1) strong processes, (2) high-quality team members, and (3) higher performance in general on team-related success factors. Surprising was the heavy importance placed on process and team-related success factors (e.g., having clear job descriptions, strong management, trust and cooperation among team members, multiple perspectives represented on the team), compared with the significantly lesser importance placed on having the latest communications technology. A significant issue with the latest technology was reliability; many middle-aged workers would rather use conference calls or e-mail than spend one-third of a meeting trying to get a multi-national team connected into the same computer-based conference. Regardless of what technology you choose to use for your virtual team, make sure to support it with strong team processes to be successful!

Shawn Jordan

Figure 1.1 Virtual Cross-Disciplinary Engineering Design Team Success Factors*

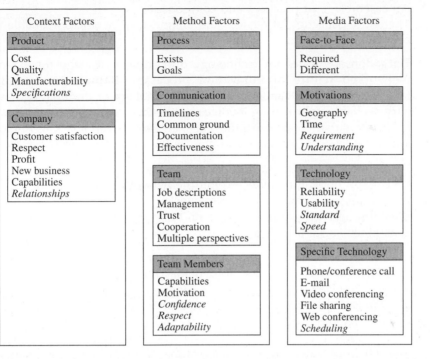

*Factors (except those in italics) were independently identified in all three team cases in the study. Factors in italics were independently identified by one or more team cases in the study.

Innovation and creativity are getting a lot of attention in engineering circles. Van de Ven, Polley, Garud and Venkataraman's (1999) research indicates that "The innovation journey is a nonlinear cycle of divergent and convergent activities that may repeat over time and at different organizational levels if resources are obtained to renew the cycle" (p. 16). Their view is similar to the divergent (brainstorming) and convergent (selecting among alternative prototypes, needs, constraints, etc.) cycles portrayed in the IDEO Deep Dive video. My current favorite definition of innovation is the one offered by Denning and Dunham (2010), in which they describe innovation "as the art of getting people to adopt change" and offer the following definition: "Innovation is the adoption of new practice in a community."

Andrew Hargadon (2003) argues that "Extraordinary innovations are often the results of recombinant invention" (p. viii, ix). He cites science fiction writer William Gibson, "The future is already here, it's just unevenly distributed," to help make his point. Brian Arthur argues in his 2009 book *The Nature of Technology: What It Is and How It Evolves* that there are three fundamental principles of technology:

1. All technologies are combinations.
2. Each component of technology is itself in miniature a technology.
3. All technologies harness and exploit some effect or phenomena, usually several.

And he offers three related definitions of technology:

1. A means to fulfill a human purpose.
2. An assemblage of practices and components.
3. The entire collection of devices and engineering practices available to a culture.

Hargadon advocates for technology brokering, a strategy for exploiting the networked nature of innovation processes. Rather than producing fundamentally novel advances in any one technology or dominating any one industry, technology brokering involves combining existing objects, ideas, and people in ways that create breakthroughs, and may even spark technological revolutions. Technology brokering involves the concept of bridging:

1. Breakthrough innovation depends on exploiting the past.
2. Successful innovators better exploit the networked structure of ideas within unique organizational frameworks.
3. Breakthrough innovations depend on building communities—innovation is as much social as it is technical.

Edgar Schein (2003), who served as a consultant to Digital Equipment Corporation (DEC) for over 20 years, argued that innovation is predominantly a cultural artifact. He wrote "Culture is a complex force field that influences all of an organization's processes. We try to manage culture but, in fact, culture manages us far more than we manage it, and it happens largely outside of awareness" (p. 31).

Regardless of how you frame innovation and creativity it is likely to be of great importance to your success in engineering. Also, since innovation has become such an important and timely topic, a new chapter, Innovation in a Team Environment (Chapter 7), written by Senay Purzer and Nicholas Fila, is now a part of this book.

Now that we've explored engineering and the role of design, let's turn to the role of teamwork and project management in engineering.

Teamwork and Engineering

 REFLECTION What have been your own personal experiences in working on a team (or group)? Were these good or bad experiences? Have you worked as a member of a project team (in school or otherwise)? Can you recall any particular reason why you needed to work as a team (or group)? What were the benefits (or the drawbacks)? Why do you think teamwork is (or is not) important in the practice of engineering? Take a moment to reflect on your experiences with teamwork and then think about the importance and role of teamwork in engineering practice.

How important is teamwork in the practice of engineering? National leaders in engineering and engineering education are advocating increased emphasis on teamwork and leadership skills as outlined in this book's Preface.

Table 1.1 Proportion of Employers Who Say Colleges and Universities Should Place More Emphasis than They Do Today on Selected Learning Outcomes

Selected Learning Outcomes	%
Concepts and new developments in science and technology	82
Teamwork skills and the ability to collaborate with others in diverse group settings	76
The ability to apply knowledge and skills to real-world settings through internships or other hands-on experiences	73
The ability to effectively communicate orally and in writing	73
Critical thinking and analytical reasoning skills	73
Global issues and developments and their implications for the future	72

Similarly, business leaders are stressing the importance of developing a broad range of skills. The 2003 Business–Higher Education Forum report, *Building a Nation of Learners*, listed the following skills and attributes of a nation of learners: leadership, teamwork, problem solving, time management, self-management, adaptability, analytical thinking, global consciousness, and basic communication (listening, speaking, reading, and writing). The quotes from Rockefeller and Welch that open Chapter 4 of this text (please turn to the first page of Chapter 4 and read them) stress the importance of teamwork from the perspective of a corporate chief executive officer (CEO), but what about its importance for engineering graduates?

The AAC&U *College Learning for the New Global Century* study included the results of an employer survey conducted by Peter D. Hart Research Associates (2006). The top two responses to the question, "Most important skills employers look for in new hires" were teamwork and critical thinking and reasoning. Areas where employers noted that more emphasis is needed in colleges and universities are show in Table 1.1.

Teamwork and project management are central to engineering. Learning how to organize and manage projects, and to participate effectively in project teams, not only will serve you well in engineering school, where there are lots of group projects, but also will be critical to your success as a professional engineer. The Boeing Company uses the checklist shown below when considering new applicants for employment.

Employer's Checklist—Boeing Company

✔ A good grasp of these engineering fundamentals:
Mathematics (including statistics)
Physical and life sciences
Information technology
✔ A good understanding of the design and manufacturing process (i.e., an understanding of engineering)
✔ A basic understanding of the context in which engineering is practiced, including:
Economics and business practice
History
The environment
Customer and societal needs

✔ A multidisciplinary systems perspective
✔ Good communication skills
    Written
    Verbal
    Graphic
    Listening
✔ High ethical standards
✔ An ability to think critically and creatively as well as independently and cooperatively
✔ Flexibility—an ability and the self-confidence to adapt to rapid/major change
✔ Curiosity and a lifelong desire to learn
✔ A profound understanding of the importance of teamwork

Source: Briefings ASEE Prism, December 1996, p. 11.

The Boeing Company checklist has been undergoing updates and refinements, and the following were added (or revised extensively) in a list titled "Desired Attributes of a Global Engineer":

- An awareness of the boundaries of one's knowledge, along with an appreciation for other areas of knowledge and their interrelatedness with one's own expertise.
- An awareness and strong appreciation for other cultures and their diversity, their distinctiveness, and their inherent value.
- A strong commitment to teamwork, including extensive experience with and understanding of team dynamics.
- An ability to impart knowledge to others.

The emphasis on teamwork is not entirely new, as shown in the following 1988 list of skills employers wanted their employees to have.

What Employers Want

- Learning to learn
- Listening and oral communication
- Competence in reading, writing, and computation
- Adaptability: Creative thinking and problem solving
- Personal management: Self-esteem, goal setting/motivation, and personal/career development
- Group effectiveness: Interpersonal skills, negotiation, and teamwork
- Organizational effectiveness and leadership

Source: Workplace Basics: The Skills Employers Want. 1988. American Society for Training and Development and U.S. Department of Labor.

The importance of teamwork in business and industry is also embedded in the concepts of concurrent (or simultaneous) engineering and total quality management. The following quote elaborates on this point:

> In concurrent engineering (CE), the key ingredient is teamwork. People from many departments collaborate over the life of a product—from idea to obsolescence—to ensure that it reflects customers' needs and desires. . . . Since the very start of CE, product development must involve all parts of an organization. Effective teamwork depends upon sharing ideas and goals

beyond immediate assignments and departmental loyalties. Such behavior is not typically taught in the engineering schools of U.S. colleges and universities. For CE to succeed, teamwork and sharing must be valued just as highly as the traditional attributes of technical competence and creativity, and they must be rewarded by making them an integral part of the engineer's performance evaluation. (Shina, 1991, p. 23)

The increased emphasis on teamwork in engineering classes is partly due to the emphasis by employers, but it is also due to engineering education research on active and cooperative learning, and the emphasis of ABET. To maintain ABET accreditation, engineering departments must demonstrate that all of their graduates have the following 11 general skills and abilities (ABET, 2000):

1. An ability to apply knowledge of mathematics, science, and engineering
2. An ability to design and conduct experiments, as well as to analyze and interpret data
3. An ability to design a system, component, or process to meet desired needs
4. An ability to function on multidisciplinary teams
5. An ability to identify, formulate, and solve engineering problems
6. An understanding of professional and ethical responsibility
7. An ability to communicate effectively
8. The broad education necessary to understand the impact of engineering solutions in a global and societal context
9. A recognition of the need for, and an ability to engage in, lifelong learning
10. A knowledge of contemporary issues
11. An ability to use the techniques, skills, and modern engineering tools necessary for engineering practice

As you no doubt have recognized, a confluence of pressures emphasizes teamwork in engineering education and practice. We need to leave room for the "maverick," but most, if not all, engineering graduates need to develop skills for working cooperatively with others—as indicated by the lists of the top three engineering work activities.

Top Three Main Engineering Work Activities

Engineering Total	Civil/Architectural
• Design—36%	1. Management—45%
• Computer applications—31%	2. Design—39%
• Management—29%	3. Computer applications—20%

Source: Burton, Parker, and LeBold, 1998.

The full list of work activity reported by engineers is shown in Table 1.2. Note that 66 percent mentioned design and 49 percent mentioned management.

Table 1.2 Rank Order of Work Activities, 1993

Activity	% Mentioning
1. Design	66
2. Computer applications	58
3. Management	49
4. Development	47
5. Accounting, etc.	42
6. Applied research	39
7. Quality or productivity	33
8. Employee relations	23
9. Sales	20
10. Basic research	15
11. Production	14
12. Professional services	10
13. Other work activities	8
14. Teaching	8

Source: Burton, Parker, and LeBold, 1998, p. 19.

Numerous surveys of employers highlight the top skill needs. Below is a list from an Employer Evaluation of Employee Attributes, 2008–2009, Employer Survey from Minnesota Measures, 2009 (also cited in Sparks and Waits, 2011).

Top Attributes (most frequent ratings of "very important" by employers; top five):

- Professionalism (punctuality, time management, attitude)
- Self-direction, ability to take initiative
- Adaptability, willingness to learn
- Professional ethics, integrity
- Verbal communication skills

Middle Attributes between top five and bottom five:

- Capability for promotion
- Creativity
- Ability to work in a culturally diverse environment
- Ability to work in teams
- Written communication skills
- Basic mathematical reasoning (arithmetic, basic algebra)
- Critical thinking and analysis
- Problem solving, application of theory
- General computer skills (word processing, spreadsheets)
- Knowledge of technology/equipment required for the job

Bottom Attributes (most frequent ratings of "not at all" or "not very important"; bottom five):

- Advanced mathematical reasoning (linear algebra, statistics, calculus)
- Technical communication
- Fluency in a language other than English
- Knowledge of specific computer applications required for the job
- Application of knowledge from a particular field of study

Employers' wish lists are making it into popular guides for college students. For example, Bill Coplin's (2003) *10 Things Employers Want You to Learn in College* are Establishing a Work Ethic, Developing Physical Skills, Communicating Verbally, Communicating in Writing, Working Directly with People, Influencing People, Gathering Information, Using Quantitative Tools, Asking and Answering the Right Questions, and Solving Problems.

A few guides are available specifically for engineering students and graduates entering the engineering workforce. Krista Donaldson's (2005) *The Engineering Student Survival Guide* has lots of terrific suggestions for making the most of your undergraduate engineering education, tips that will help you thrive, not just survive. Carl Selinger's (2004) *Stuff You Don't Learn in Engineering School* provides similar guidance to graduates entering the engineering workforce.

Some of this advice is based on research on what it takes to succeed in college. Richard Light's research with students, for example, revealed the following keys to making the most of college (Light, 2001):

1. Meet the faculty.
2. Take a mix of courses, especially early on.
3. Study in groups.
4. Write, write, write.
5. Speak another language
6. Consider time—successful students manage their time effectively.
7. Hold the drum—get involved in professional and social activities.

 REFLECTION What is your plan for developing a broad range of skills? How about for making the most of your engineering education? Take a moment and reflect on your plan and your progress to date.

Fundamental Tools for the Next Generation of Engineers and Project Managers

I've stressed the importance of teamwork for engineering education and practice, but teamwork isn't all that's needed. If engineers are going to become "the master integrators," as emphasized by Joe Bordona (1998), three additional tools are fundamental:

- Systems/systems thinking/systems engineering
- Models, modeling, and heuristics
- Quality (I defer this discussion to Chapter 12)

The Systems Approach

Employer checklists like Boeing's and the new ABET accreditation criteria emphasize systems and the systems approach.

A system is a whole that cannot be divided up into independent parts (Ackoff, 1994). Systems are made up of sets of components that work together for a specified overall objective. The systems approach is simply a way of thinking about total systems and their components.

The Art and Practice of the Learning Organization

1. *Building shared vision.* The idea of building shared vision stresses that you never quite finish it—it's an ongoing process.
2. *Personal mastery.* Learning organizations must be fully committed to the development of each individual's personal mastery—each individual's capacity to create their life the way they truly want.
3. *Mental models.* Our vision of current reality has everything to do with the third discipline—*mental models*—because what we really have in our lives is constructions, internal pictures that we continually use to interpret and make sense out of the world.
4. *Team learning.* Individual learning, no matter how wonderful it is or how great it makes us feel, is fundamentally irrelevant to organizations, because virtually all important decisions occur in groups. The learning units of organizations are "teams," groups of people who need one another to act.
5. *Systems thinking.* The last discipline, the one that ties them all together, is *systems thinking.*

Source: Senge, 1993.

Five basic considerations must be kept in mind when thinking about the meaning of a system: (1) the total system's objectives and, more specifically, the performance measures of the whole system; (2) the system's environment: the fixed constraints; (3) the resources of the system; (4) the components of the system, their activities, goals, and measures of performance; and (5) the management of the system (Churchman, 1968).

Systems thinking is a discipline for seeing wholes—a framework for seeing interrelationships rather than things, for seeing patterns of change rather than static "snapshots." It is a set of principles and a set of specific tools and techniques (Senge, 1990). An implication of the systems approach is that it is important to get everybody involved to improve whole systems (Weisbord, 1987). The systems approach is commonly implemented through learning organizations (see the box "The Art and Practice of the Learning Organization").

A systems theme is one of the integrating threads in this book. The concepts of systems and of the learning organization are important not only to your study of teamwork and project management but to many other things you will be studying in engineering. Here, for example, are eight principles for learning from Xerox (Jordon, 1996, p. 116):

1. Learning is fundamentally social.
2. Cracking the whip stifles learning.
3. Learning needs an environment that supports it.
4. Learning crosses hierarchical bounds.
5. Self-directed learning fuels the fire.
6. Learning by doing is more powerful than memorizing.
7. Failure to learn is often the fault of the system, not the people.
8. Sometimes the best learning is unlearning.

This list from Xerox indicates that the ideas in this book are important not only for your project work but also for your day-to-day work in engineering school.

Nelson and Stolterman's (2003) *The Design Way* provides many connections to systems and systems thinking as well as a sound foundation and fundamentals of design competence. The authors' adamancy about design is regularly revealed in provocative statements such as "Humans did not discover fire—they designed it. The wheel was not something our ancestors merely stumbled over in a stroke of good luck; it, too, was designed. The habit of labeling significant human achievements as 'discoveries,' rather than 'designs,' discloses a critical bias in our Western tradition."

Nelson and Stolterman (2003) make many connections between design and systems thinking. For example they write: "The systems approach is the logic of design. Such an approach requires that close attention be paid to relationships and the phenomenon of emergence when evaluating any subset of existence. If the designer's intention is to create something new, not to just describe and explain, or predict and control, it is especially important to take a systems approach" (p. 74). I recommend this book to help deepen your understanding of systems and design, and I'm confident that deep understanding of both these concepts as well as the interaction between them is essential for success in engineering in the twenty-first century.

An emerging area of systems that is gaining momemtum is complexity and complex adaptive systems (Axelrod and Cohen, 2001; Miller and Page, 2007). Page (2009) claims that a "system can be considered complex if its agents meet four qualifications: diversity, connection, interdependence, and adaptation" (p. 4) and "the attributes of interdependence, connectedness, diversity, and adaptation and learning generate complexity" (p. 10). Furthermore, Page (2009) notes that "interdependence refers to whether other entities influence actions, whereas connectedness refers to how many people a person is connected to" (p. 11). Preparing students with a deeper understanding of complex systems is essential, since complex systems (1) are often unpredictable and can produce large events as well as withstand trauma, (2) produce bottom-up emergent phenomena, and (3) produce amazing novelty (Page, 2009).

Systems, systems thinking, and especially complex adaptive systems will be revisited in Chapter 15.

Models, Modeling, and Heuristics

Modeling in its broadest sense is the cost-effective use of something in place of something else for some cognitive purpose (Rothenberg, 1989). A model represents reality for the given purpose; the model is an abstraction of reality, however, in the sense that it cannot represent all aspects of reality. According to Rothenberg, models are characterized by three essential attributes:

1. *Reference:* A model is of something (its *referent*).
2. *Purpose:* A model has an intended cognitive *purpose* with respect to its referent.
3. *Cost-effectiveness:* A model is more *cost-effective* to use for this purpose than the referent itself would be.

I often give students this problem that I first learned about from Billy Koen to help them learn about these attributes of modeling: Determine the maximum number of Ping-Pong balls that could fit in the room you're sitting in.

First I give them about 20 seconds and ask each person to guess. Next I ask them to work in groups for 10 or 15 minutes to develop not only a numerical estimate but also a description of the model they use and the assumptions they specified. At this stage, students typically model the room as a rectangular box and the ball as a cube. They then determine the number by dividing the volume of the room by the volume of a ball. I ask them what they would do if I gave them the rest of the class period to work on the problem. They report that they need measuring tools and a container of Ping-Pong balls, and after receiving these materials, set off to work. Sooner or later a student says, "Who cares how many Ping-Pong balls could fit in the room!" I thank that student and report that we can now stop. In any problem that involves modeling, the purpose must be specified. Without knowing the purpose, we don't know how exact an answer must be or how to use the model. In fact, the 20-second answer might be good enough. This problem is also featured in our book *How to Model It: Problem Solving for the Computer Age* (Starfield, Smith, and Bleloch, 1990).

An essential aspect of modeling is the use of heuristics (Starfield, Smith, and Bleloch, 1994), which may be generally defined as methods or strategies that aid in discovery or problem solving. Although difficult to define, heuristics are relatively easy to identify using the characteristics listed by Koen (1984, 1985, 2003):

1. Heuristics do not guarantee a solution.
2. Two heuristics may contradict each other or give different answers to the same question and still be useful.
3. Heuristics permit the solving of unsolvable problems or reduce the search time to a satisfactory solution.
4. The heuristic depends on the immediate context instead of absolute truth as a standard of validity.

Thus, a heuristic is anything that provides plausible aid or direction in the solution of a problem but is in the final analysis unjustified, incapable of justification, and fallible. It is used to guide, to discover, and to reveal. Heuristics are also a key part of Koen's definition of the engineering method:

> The engineering method is the use of heuristics to cause the best change in a poorly understood situation within the available resources. (p. 70)

Typical engineering heuristics include (1) rules of thumb and orders of magnitude, (2) factors of safety, (3) circumstances that determine the engineer's attitude toward his or her work, (4) procedures that engineers use to keep risk within acceptable bounds, and (5) rules of thumb that are important in resource allocation.

My colleague and coauthor, Tony Starfield, has been thinking, teaching, and writing about heuristics for many years and his reflection in the nearby box provides his collected wisdom (Starfield, 1999, 2005).

Modeling Heuristics

1. Keep it simple. Use the leanest model for the purpose at hand.
2. Be sure you've defined your objectives clearly.
3. Think yourself into the problem. Plan your output. What will you do with it and how do you expect it to look? For example, do you need numbers out to three decimal places?
4. Be prepared to explain your model. Graphs, pictures, and histograms are better than words or numbers to explain model results.
5. Anticipate your results. If you get what you anticipate—good! If actual results do not agree with anticipated results, make sure you understand why.
6. Look for upper and lower bounds. What is the biggest number? Smallest number? If they are close, there may be no need to look further. If not, you need to study further.
7. Choose appropriate spatial and temporal scales. What do you see or not see at a particular step in building the model?
8. Choose suitable time/space steps. Look for magic numbers (time or spatial scales that simplify and suit the structure of the problem).
9. Keep a list of assumptions and review them frequently. Have the "guts" to make assumptions. List your assumptions as you develop the model.
10. Think about what level of detail you will need to meet the purpose of the model. If in doubt, leave it out. Make assumptions. Revisit those assumptions later.
11. Cut through "Gordian" knots. Gordian knots are things that are messy. There are no clear means to untie them easily (they are also called a can of worms). Either leave it out or find a simple way through it. Make simplifying assumptions. Build your model around your purpose not around knots.
12. Don't be held up (stymied) by lack of data.
13. Plan for a sensitivity analysis (i.e., vary the values of parameters). What things do I need to change to see how sensitive the model is to changes in the data or assumptions? Get a series of answers for a feel of how the model works.
14. Finding the right notation (i.e., numbers or symbols to represent model formulas or calculations) helps you think through the model. This is a way for you to describe your model.
15. If a formula is used, be sure to understand why it fits. Be cautious of pulling formulae out of books and using them without understanding them. All have baggage and assumptions, including statistics.
16. Never write down a formula without first writing it down in words so that you understand the process. Then write it as a mathematical equation. If you need to add to or adjust a formula, never try to just "fix it." Go back to the statement in words and redevelop it.
17. Write parameters into a model as symbols, not numbers, so you can change their values easily (i.e., sensitivity analysis).
18. Use prototypes.
19. Consider using salami tactics. You can't get the whole salami at once nor can you solve the whole problem at one time. Ask for one slice of the salami then ask for another one. Slice the problem and solve it as a series of steps. Get a whole model (or a whole salami) one slice at a time. (Besides, if you try to eat a whole salami at one time you will probably get a stomachache. If you try to solve the whole model at one time you will probably get a headache.) Keep in mind that your objective is the whole salami.
20. Maintain intellectual control. You control your model, so don't let the model control you. (If you don't understand the model, you cannot expect others to understand it.)
21. Press ahead. Don't get bogged down. Get something working as soon as possible. When you start seeing what your model does, you can see what your model does right and wrong. Be prepared that some models may just have to be abandoned. This concept is called rapid prototyping.

Tony Starfield

As you can no doubt tell, Tony Starfield has been thinking and writing about and teaching models and modeling for a long time. His university courses and workshops with professionals focus on helping people learn how to model complex phenomena, mainly ecological modeling. He stresses heuristics in his courses and workshops and encourages students and workshop participants to be on the lookout for heuristics in all aspects of their lives.

Here's a complementary set of modeling heuristics from an operations research textbook (Ravindran, Phillips, and Solberg, 1987):

1. Do not build a complicated model when a simple one will suffice.
2. Beware of molding the problem to fit the technique.
3. The deduction phase of modeling must be conducted rigorously.
4. Models should be validated prior to implementation.
5. A model should never be taken too literally.
6. A model should neither be pressed to do, nor criticized for failing to do, that for which it was never intended.
7. Beware of overselling a model.
8. Some of the primary benefits of modeling are associated with the process of developing the model.
9. A model cannot be any better than the information that goes into it.
10. Models cannot replace decision makers.

Some of my favorites from this list are number 2 because you learn powerful tools and techniques in engineering school but not necessarily the understanding of where and how to use them; number 8 because I've seen an enormous amount of learning as I've observed students building models; and number 9 because I've seen too many examples of GIGO (garbage in, garbage out).

A more recent definition from researchers who design activities and environments to help people learn to model is: Modeling, at its core, is a way of thinking used in order to represent, describe, or explain a system with another system for a purpose (Lesh and Doerr, 2003; Moore, 2008).

Tamara Moore's reflections in the nearby box on developing modeling thinking provides insights into how to advance your understanding.

Modeling Thinking

Modeling abilities play an important role in engineering. So, engineering educators are interested in facilitating students' development of these abilities. Model-Eliciting Activities (MEAs) are client-driven, team-based tasks that we've been using in undergraduate engineering education to help students build competent modeling abilities. MEAs allow participants to demonstrate their knowledge in multiple ways. Solution processes in MEAs often involve shifting back and forth among a variety of relevant representations or models. Within MEAs, students develop, construct, describe, or explain engineering systems.

As Karl and I have been working together over the last several years, we have begun to think about why modeling is so important to engineers and STEM professionals in general. These conversations have led to us thinking deeply about what are the most important skills for engineers to know. At the top of our list is modeling . . . why is this? Because, engineering is a field (along with finance, business, agriculture, etc.) that relies on modeling to make many important decisions about how systems are performing. MEAs were created to focus on the modeling abilities (mathematical and otherwise) that are needed in this environment—especially as our technology-based age of information is changing so rapidly. If we spend too much time teaching specific skills, in just a few short years after a student graduates, that skill is likely to be outdated. However, modeling is more robust. It is a way of thinking that is adaptable to new situations and new technologies.

MEAs create learning environments in which it is safe to explore these skills that are beyond just pure mathematical or science abilities. Teamwork, communication, and ethical considerations are all examples of skills that you need to be comfortable working with and in. Work on MEAs can help you construct, describe, and explain complex systems in ways that are reusable and shareable while at the same time honing your teamwork, communication, and other relevant skills.

The NanoRoughness Problem is an example of an MEA. Generally, MEAs start with some type of background reading to introduce students to the problem and its context. In the NanoRoughness Problem, there are three types of short introduction activities for students to complete as individuals. Before the problem, there is a one-page information sheet provided as background on the Atomic Force Microscopy (AFM) machine and how it works. This is important because most students are not familiar with this technology or how it works, and the product of the AFM machine is integral to the problem. Second, the students are asked to think about roughness by answering the following prompts:

- How do you define roughness?
- What procedure might you use to measure the roughness of the pavement on a road?
- Give an example of something for which degree of roughness matters. For your example, why does the degree of roughness matter? How might you measure the roughness (or lack of roughness) of this object?

Third, the students read a profile on the company that they are working for which is a company that develops coatings for orthopedic and biomedical implants. This sets the context for the problem. This individual work is important because all students need to be able to enter into the problem meaningfully, and we all process information at different rates. Have you ever been in a team where one person was off and running before the others really even understood what was being asked? This is a common problem in teaming. Getting everyone on even ground before beginning is important, both when learning about teaming and when you are out in the workforce working with your colleagues.

Next, student teams of three to four students work together on the modeling part of the problem. In the NanoRoughness Problem, the teams of students are asked to develop a procedure to measure roughness given AFM images of three different samples of gold. In order to motivate the problem, a realistic context in which a company specializing in biomedical applications of nanotechnology wishes to start producing synthetic diamond coatings for joint replacements is provided. The company intends to extend its experience with gold coatings for artery stents to this new application. They want to use the model for roughness on this new application, thus the need for the model to measure roughness. The company only has AFM samples of gold that students can use to develop the procedure for measuring roughness, but later the company intends on using the procedure to measure the roughness of gold. Figure 1.2 is an example of one of these images.

The teams must communicate their model back to the company providing explicit details about their procedure. I have written an article that details this MEA and another called the Aluminum Bat Problem. If you are interested, you can find it at http://matdl.org/jme/files/2008/06/moore_jme_model_eliciting_activities.pdf.

When thinking about a problem that is as complex as this one, I bet you can imagine that, in order to get a good solution to this, different perspectives are valued. You want to think about this problem from many different aspects and consider many different ways of attacking this problem. Considering that a diversity of thought will strengthen the model, it makes sense then that when you build a team, varied

Figure 1.2 Electron Photomicrograph of Gold Coating

backgrounds and different strengths are likely to make the product better. Consider Karl's section on the importance of diversity in Chapter 3. We have found that teams do better on MEAs when the teams are more diverse in thought and background, as long as they are willing to work together. We also know that all types of students are more likely to deeply engage in these types of problems than in the more traditional book problems.

So, what do you need to know about modeling? When you interpret a situation, you do not simply apply logical mathematical and scientific models to the system. You also engage feelings, values, dispositions, beliefs, and many other personal ways of thinking to the problem. These different ways of thinking can both strengthen and bias your models. So learn to think about what you bring to the table and use it to the best advantage. Problem solving is difficult, but also incredibly rewarding. Modeling is a form of problem solving, and as such, people who are good at it use tools to help them when they get stuck. These tools are often referred to as the

heuristics that are described earlier in this chapter. Something to think about with heuristics is that problem-solving heuristics must be learned through the process of solving problems. It won't be effective for you to take this list and just try to implement them. We know. We've tried to get students to learn it that way starting over 50 years ago to no avail. However, once you have had a chance to work on complex modeling problems, like MEAs, reflecting about what you did and about the heuristics allows you to make meaning about your process and therefore be able to generalize it. Once you have generalized some of your processes, you have begun building your own set of heuristic tools. And as you encounter the next problem, think back to your tools and look for similar structure in the problems.

I hope the ideas presented here will help you in your journey to developing systems thinking, modeling, and problem-solving skills. These are so important to your career and to life.

Tamara Moore

We encourage you to be on the lookout for heuristics in the courses and projects you encounter, and most importantly, to develop your own heuristics.

Models and heuristics will constitute a major part of this book. The critical path method (CPM) is a procedure for modeling complex projects with interdependent activities. Visual representations include Gantt charts and precedence network diagrams. My goal is for you to develop the skills and confidence necessary to organize, manage, be a participant in, and lead project teams. This goal is consistent with current thinking about the purpose of engineering schools. Deming associate and engineering educator Myron Tribus (1996) summarized the purpose of engineering schools as follows:

> The purpose of a School of Engineering is to teach students to create value through the design of high quality products and systems of production, and services, and to organize and lead people in the continuous improvement of these designs. (p. 25)

Notice that Tribus considers management an integral part of engineering. He also elaborates on the importance of group work for learning to engineer:

> The main tool for teaching wisdom and character is the group project. Experiences with group activities, in which the members of the groups are required to exhibit honesty, integrity, perseverance, creativity and cooperation, provide the basis for critical review by both students and teachers. Teachers will need to learn to function more as coaches and resources and less as givers of knowledge. (p. 25)

We've covered a lot of ground in this chapter and have hopefully given you a lot to think about as you learn more about teamwork and project management in engineering. We encourage you to stop and reflect periodically (as we are encouraging you to do in this book). Remember to assess both your strengths and your weaknesses, celebrate your accomplishments and recognize and plan the things you need to improve.

A Reflection on Teamwork and Project Management in Engineering

As I finished writing the first edition of this book in 1999, I was reminded of a book from 1978 that I read more than 20 years earlier—*Excellence in Engineering* by W. H. Roadstrum. I was unable to locate my copy (I probably loaned it out) but did find the second edition, *Being Successful as an Engineer* (Roadstrum, 1988). In this edition, Roadstrum remarks, "Engineering is almost completely divorced from this concept of routine and continuous. Engineering work is project work" (p. 7). Engineering is project work! This is the essence of Roadstrum's book. The first two chapters, "What Engineering Is" and "The Engineer," cover ground similar to the material presented in this chapter, but from a perspective from many years ago. Chapters 3 and 4 are "The Project and the Project Team" and "Project Control." Although I had not looked at Roadstrum's book for several years, I was struck by the overlap between his book and mine.

Being Successful as an Engineer addresses a broad range of topics, including problem solving, laboratory work, design, research and development, manufacturing and quality control, systems, proposal work, human relations, and creativity. Roadstrum writes, "Design is the heart of the engineering process—its most characteristic activity." Furthermore, he states, "If you and I are going to understand engineering, we'll have to understand design" (p. 97).

Roadstrum further elaborates on the role of the project engineer:

> Every engineer looks forward to the time when he can have a project of his own. A project engineer has the best job in the business. He has ultimate responsibility for the work as a whole. He is the real architect of the project solution. Even more than his colleagues, he looks at the job as a whole from the beginning. He watches carefully to make all details come together into a timely, economical, fresh, and effective meeting of the need. (p. 166)

Roadstrum's book and ideas no doubt influenced my decision to develop skills and expertise in teamwork and project management; however, the specific reference lay dormant until now. I hope my book will influence your experience and practice of teamwork and project management in engineering.

A final note: This chapter opened with a discussion of Professor Billy Koen's probing questions. Koen's fourth question is this: "Lacking a ready answer [to the third question, What is the engineering method?], can you then name a nationally known engineer who is wise, well-read, and recognized as a scholar in the field of engineering—one to whom I can turn to find out what engineering really is?" To whom would you turn? Difficult, isn't it? No other profession lacks knowledgeable, clearly recognized spokespersons. I sincerely hope you'll help provide the leadership to make engineering better known.

Questions

1. What is engineering? How does engineering differ from science? What role does design play in engineering?
2. What is a model? Why are models useful in teamwork and project management and in engineering?
3. What is a system? Why are many books on teamwork and project management organized around a systems approach?

Exercises

1. Summarize your course work and experiences with engineering and design. What are some of the key things you've learned about engineers and engineering? Do you have relatives or friends who are project managers or engineers? If so, talk with them.
2. Why should you, as a first-year engineering student, be interested in teamwork and project management? Take a minute and reflect. Jot down at least three reasons why a first-year engineering student should be interested in these practices. What did you come up with? Did you say, for instance, that teamwork and project management are integral to professional engineering practice?

3. List your good experiences with projects and teamwork. Have you ever been on a team that had extraordinary accomplishments? If so, describe the situation, especially the characteristics of the team and project that led to extraordinary success. What were some of the factors? A sense of urgency? A project too complex or timeline too short for one person to complete? A need for synergistic interaction?

References

Accreditation Board for Engineering and Technology (ABET). 2000. *Criteria for accrediting engineering programs.* Baltimore, MD: Engineering Accreditation Commission of the Accreditation Board for Engineering and Technology.

Ackoff, Russell L. 1994. *The democratic corporation: A radical prescription for recreating corporate America and rediscovering success.* Oxford: Oxford University Press.

Adams, James L. 1991. *Flying buttresses, entropy, and o-rings: The world of an engineer.* Cambridge, MA: Harvard University Press.

Arthur, W. Brian. 2009. *The nature of technology: What it is and how it evolves.* New York: The Free Press.

Auyang, Sunny Y. 2004. *Engineering: An endless frontier.* Cambridge, MA: Harvard University Press.

Axelrod, R., and M. D. Cohen. 2001. *Harnessing complexity: Organizational implications of a scientific frontier.* New York: Simon & Schuster.

Bennis, W. G., and P. E. Slater. 1968. *The temporary society.* New York: Harper & Row.

Billington, David P. 1985. *The tower and the bridge: The new art of structural engineering.* Princeton, NJ: Princeton University Press.

———. 1986. In defense of engineers. *The Wilson Quarterly*, January.

Bordogna, Joseph. 1998. *Realizing the new paradigm for engineering education: The professional engineer in 2010.* Engineering Foundation Conference, Baltimore, MD, June 4.

Brown, Tim. 2009. *Change by design: How design thinking transforms organizations and inspires innovation.* New York: Harper Business.

Bucciarelli, Louis. 1994. *Designing engineers.* Cambridge, MA: MIT Press.

Burton, Lawrence, Linda Parker, and William K. LeBold. 1998. U.S. engineering career trends. *ASEE Prism* 7(9), 18–21.

Business–Higher Education Forum. 2003. *Building a nation of learners: The need for change in teaching and learning to meet global challenges.* Washington, DC: Business–Higher Education Forum.

Chapman, William L., A. Terry Bahill, and A. Wayne Wymore. 1992. *Engineering modeling and design.* Boca Raton, FL: CRC Press.

Churchman, C. West. 1968. *The systems approach.* New York: Laurel.

Coplin, Bill. 2003. *10 things employers want you to learn in college: The know-how you need to succeed.* Berkeley, CA: Ten Speed Press.

Davis, Michael. 1998. *Thinking like an engineer: Studies in the ethics of a profession.* Oxford: Oxford University Press.

Denning, Peter J., and Robert Dunham. 2010. *The innovator's way: Essential practices for successful innovation.* Cambridge, MA: MIT Press.

Donaldson, Krista. 2005. *The engineering student survival guide,* 3rd ed. New York: McGraw-Hill.

Dym, Clive L., Alice M. Agogino, Ozgur Eris, Daniel D. Frey, and Larry J. Leifer. 2005. Engineering design thinking, teaching, and learning. *Journal of Engineering Education* 94(1), 103–120.

Employer's Checklist—Boeing Company. 1996. Briefings. *ASEE Prism* 6(4), 11.

Ferguson, Eugene S. 1992. *Engineering and the mind's eye*. Cambridge, MA: MIT Press.

Friedman, Thomas L. 2000. *The Lexus and the olive tree: Understanding globalization*. New York: Anchor Books.

———. 2004. Commencement address. Washington University, St. Louis, May 21, http://news-info.wustl.edu/news/page/normal/887.html (accessed 4/14/05).

———. 2005. *The world is flat: A brief history of the 21st century*. New York: Farrar, Straus and Giroux.

——— and Michael Mandelbaum. 2011. *That used to be us: How America fell behind in the world it invented and how we can come back*. New York: Farrar, Straus and Giroux.

Gabriele, Gary A. 2005. Advancing engineering education in a flattened world. *Journal of Engineering Education* 94(3), 285–286.

Hancock, J. C., Chairman (1986). *Workshop on undergraduate engineering education*. Washington, DC: National Science Foundation.

Hapgood, Fred. 1992. *Up the infinite corridor: MIT and the technical imagination*. Reading, MA: Addison-Wesley.

Hargadon, Andrew. 2003. *How breakthroughs happen: The surprising truth about how companies innovate*. Cambridge, MA: Harvard Business School Press.

Jacobs, Jane. 1961. The death and life of great American cities. New York: Random House.

———. 2004. *Dark age ahead*. New York: Random House.

Jordon, Brigitte. 1996. 8 principles for learning. *Fast Company,* October/November, p. 116.

Kincheloe, J. L., and K. Berry. 2004. *Rigour and complexity in educational research: Conceptualizing the bricolage*. London: Open University Press.

Koen, B. V. 1971. The teaching of the engineering method to large groups of non-engineering students. Gulf-Southwest Section, American Association for Engineering Education, March 26, 1971.

———. 1984. Toward a definition of the engineering method. *Engineering Education* 75, 151–155.

———. 1985. *Definition of the engineering method*. Washington, DC: American Society for Engineering Education.

———. 2002. *Discussion of the method*. Oxford: Oxford University Press.

———. 2011. *Engineering method: What it is; what it isn't*. Philosophy of Engineering and Engineering Education Workshop. ASEE/IEEE Frontiers in Education Conference.

Kranz, Gene. 2001. *Failure is not an option: Mission Control from Mercury to Apollo 13 and beyond*. New York: Simon and Schuster.

Leifer, Larry. 1997. *A collaborative experience in global product-based learning*. National Technological University Faculty Forum. November 18.

Lesh, R., and H. M. Doerr. 2003. Foundations of a models and modeling perspective on mathematics teaching, learning, and problem solving. In *Beyond constructivism: Models and modeling perspectives on mathematics problem solving, learning, and teaching* (pp. 3–34), edited by R. Lesh and H. M. Doerr. Mahwah, NJ: Lawrence Erlbaum Associates.

Light, Richard J. 2001. *Making the most of college*. Cambridge, MA: Harvard University Press.

Martin, Douglas. 2012. Roger Boisjoly, 73, Dies; Warned of Shuttle Danger. *New York Times,* http://www.nytimes.com/2012/02/04/us/roger-boisjoly-73-dies-warned-of-shuttle-danger.html.

Martin, Roger. 2009. *The design of business: Why design thinking is the next competitive advantage*. Boston, MA: Harvard Business Press.

McDonough, W., and M. Braungart. 2002. *Cradle to cradle: Remaking the way we make things*. New York: North Point Press.

Miller, J., and S. E. Page. 2007. *Complex adaptive systems: An introduction to computational models of social life.* Princeton, NJ: Princeton University Press.

Minnesota Measures–2009. St. Paul, MN: Minnesota Office of Higher Education Performance.

Moore, T. J. 2008. Model-eliciting activities: A case-based approach for getting students interested in material science and engineering. *Journal of Materials Education* 30(5–6), 295–310.

National Academy of Engineering. 2005. *Assessing the capacity of the U.S. engineering research enterprise.* Washington, DC: The National Academy Press.

Nelson, Harold G., and Erik Stolterman. 2003. *The design way: Intentional change in a unpredictable world.* Englewood Cliffs, NJ: Educational Technology Publications.

Page, S. E. 2009. *Understanding complexity.* The Great Courses. Chantilly, VA: The Teaching Company.

Papalambros, Panos Y., and Douglass J. Wilde. 1988. *Principles of optimal design: Modeling and computation.* Cambridge: Cambridge University Press.

Perkins, David. 2002. *King Arthur's round table: How collaborative conversations create smart organizations.* New York: Wiley.

———. 2010. *Making learning whole: How seven principles of teaching can transform education.* San Francisco: Jossey-Bass.

Peter D. Hart Research Associates. 2006. *Report of findings based on focus groups among business executives.* Washington, DC: Peter D. Hart Research Associates.

Petroski, Henry. 2003. *Small things considered: Why there is no perfect design.* New York: Knopf.

———. 2003. Failure is always an option. *New York Times*, August 29.

Pink, Daniel H. 2005. *A whole new mind: Moving from the information age to the conceptual age.* New York: Riverhead Books.

Ravindran, A., Don T. Phillips, and James J. Solberg. 1987. *Operations research: Principles and practice*, 2nd ed. New York: Wiley.

Ray, Michael, and Alan Rinzler, eds. 1993. *The new paradigm in business: Emerging strategies for leadership and organizational change.* Los Angeles: Tarcher/Perigee.

Roadstrum, W. H. 1988. *Being successful as an engineer.* San Jose: Engineering Press.

Rothenberg, James. 1989. The nature of modeling. In *Artificial intelligence, simulation and modeling*, edited by L. E. Widman, K. A. Loparo, and N. R. Nielsen. New York: Wiley.

Schein, Edgar H. et al. 2003. *DEC is dead: Long live DEC—The lasting legacy of Digital Equipment Corporation.* San Francisco: Berrett-Koehler.

Selinger, Carl. 2004. *Stuff you don't learn in engineering school: Skills for success in the real world.* New York: Wiley.

Senge, Peter. 1990. *The fifth discipline: The art and practice of the learning organization.* New York: Doubleday.

———. 1993. The art and practice of the learning organization. In *The new paradigm in business: Emerging strategies for leadership and organizational change (A new consciousness reader)*, edited by Alan Rinzler and Michael Ray. Los Angeles: Tarcher.

Sheppard, Sheri, Anne Colby, Kelly Macatangay, and William Sullivan. 2005. *What is engineering practice?* Presented at 2005 Harvey Mudd Design Workshop.

Shina, S. G. 1991. New rules for world-class companies. *Special Report on Concurrent Engineering*, edited by A. Rosenblatt and G. F. Watson. *IEEE Spectrum* 28(7), 22–37.

Shulman, Lee S. 1998. Theory, practice, and the education of professionals. *The Elementary School Journal* 98(5), 511–526.

Shuman, Larry J., Mary Besterfield-Sacre, and Jack McGourty. 2005. The ABET "professional skills"—Can they be taught? Can they be assessed? *Journal of Engineering Education* 94(1), 41–56.

Sparks, E., and M. J. Waits. 2011. *Degrees for what jobs? Raising expectations for universities and colleges in a global economy.* National Governors Association.

Starfield, Anthony M. 1999. *Principles of modeling.* Unpublished workshop notes. Fort Collins, CO. May 17–24.

———. 2005. *Heuristics or rules of thumb for modeling.* Personal communication. July 14, 2005.

Starfield, Anthony M., Karl A. Smith, and Andrew L. Bleloch. 1990. *How to model it: Problem solving for the computer age.* New York: McGraw-Hill.

———. 1994. *How to model it: Problem solving for the computer age,* updated edition. Edina: Interaction Book Company.

Surowiecki, James. 2004. *The wisdom of crowds: Why the many are smarter than the few and how collective wisdom shapes business, economies, societies and nations.* New York: Doubleday.

Surowiecki, Jim. 1997. Decision time. *Rogue missives,* January 6, http://www.fool.com/Rogue/1997/Rogue970106.htm (accessed 3/9/03).

Tribus, Myron. 1996. Total quality management in schools of business and engineering. In *Academic initiatives in total quality for higher education,* edited by Harry V. Roberts, 17–40. Milwaukee: ASQC Quality Press.

Van de Ven, Andrew H., Douglas E. Polley, Raghu Garud, and Sankaran Venkataraman. 1999. *The innovation journey.* Oxford: Oxford University Press.

Weisbord, Marvin R. 1987. *Productive workplaces: Organizing and managing for dignity, meaning, and community.* San Francisco: Jossey-Bass.

CHAPTER 2

Framing and Aligning the Project and Team

"Would you tell me, please, which way I ought to go from here?"

"That depends a good deal on where you want to get to," said the Cat.

"I don't much care where—" said Alice.

"Then it doesn't matter which way you go," said the Cat.

"—so long as I get SOMEWHERE," Alice added as an explanation.

"Oh, you're sure to do that," said the Cat, "if you only walk long enough."

ALICE'S ADVENTURES IN WONDERLAND

The above quote is often mistakenly referred to as: "If you don't know where you're going, any road will get you there." It also represents conventional wisdom for project management, that is, the importance of a clear goal and deliverables. While clear goals and deliverables are essential for projects, the path to or process for achieving the goal is not always clearly specified.

The overarching purpose of Chapter 2 is to assist the reader to effectively and efficiently organize and manage projects to either (1) support ongoing operations or (2) support innovation, which are described by March (1991), Martin (2009), and Page (2009) as the explore–exploit trade-off, and by Govindarajan and Trimble (2010) as the Performance Engine vs. Innovation. This is a brief chapter; however, my sense is that it is probably one of the most important chapters in the book because it argues that the best approach to project management is IT DEPENDS.

The principal questions that need to be answered to categorize a project are: (1) how clear is the goal/task/deliverable? and (2) how clear is the path/process? Responses to these questions help guide the choice of project management approach and, in part, the type of team that is most likely to pull it off. Figure 2.1 adapted from Wysocki (2011) helps position projects:

Figure 2.1   Selecting a Project Management Approach

Process Clarity	Goal/Task/Deliverables Clarity	
	Low	**High**
High	Adaptive Project Management (APM)	Traditional Project Management (TPM)
Low	Punt	Adaptive Project Management (APM)

If the goal, task and/or deliverable is well defined and the process needed to reach it is clear, then a Traditional Project Management (TPM) approach is probably well suited. If either the goal or the process is not well defined, then an Adaptive Project Management (APM) approach is probably best. Adaptive Project Management is a relatively new idea, and is probably most often identified with the Agile Manifesto (2001) and the Declaration of Interdependence (2005).

If neither the goal nor the process is clear, then it may be best to avoid the project; or if there is a strong hunch of promising territory, then perhaps the best approach is to jump in and see what emerges.

 REFLECTION Think about the projects you've been involved in and where they fit in Figure 2.1. What proportion fall in the clear goal/clear path quadrant?

I've asked this question to students in my Management of Technology (MOT) and Infrastructure Systems Management and Engineering (ISME) MS classes as well as participants in workshops such as the MSPE Engineers Leadership Institute, and in each case the response is "About 20 percent." Figure 2.2

Figure 2.2   Distribution of PM Work—Innovation and Ongoing Operations

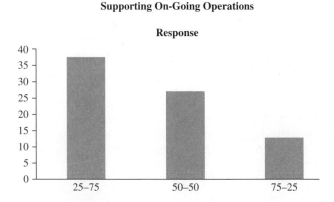

shows more detailed survey results for four groups of the participants (primarily engineers) in these classes and workshops.

These data indicate that about one-half of the respondents report that at least 50 percent of their work is focused on supporting innovation.

Additional survey results indicate that the majority of their work is project work and that most are working on five or fewer projects (Figure 2.3).

Initially, I was stunned at the class and workshop respondents' spontaneous comment that only about one in five projects fit in the clear goal/clear process quadrant, and the data in Figure 2.2 indicates that for these 80 predominantly engineers it may be higher than that. Wysocki notes in his 2011

Figure 2.3   Percentage of Project Work and Number of Projects

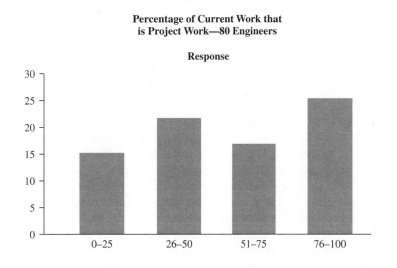

**Percentage of Current Work that
is Project Work—80 Engineers**

Response

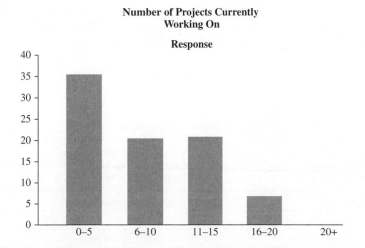

**Number of Projects Currently
Working On**

Response

Executive's Guide to Project Management that testimonial data suggests about 20 percent of all business projects fit in the TPM category. Yet the predominant project management approach is TPM.

Selecting a project management approach requires deciding if your project is focused on supporting ongoing operations (exploitation) or supporting innovation (exploration). James March (1991) described these contrasting approaches as exploitation (doing old things better) and exploration (doing new things).

Reflection on Exploration and Exploitation

I encountered James March's (1991) article many years ago and the idea lay dormant until about 10 years ago or so when I started mentioning it in my project and knowledge management graduate classes. It didn't seem to resonate with the students. I summarized the idea in this book's third edition, but almost gave up on the idea and was considering removing it from my project and knowledge management courses and books. In 2009 and 2010 the floodgates opened and numerous authors embraced March's idea. The explore–exploit trade-off is back and is an organizing feature of the fourth edition.

March's (1991) distinction between exploitation and exploration, summarized in Table 2.1, provides some guidance on differences.

Roger Martin elaborated on the characteristics of exploration and exploitation in his 2009 book *Design of Business* (Table 1-1, p. 20). Martin's comparison, shown in Table 2.2, provides deeper insight into the nature of projects in these two domains, especially the contrast between the two in "overriding goal," "driving forces," "progress," and "risk and reward." He also highlights the potential challenge if there is too much emphasis on either.

Complexity theorist and author Scott Page argues in his 2009 *Understanding Complexity* Lecture 5, Explore–Exploit: The Fundamental Trade-Off, that to succeed in a complex environment requires balancing exploration and exploitation. He highlights the need for both and, as with Martin, suggests potential catastrophic consequences of overemphasis on either. Complexity and complex adaptive systems are discussed further in Chapter 15, Teamwork for the Future.

Govindarajan and Trimble (2010) in *The Other Side of Innovation* articulate key differences between typical planning processes for the Performance Engine and best practices for innovation (Table 4.1, p. 99). Similar to Martin (2009)

Table 2.1 Exploiting Old Ways vs. Exploring New Ways

Exploiting Old Ways: Organizing for Routine Work	Exploring New Ways: Organizing for Innovative Work
Drive out variance	Enhance variance
See old things in old ways	See old things in new ways
Replicate the past	Break from the past
Goal: Make money now	Goal: Make money later

Table 2.2 Martin, Design of Business (2009), Table 1-1

	Exploration	**Exploitation**
Organizational focus	The invention of business	The administration of business
Overriding goal	Dynamically moving from the current knowledge stage to the next	Systematically honing and refining within the current knowledge stage
Driving forces	Intuition, feeling, hypotheses about the future, originality	Analysis, reasoning, data from the past, mastery
Future orientation	Long-term	Short-term
Progress	Uneven, scattered, characterized by false starts and significant leaps forward	Accomplished by measured, careful incremental steps
Risk and reward	High risk, uncertain but potentially high reward	Minimal risk, predictable but smaller rewards
Challenge	Failure to consolidate and exploit returns	Exhaustion and obsolescence

and Page (2009), Govindarajan and Trimble argue that both are important and must be balanced in order to succeed. Their comparison of planning processes summarized in Table 2.3 is an excellent guide to thinking about an appropriate approach to project management.

As you can see from these representations and comparisons of exploration and exploitation, and all the varieties of descriptions, the most effective approach to project management and teamwork depends to a great extent on which of these best describes your situation. Furthermore, it is important to develop a repertoire of skills for working on as well as organizing, managing and leading both (all) types of projects.

Table 2.3 Typical Planning Processes for the Performance Engine and Best Practices for Innovation (Govindarajan and Trimble, 2010, Table 4.1)

Planning Principles for Innovation	**Norm in Performance Engine**
Invest heavily in planning	Invest in proportion to budget
Create the plan and the scorecard from scratch	Just modify last year's plan
Discuss data and assumptions	Focus on data
Document a clear hypothesis of record	Document clear expectations
Find ways to spend a little, learn a lot	Be on budget, on time, and on spec
Create a separate forum for discussing results	Separate forums are unnecessary
Frequently reassess the plan	Deliver the results in the plan
Analyze trends	Analyze totals
Allow formal revisions to predictions	Revisions frowned on
Evaluate innovation leaders subjectively	Evaluate based on results

GROUP REFLECTION Discuss and develop a strategy for identifying project features (based on the comparisons of March, Martin, Page, and Govindarajan and Trimble) that you can use to guide your approach to organizing and managing new projects. Additionally, start to identify specific projects that fit into each of these categories.

Routine, ongoing operations such as assembly, fabrication, food service, hotel management, purchasing and payroll fit fairly well in the exploitation category and can be managed via traditional project management strategies.

More complicated and complex operations such as logistics and supply chain, computer and IT services, and construction may be approached via traditional project management; however, a combination of traditional and adaptive approaches might be more effective.

Innovative operations such as design and development of new products or services, research and development, and program development likely can be approached most effectively with adaptive or agile project management strategies.

Amy Edmondson provides a different perspective in her book on teaming on the contrasting approaches involved in exploration versus exploitation projects. She describes the contrast as organizing to execute versus organizing to learn (Edmondson, 2012), which will be elaborated on in Chapter 15.

The Waterfall Model Is Wrong and Harmful; We Must Outgrow It—Fred Brooks

Fred Brooks, author of the famous project management book, *The Mythical Man-Month: Essays on Software Engineering* (Brooks, 1975, 1995), argues in his recent book *The Design of Design: Essays from a Computer Scientist* (Brooks, 2010): "A design is a created object, associated with a design process, which I shall call design, without any article. Then there is the verb to design." He contrasts *original design* (the design of complex systems in which his viewpoint is that of the engineer who is focused on utility and effectiveness but also on efficiency and elegance) with the *routine redesign* of an object with changed parameters and *adaptive design*, which is essentially the modification of a preceding design or object to serve new purposes.

Traditional project management approaches are suitable for routine design and to some extent for adaptive design; however, a different approach is needed for original design. Approaches for original design are presented in Chapters 8 and 15.

References

Agile Manifesto. 2001. *Manifesto for Agile Software Development*, ©2001, http://agilemanifesto.org/principles.html.

Brooks, Frederick P. 1975, 1995. *The mythical man-month: Essays on software engineering.* Upper Saddle River, NJ: Addison-Wesley.

Brooks, Frederick P. 2010. *The design of design: Essays from a computer scientist*. Upper Saddle River, NJ: Addison-Wesley.

Declaration of Interdependence. 2005. *Agile and adaptive approaches for linking people, projects and value*, http://pmdoi.org/.

Edmondson, A. C. 2012. *Teaming: How organizations learn, innovate, and compete in the knowledge economy*. San Francisco: Jossey-Bass.

Govindarajan, Vijay, and Chris Trimble. 2010. *The other side of innovation: Solving the execution challenge*. Cambridge, MA: Harvard Business School Press.

March, James G. 1991. Exploration and exploitation in organizational learning. *Organization Science* 2(1), 71–87.

Martin, Roger. 2009. *The design of business: Why design thinking is the next competitive advantage*. Boston, MA: Harvard Business Press.

Page, S. E. 2009. *Understanding complexity*. The Great Courses. Chantilly, VA: The Teaching Company.

Wysocki, Robert K. 2011. *Executive's guide to project management: Organizational processes and practices for supporting complex projects*. New York: Wiley.

CHAPTER 3

Teamwork Basics

*Everyone has to work together; if we can't get everybody working toward
common goals, nothing is going to happen.*

HAROLD K. SPERLICH,
Former President, Chrysler Corporation

Coming together is a beginning;
Keeping together is progress;
Working together is success.

HENRY FORD

 REFLECTION Think about a really effective team you've been a member of, a team that accomplished extraordinary things and perhaps was even a great place to be. Start by thinking about teams in an academic, professional, or work setting. If no examples come to mind, then think about social or community-based teams. If again you don't conjure up an example, then think about sports teams. Finally, if you don't come up with a scenario from any of these contexts, then simply imagine yourself as a member of a really effective team. OK, do you have a picture of the team in mind? As you recall (or imagine) this highly effective team experience, try to identify the specific characteristics of the team that made it so effective. Please list these characteristics. Now that you have made a list of characteristics for a highly effective team, what attributes do you think describe a really *in*effective team? As you did above, recall (or imagine) a team you were on that you considered to be highly *in*effective. What characteristics do you believe made the team ineffective? Again, please make a list.

Look over the lists you made for the Reflection. What were the key characteristics that defined an effective and ineffective team? Sometimes it is as important for you to simply think about attributes of an ineffective team, so that as you begin to learn about characteristics of effective teams, you will understand their importance. Did you preface either of your lists with "It depends"? The characteristics of an effective team depend, of course, on the purpose of the team. In large measure they depend on goals related to the team's task (what the team is to do) and maintenance (how the team functions). Michael Schrage (1991) states emphatically:

> People must understand that real value in the sciences, the arts, commerce, and, indeed one's personal and professional lives, come[s] largely from the process of collaboration. What's more, the quality and quantity of meaningful collaboration often depend upon the tools used to create it. . . . Collaboration is a purposive relationship. At the heart of collaboration is a desire or need to: solve a problem, create, or discover something. (pp. 27, 34)

Let's assume that an effective team has both task goals and maintenance goals, because most effective teams not only have a job to do (a report to write, a project to complete, a presentation to give, etc.) but also a goal of getting better at working with one another.

I've used the Reflection that started the chapter with hundreds of faculty and students in workshop and classroom settings. Here is a typical list of the characteristics of effective teams:

Good participation	Common goal
Respect	Sense of purpose
Careful listening	Good meeting facilitation
Leadership	Empowered members
Constructively managed conflict	Members take responsibility
Fun, liked to be there	Effective decision making

My goal for this chapter is to help you get a sense of the essential characteristics of teams that perform at a high level by drawing on your experience (as I have tried to do above) and introduce you to some of the rapidly expanding literature in this area. I will remind you of the importance of maintaining a team climate that embraces and celebrates diversity, then summarize some of the classic work on stages of team development. Finally, I aim to acquaint you with emerging notions, such as "communities of practice," "network quotient," and "emotional intelligence."

Definition of a Team

Katzenbach and Smith (1993) studied teams that performed at a variety of levels and came up with four categories:

> *Pseudo teams* perform below the level of the average member.
> *Potential teams* don't quite get going but struggle along at or slightly above the level of the average member.
> *Real teams* perform quite well.
> *High-performing teams* perform at an extraordinary level.

Katzenbach and Smith then looked for common characteristics of real teams and high-performing teams. All real teams fit this description: a small number of people with complementary skills who are committed to a common purpose, performance goals, and approach for which they hold themselves mutually accountable. High-performing teams met all the conditions of real teams and, in addition, had members who were deeply committed to one another's personal growth and success.

 REFLECTION Now think about the teams in your engineering classes. Think about your most successful and effective team project experience. What were the characteristics of the team? What were the conditions? Are they similar to those of your most effective teams? Describe the team development process.

Types of Learning Teams

There is nothing magical about teamwork in engineering classes. Some types of learning teams increase the quality of classroom life and facilitate student learning. Other types of teams hinder student learning and create disharmony and dissatisfaction with classroom life. To use teamwork effectively, you must know what is and what is not an effective team.

There are many types of teams that can be used in classrooms. Formal cooperative learning groups are just one of them, although they are becoming quite common (Johnson, Johnson, and Smith, 1998a, 1998b, 2007; Smith, Sheppard, Johnson, and Johnson, 2005). When you choose to use (or are required to use) groups as part of a course, you must ask yourself, What type of group or team am I involved in? Figure 3.1 and the following descriptions of groups may help you answer that question.

Figure 3.1 Group Performance

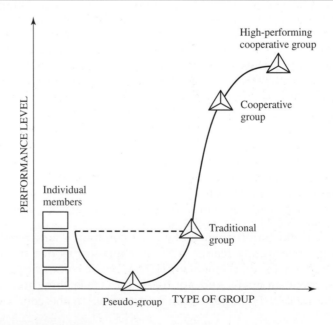

Pseudo Learning Group

Students in a pseudo learning group are assigned to work together but they have no interest in doing so. They believe they will be evaluated by being ranked in terms of highest performer to lowest performer. On the surface these students talk to each other, but under the surface they are competing. They see each other as rivals who must be defeated, and they block or interfere with each other's learning, hide information from each other, attempt to mislead and confuse each other, and distrust each other. These students would achieve more if they were working alone.

Traditional Classroom Learning Group

Students in a traditional classroom learning group are assigned to work together and accept that they must do so. But because assignments are structured, very little joint work is required. These students believe that they will be evaluated and rewarded as individuals, not as members of the group, so they interact primarily to clarify how assignments are to be done. They seek each other's information, but have no motivation to teach what they know to their groupmates. Helping and sharing is minimized. Some students loaf, seeking a free ride on the efforts of their more conscientious groupmates. The conscientious members feel exploited and do less. The result is that the sum of the whole is more than the potential of some of the members, but the harder working, more conscientious students would perform better if they worked alone.

Cooperative Learning Groups

Students in cooperative learning groups are assigned to work together and, given the complexity of the task and the necessity for diverse perspectives, most members are relieved to do so. They know that their success depends on the efforts of all group members. The group format is clearly defined: (1) The group goal of maximizing all members' learning provides a compelling common purpose that motivates members to roll up their sleeves and accomplish something beyond their individual achievements. (2) Group members hold themselves and each other accountable for doing high-quality work to achieve their mutual goals. (3) Group members work face-to-face to produce joint work-products. They do real work together. Students promote each other's success through helping, sharing, assisting, explaining, and encouraging. They provide both academic and personal support based on a commitment to and caring about each other. (4) Group members are taught teamwork skills and are expected to use them to coordinate their efforts and achieve their goals. Both task and team-building skills are emphasized. All members share responsibility for providing leadership. (5) Groups analyze how effectively they are achieving their goals and how well members are working together. There is an emphasis on continual improvement of the quality of learning and teamwork processes.

High-Performance Cooperative Learning Group

A high-performance cooperative learning group meets all the criteria for being a cooperative learning group and outperforms all reasonable expectations, given its membership. What differentiates the high-performance group from the cooperative learning group is the level of commitment members have to each other and the group's success. Jennifer Futernick, who is part of a high-performing, rapid-response team at McKinsey & Company, calls the emotional binding together of her teammates a form of love (Katzenbach and Smith, 1993). Ken Hoepner of the Burlington Northern Intermodal Transport Team, stated: "Not only did we trust each other, not only did we respect each other, but we gave a damn about the rest of the people on this team. If we saw somebody vulnerable, we were there to help" (Katzenbach and Smith, 1993). Members' mutual concern for each other's personal growth enables high-performance cooperative groups to perform far above expectations, and also to have lots of fun. The bad news about extraordinarily high-performance cooperative learning groups is that they are rare. Most groups never achieve this level of development.

J. Richard Hackman (2002) has done extensive research on teams and argues in his book *Leading Teams: Setting the Stage for Great Performances* that there are five key elements:

- Real Team
- Compelling Direction
- Enabling Structure
- Supportive Organizational Context
- Available Expert Coaching

A "real team" is characterized by the following features:

- Clear boundaries.
- Team members are interdependent for some common purpose, producing a potentially assessable outcome for which members bear collective responsibility.
- At least moderate stability of membership.

A team with "compelling direction" has good team direction, which is:

- Challenging (which energizes members)
- Clear (which orients them to their main purposes)
- Consequential (which engages the full range of their talents)

And a team with "enabling structure" has key structural features in fostering competent teamwork, including:

- Task design: The team task should be well aligned with the team's purpose and have a high standing on "motivating potential."
- Team composition: The team size should be as small as possible given the work to be accomplished, should include members with ample task and interpersonal skills, and should consist of a good diversity of membership.
- Core norms of conduct: Team should have established early in its life clear and explicit specification of the basic norms of conduct for member behavior.

Hackman also developed an excellent team survey, the Team Diagnostic Survey (TDS), which will be described in more detail in Chapter 12.

Amy Edmondson claims in a 2011 interview that "it is the end of the team as we know it" (http://www.forbes.com/sites/karlmoore/2011/07/19/hbss-amy-edmondson-on-the-death-of-teams/). In her 2012 book, *Teaming: How Organizations Learn, Innovate, and Compete in the Knowledge Economy*, Edmondson writes that "teaming, coined deliberately to capture the activity of working together, presents a new, more flexible way for organizations to carry out interdependent tasks" (p. 2). Prior work, Hackman, for example, treated "team" as a noun; whereas Edmondson argues that teaming is a verb.

Groups and Teams

I've been using the term *team* in reference to projects and *group* in reference to learning, but I will use these two terms interchangeably throughout this book. Though the traditional literature focuses on groups, recently some writers have been making distinctions between groups and teams. For example, Table 3.1 presents Katzenbach and Smith's (1993) summary of the major differences between working groups and teams.

Are there any surprises in this list, from your perspective? Many students emphasize the importance of a strong leader, but Katzenbach and Smith indicate that real teams, as opposed to working groups, have shared leadership roles. Also, the literature on high-performance teams indicates that they are composed of members with complementary skills; that is, they're diverse.

Regardless of whether you call them groups or teams, as we move from the information age (where knowledge workers ruled) to the conceptual age (where creators and empathizers will rule), the horizontal element of the T-shaped person will become more and more important. Expertise involving analysis is still important of course, but only provides one pillar (or column in engineering terminology) of the T-shaped person.

David Radcliffe's reflection in the nearby box on Reid Hoffman's book *The Start-up of You* provides deeper insight into the need for dynamic and adaptive teamwork.

Table 3.1 Not All Groups Are Teams: How to Tell the Difference

Working Group	Team
Strong, clearly focused leader	Shared leadership roles
Individual accountability	Individual and mutual accountability
The group's purpose is the same as the broader organizational mission	Specific team purpose that the team itself delivers
Individual work-products	Collective work-products
Runs efficient meetings	Encourages open-ended discussion and active problem-solving meetings
Measures its effectiveness indirectly by its influence on others	Measures performance directly by assessing collective work-products
Discusses, decides, and delegates	Discusses, decides, and does real work together

Source: Katzenbach and Smith, 1993.

Agile Careers in "Permanent Beta"

As a pioneering school in a new discipline, there is considerable uncertainty about how our chosen field will develop and what career opportunities will emerge. Unlike established disciplines, we do not have 50 or 100 years of history to examine as we think about and plan our future, individually or collectively, nor even exemplars or role models to emulate. But given the current level of volatility in many established industries and professions, maybe there is a distinct advantage to being in a new and emergent discipline. Many traditional assumptions about career paths no longer hold; jobs for life and earnestly climbing the corporate ladder are things of the past. Even in the relatively stable world of higher education, many long-held assumptions are being questioned, and traditional ways of operating may be subject to *disruptive change*.

Reid Hoffman, co-founder and CEO of LinkedIn and member of the "PayPal mafia," has co-authored a book on career planning for these uncertain times and unpredictable job prospects. Drawing parallels between entrepreneurial ventures and individual careers, he argues that as we plan for possible futures we should be prepared to be in permanent beta mode, much as products from technology companies are always in a state of continuous development, never quite finished. In a discussion with Tom Friedman on the book, Hoffman states that "for entrepreneurs *finished* is an F-word," and just as great companies are always evolving, so will future careers, and thus "*finished* ought to be an F-word for all of us."

He argues that there are three factors that comprise our individual competitive advantage as we each craft a career in volatile times: our assets, our aspirations and the market realities. We each have two kinds of assets, soft and hard, and it is our soft assets in which we should invest strategically. Our aspirations are our interests, passions, desires, and values. But just having excellent assets and clear aspirations is not sufficient; these have to be operationalized in the prevailing "market realities," which can either limit or enhance our career plans.

Rather than having a rigid, long-term plan that you play out, Hoffman argues that future career success depends on being "both persistent *and* flexible"; i.e., be short term *and* long term in your thinking. He introduces the idea of ABZ planning. Plan A is what you are doing now, the current implementation of your competitive advantage. Plan B is what you pivot into when Plan A is no longer working or if you find a better path towards your goal. Of course we all need a Plan Z, the lifeboat that we can revert to if things go bad; it is Plan Z that enables us to take on uncertainty in Plan A and B. This way of approaching an emergent, contingent career aligns perfectly with the thinking behind the reflexive portfolio we ask our PhD students to initiate and hopefully continue for the rest of their life as a critical navigation tool for uncertain times and places: *permanent beta*. I am reminded of Lucy Suchman's book from the late 1980s, *Plans and Situated Actions*, and the story of the Trukese navigators.

Another interesting idea put forward by Hoffman is that of I^{We}—that is to say, "I" to the power "We." As co-founder of LinkedIn, it is not surprising that he stresses the importance of professional networking. That said, the concept of I^{We} places the focus on "how you and your network, *working together*, can achieve amazing things," not simply how you can leverage others for your personal advantage. This is worth some deeper thought.

The more alumni from Purdue's Interdisciplinary Engineering (IDE) program that I meet, the more impressed I am at the diverse, unpredictable yet amazing careers these people have created over the past three or four decades. Being pioneers in an out-of-the-ordinary and hard-to-explain major, they had no choice but to make their own way. They did not have a guidebook, but nevertheless they somehow figured it out for themselves and used very similar strategies to those that Hoffman has distilled. Similarly, our engineering education (ENE) PhD graduates and current graduate students are embarking with agility on emergent careers that may never be quite finished, imagined through *flexible persistence*. Becoming a faculty member in ENE typically involved pivoting from Plan A to Plan B, which then became the new Plan A.

Reid Hoffman's book is *The Start-up of You*. I heard about this new release from our recent outstanding alumna, Leslie Bottorff, a venture capitalist who works in Silicon Valley and who personifies an agile career, always learning, willing to take *intelligent risks* and bold enough to *pivot to Plan B* to grasp *breakout opportunities*.

David Radcliffe

Teams at the undergraduate level are typically structured and sometimes organized by the faculty, and hopefully the structure and organization is based on research on effective teams.

 REFLECTION Take a moment to reflect on the structure and organization of teams you've been a part of. How were they formed? How large were they? How was diversity managed? How long did you work together? Did you create a team charter? Were there assigned roles?

There are several ways of forming teams. One of the most common at the undergraduate level is letting the participants decide, that is, asking members to form the teams themselves. Although this approach is common, it can be awkward and ineffective, especially if the participants in the class don't know one another or, worse still, if some people know one another and others don't. More effective ways of forming teams for achieving both individual learning and team performance are (1) identifying common interests, in terms of the project for example; (2) distributing relevant prior experience and expertise; (3) assessing and then distributing students with different levels of motivation and prior team experience; (4) maintaining academic and social support networks within teams (but making sure people have access to peer support); and (5) if time is short and the teams will not be together for too long, form them randomly.

Holly Matusovich's reflection in the nearby box on her engineering experience and her research on motivation provides insights into many essential aspects of effective teams.

Value the Differences That Motivate People and Harness Them for Maximal Engagement

As a practicing engineer, I learned an important lesson. People are different and there is no more important time to remember and value this than when working on teams. Sure we know that people have different likes and dislikes. We see this in the ways that people make different choices about what car to buy or what to eat for lunch. In these settings it seems obvious. However, in working on teams, with a common goal, it is easy to forget that people engage in their work in different ways and for different reasons. It is easy to assume that everyone wants to be part of the team for the same reasons or that everyone sees the project moving in the same direction. However, this is often not the case nor perhaps should it be

the case because it is variation in perspectives that makes truly collaborative team products better; individual differences allow people to view the product differently. It is also this variation that can lead to team conflict.

Since becoming an academic, I have found that Expectancy-Value Theory of Motivation provides a useful way to think about being a member of a team or even leading a team. This theory suggests that people engage in activities that they think they *can* do and that they *want* to do. How does this relate to teamwork? First, team members could strive to help each other feel competent. For example, don't laugh at ideas. Encourage people to be creative and draw on their individual strengths and abilities. This goes for skills that may not seem immediately relevant to the project too. Good, creative ideas come from thinking outside the box. Team members could also strive to make the team activity something that everyone wants to do. This means remembering that people have different interests and find different things important. This means remembering that everyone has many things pulling on their time and choosing to participate in the team often means not doing something else. Importantly, this means talking to people; in work or in school, we sometimes do not know what motivates our colleagues and engaging in conversation is a really good way to find out.

Holly Matusovich

Team size is another area where care and attention during formation and structuring is needed. Team size needs to be appropriate for the task as well as the teamwork skills of the members, neither too small nor too large. David Perkins' (2002, p. 76) figure plotting Group IQ as a function of the Group size shows maximum Group IQ between 3 and 4 heads. Steiner's (1972) research, reported in Hackman (2002, pp. 116–117) notes that Potential Productivitiy increases with the number of members (but levels off), whereas Process Losses also increase but at an accelerating rate. Steiner's research indicates that Actual Productivity reaches a peak between four and five members. Hackman (2002, p. 115) notes that the three biggest mistakes people make when they compose a team are:

1. They assume "the more the better" and therefore put too many people on the team.
2. They assume that people who are similar to one another will get along better, and therefore compose a team that is too homogeneous.
3. They assume that everyone knows how to work in a group, and therefore pay too little attention to the interpersonal skills of prospective members.

Team diversity is another challenging area, since we often must work with people who are different from us or difficult to work with but whose skills, talents, expertise, and experience are essential to the project. Working with a diverse group may seem impossible at times, but look at the example of Phil Jackson, former head coach of the Chicago Bulls basketball team. Can you imagine a more diverse group than one made up of Dennis Rodman, Michael Jordan, and Scottie Pippin, along with the rest? Phil Jackson is an expert at managing diversity, as his success throughout his career testifies.

Diversity has many faces, including preferred learning preference (visual, auditory, kinesthetic); social background and experience; ethnic and cultural heritage; gender; and sexual orientation. The evidence from effective groups is that diversity is important—that is, the better the group represents the broader community, the more likely it is to make significant, creative, and desired contributions. Participating in and managing diverse groups is not always easy, because diverse groups usually bring a diversity of ideas and priorities. Here are some considerations that may help you learn to manage diverse groups more effectively (Cabanis, 1997; Cherbeneau, 1997):

1. Learn skills for working with all kinds of people.
2. Stress that effective teams are diverse.

3. Stress the importance of requirements.
4. Emphasize performance.
5. Develop perspective-taking skills (i.e., put yourself in others' shoes).
6. Respect and appreciate alternative perspectives.

The Chicago Bulls' former head coach Phil Jackson argued that "Good teams become great ones when the members trust each other enough to surrender the 'me' for the 'we.'" In his 1995 book (coauthored by Hugh Delehanty) *Sacred Hoops: Spiritual Lessons of a Hardwood Warrior,* Jackson offers terrific advice on organizing and managing extraordinarily high-performing teams.

Reflection on Diversity

As a faculty member concerned with preparing students to work effectively with other people and in a variety of settings, I've grappled with the question, "Why bother?" Why should we be concerned about the diversity of student team members' experiences? Here are the reasons I've identified.

First, little attention is paid to the fact that not all students are the same. University of Minnesota astronomy professor Larry Rudnick once said, "I used to think all students learn exactly the same way I do; perhaps a little slower." It seems that many faculty assume that students are basically like themselves, not only in learning styles but in many other characteristics as well—outlook, cultural or ethnic background, experience, motivation, expectations, sexual orientation. This "sameness" approach is simpler, easier, and safer for faculty. If faculty need to design only a single, one-size-fits-all instructional system (probably the one they experienced as a student), they'll have a system that they find familiar and manageable. Faculty who acknowledge that learners are different must face lots of unknowns, and more work. But when faculty don't provide students with opportunities for diverse experiences in the classroom, students are less likely to learn the skills and knowledge they will need to work in teams with diverse membership.

The consequences of ignoring differences can be enormous. For example, they affect simple testing situations. Students from some cultures (some Native Americans and Asians, for example) are reluctant to correct others or to make them look bad in front of their peers. When there is an individual test followed by a group test format, such students might get a higher individual score but won't contradict the group during the group exam portion. Typically such a student will explain such behavior by saying that in their culture it's unacceptable to correct another person. One group dealt with this difference by always having the Asian-American students go first during the group exam portion.

Second, U.S. demographics are changing very rapidly, and undergraduate engineering enrollments don't reflect the broader diversity. Many students will choose to avoid fields of study where they don't see students like themselves enrolled, partly because they feel unwelcome.

William A. Wulf (1998), former president of the National Academy of Engineering, stressed this point in his article "Diversity in Engineering":

Every time an engineering problem is approached with a pale, male design team, it may be difficult to find the best solution, understand the design options, or know how to evaluate the constraints. (p. 8)

Wulf also made a case for the connection between diversity and creativity:

Collective diversity, or diversity of the group—the kind of diversity that people usually talk about—is just as essential to good engineering as individual diversity. At a fundamental level, men, women, ethnic minorities, racial minorities, and people with handicaps, experience the world differently. Those differences in experience are the "gene pool" from which creativity springs. (p. 11)

People who don't see themselves represented can find it hard to be interested in the designs, products, and services created by engineers, and engineering in turn is deprived of their marvelous talents.

Third, the trend toward globalization as described in the Preface and Chapter 1 means that engineering graduates will likely be working for international companies and on globally distributed teams. The more extensive and deeper the understanding of people from other countries and especially other languages, the easier it will be to work in the global workplace.

Fourth, diversity is the law of the land. At least three times (in *Brown v. Board of Education,* Title IX, and PL 94-142), the United States Supreme Court and Congress have reemphasized that all citizens have equal rights and opportunities—in particular, that all individuals, regardless of differences, have a right to access to the broader peer group.

Finally, a compelling argument for the importance of diversity comes from complexity theory and complex adaptive systems (Axelrod and Cohen, 2001; Miller and Page, 2007). Page (2009) claims that a "system can be considered complex if its agents meet four qualifications: diversity, connection, interdependence, and adaptation" (p. 4). Furthermore, he argues that "the attributes of interdependence, connectedness, diversity, and adaptation and learning generate complexity" (p. 10). In terms of diversity, Page (2009) argues that "progress depends as much on our collective differences as it does on our individual IQ scores."

How long to leave teams together is the next dimension of team structure and organization to consider, and there is some disagreement in the literature. Hackman (2002) argues, as noted earlier in this chapter, that "real teams" have at least moderate stability of membership. Edmondson (2012) argues that teaming is essential, that is, readily being able to move in and out of teams effectively and efficiently.

From a learning perspective it is essential to keep teams together long enough for them to succeed, that is, complete the task and help each member learn; and to provide opportunities for each student to work with as many other students as practical.

A Theory of Effective Teams

There is an extensive literature on highly effective teams in the workplace (Bennis and Biederman, 1997; Edmondson, 2012; Hackman, 2002; Hargrove,

work lacks a theoretical foundation. An exception is the research on cooperative learning, which is primarily classroom based (Johnson, Johnson, and
Smith, 1991, 1998a, 1998b, 2007; Smith, Sheppard, Johnson, and Johnson,
2005). Cooperative learning is based on Social Interdependence Theory
(Lewin, 1935; Johnson and Johnson, 2005) and the practice and implementation is described by these five Essential Elements of Cooperative Learning
(Johnson and Johnson, 2005):

1. *Positive interdependence.* The team focuses on a common goal or single
   product.
2. *Individual and group accountability.* Each person takes responsibility for
   both her or his own work and the overall work of the team.
3. *Promotive interaction.* The members do real work, usually face to face.
4. *Teamwork skills.* Each member has the skills for and practices effective
   communication (especially careful listening), decision making, problem
   solving, conflict management, and leadership.
5. *Group processing.* The team periodically reflects on how well the team is
   working, celebrates the things that are going well, and corrects the
   things that aren't.

Teams have become commonplace in engineering practice and are making inroads in engineering education. The immense literature on teams and
teamwork ranges from very practical guides (e.g., Scholtes, Joiner, and
Streibel, 1996; Brassand, 1995) to conceptual and theoretical treatises
(e.g., Johnson and Johnson, 1991; Hackman, 1990, 2003). Check out one of
these to broaden and deepen your understanding of teamwork. Four books
were highlighted in this chapter—*Shared Minds: The New Technologies of Collaboration* (Shrage, 1991); *The Wisdom of Teams: Creating the High-Performance
Organization* (Katzenbach and Smith, 1993); *Organizing Genius: The Secrets of
Creative Collaboration* (Bennis and Biederman, 1997); and *Mastering the Art of
Creative Collaboration* (Hargrove, 1998). These four books focus on extraordinary teams, teams that perform at unusually high levels and whose members
experience accomplishments through synergistic interaction that they rarely
experience in other settings. They provide lots of examples and insights into
high-performance teams.

Building Team Performance

- Establish urgency and direction.
- Select members based on skill and potential, not personalities.
- Pay attention to first meeting and actions.
- Set clear rules of behavior.
- Set some immediate performance-oriented tasks and goals.
- Challenge the group regularly with fresh information.
- Spend lots of time together.
- Exploit the power of positive feedback, recognition, and reward.
  (Katzenbach and Smith, 1993)

Stages of Team Development

Teams often progress through a series of stages. One of the most common "sequential-stage theories" was formulated by Bruce W. Tuckman (Tuckman, 1965; Tuckman and Jensen, 1977). According to Tuckman, teams develop through five sequential stages: forming, storming, norming, performing, and adjourning. Members get to know one another and start to learn to work together in the forming stage. Differences and conflicts appear during the storming stage, and much of the team's focus in the norming stage is on managing conflict. The team works together to accomplish the goals during the performing stage. The group dissolves during the adjourning stage.

An alternative to stage theory was developed by Robert Bales (1965), who argued that there must be an equilibrium between the team's focus on its task and its focus on its working relationships; that is, there must be a team maintenance orientation. Teams oscillate between focusing on achieving their goals and focusing on maintaining good working relationships.

Both these perspectives are valuable for understanding team development. Teams move through stages while dealing with issues that emerge. Additional perspectives on team development and the task-relationship dimensions are provided in Chapter 4. Further information on team development is also available in *The Team Developer* (McGourty and DeMeuse, 2001), *Joining Together* (Johnson and Johnson, 1991, 2013), and *The Team Handbook* (Scholtes, Joiner, and Streibel, 1996).

Balancing Challenge and Support

Just as effective teams balance task and relationship activities, there is a growing body of evidence that effective individuals as well as effective teams balance challenge and support. Pelz and Andrews (1966) and Pelz (1976) describe the balance as "maintaining a creative tension between challenge and security." Their initial study (Pelz and Andrews, 1966) was focused on scientists and identifying productive climates for research and development. Pelz's (1976) study was focused on environments for creative performance within universities. A common finding was that the most creative environments had a balance between challenge and support. Their work reminds me of the Yerkes-Dobson law, which states "performance increases with physiological or mental excitement, but only up to a point. When levels of arousal/ excitement become too high, performance decreases. The process is often illustrated graphically as a curvilinear, inverted U-shaped curve which increases and then decreases with higher levels of arousal" (Yerkes and Dobson, 1908).

Recently, Amy Edmondson (2008) added to this argument by noting that both psychological safety and accountability for meeting goals are essential for effective organizations (and teams) as shown in the Table below.

	Accountability for Meeting Demanding Goals	
Psychological Safety	**Low**	**High**
High	Comfort zone	Learning zone
Low	Apathy zone	Anxiety zone

Part of the basis for this claim about the importance of the simultaneous presence of safety and accountability is Edmondson's (1999) study of psychological safety and learning in work teams.

Social interdependence theory (Lewin, 1935; Johnson and Johnson, 2005) provides further support for the simultaneous presence of

1. Interdependence among members (created by common goals) which results in the group being a "dynamic whole" so that a change in the state of any member or subgroup changes the state of any other member or subgroup.
2. An intrinsic state of tension within group members that motivates movement toward the accomplishment of the desired common goals.

The conceptual cooperative learning model, which is based on social interdependence theory and is integral to this book, argues that for optimal learning we must balance (Johnson, Johnson, and Smith, 2006):

1. Academic Challenge: An academic demand that may be beyond the student's capacity to achieve.
2. Social Support: Significant others helping a student mobilize her or his resources to advance on the challenges.

And there are two types of support:

1. Academic Support: Classmates and faculty provide the assistance and help students to succeed academically.
2. Personal Support: Classmates and faculty care about and are personally committed to the well-being of each student.

Maximizing team performance and individual learning requires continual attention to maintaining this critical balance between challenge and support.

Emerging Ideas

Other exciting developments in the area of teamwork include the emerging ideas of communities of practice, emotional intelligence, and network quotient. Communities of practice are essential in many companies (e.g., Boeing, Daimler Chrysler) for managing and developing knowledge. Here's a definition of such communities:

> Communities of practice are groups of people who share a concern, a set of problems, or a passion about a topic, and who deepen their knowledge and expertise in this area by interacting on an ongoing basis. (Wenger, McDermott, and Snyder, 2002, p. 4)

The concept of emotional intelligence is also being heralded as important for team and project success. Daniel Goleman (1998) defines emotional intelligence as "the capacity for recognizing our own feelings and those of others, for motivating ourselves, and for managing emotions well in ourselves and in our relationships" (p. 24).

A related idea is that of NQ, or network quotient. Tom Boyle of British Telecom, who calls this the age of interdependence, says that people's NQ— their capacity to form connections with one another—is now more important than IQ, the measure of individual intelligence (Cohen and Prusak, 2001).

These emerging ideas indicate that teamwork, project management, and knowledge management are dynamic areas where there is a lot of innovation. So, stay posted and stay alert.

Effective teamwork is not easy to accomplish. Engineering professor Douglas J. Wilde said, "It's the soft stuff that's hard, the hard stuff is easy" (Leifer, 1997). Larry Leifer (1997), director of the Stanford Center for Design Research, reports, "Design team failure is usually due to failed team dynamics." However, if you work at it, continue to study and learn about effective teamwork, and attend to the skills and strategies needed for effective teamwork described in Chapter 3, you will very likely have many positive team experiences.

Chapter 15, Teaming for the Future, by Curt McNamara provides extensive elaboration on emerging ideas.

 REFLECTION How are you documenting the skills and knowledge you're acquiring? How about the products, documents, and artifacts you're creating? Are you keeping a portfolio? Tom Peters (whose ideas occur frequently in this book) argues that "Your projects are *you*!" A portfolio is a good way to collect evidence of your development as a T-shaped person. Consider saving your problem-based and project-based learning projects, peer mentoring and teaching experiences, co-op and internship experiences, as well as your written work, observations, designs, and especially your reflections on your learning and experiences.

Reflection on Interdependence and Teamwork

I've been a student of interdependence and teamwork ever since I took a course on the social psychology of education in about 1974. Prior to that I had predominantly thought of learning (and work, for that matter) as an individual endeavor. The instructor of that course, Dennis Falk, one of David Johnson's graduate students, had us working together, cooperatively; and he emphasized positive interdependence. I had an epiphany! I thought, This is the way I worked as an engineer—why isn't the classroom organized in this way? I elaborated on this story in detail in a 2011 article, "Cooperative Learning: Lessons and Insights from Thirty Years of Championing a Research-Based Innovative Practice" (Smith, 2011). Numerous resources are available to help faculty organize and manage learning teams.

I've often wondered why there was such an emphasis on interdependence in Minnesota. I haven't discovered the answer yet, but it might be due to the Lakota presence in Minnesota. One of the cornerstones of Lakota culture is the phrase used in all their ceremonies—*mitakuye oyasin* ("We are all related") (Marshall, 2001). According to Medearis and White Hat (1995), the connection between *mitakuye oyasin* and education is this: "Education is an art of process, participation, and making connection. Learning is a growth and life process; and life and Nature are always relationships in process" (p. 1).

Questions

1. What are the characteristics of effective teams? How do you help promote them?
2. Where and how have teamwork skills been taught or emphasized to you? in school? in social groups? in professional groups? in your family? Describe two or three instances where teamwork skills were emphasized.
3. How is increasing ethnic diversity affecting project teams? What are some strategies for effectively participating on and managing diverse teams?
4. Students often say that groups in school are different from groups in the workplace, giving this as a reason for not using groups in school. Is it a valid excuse? Summarize the major differences between groups in school and groups in the workplace. How are these differences beneficial or harmful to the work of the group? What are some things you can do to improve the school groups?

Exercises

1. Check out a study of teams that have performed at extraordinary levels. Some of the books listed in the references for this chapter have terrific stories of stellar teams (see, e.g., Hargrove, 1998; Bennis and Biederman, 1997; Schrage, 1991, 1995). You may want to check the library or do an electronic search of the literature. Summarize the features of these extraordinary teams. How does your summary compare with the list provided in this chapter? Remember, this is a dynamic area of research with lots of new books and articles appearing each year.
2. Look for opportunities to participate on a superb team. Make a plan for participating on a high-performance team.
3. Study the diversity of teams in your school or workplace and note strategies for recognizing, valuing, and celebrating diversity.

References

Axelrod, R., and M. D. Cohen. 2001. *Harnessing complexity: Organizational implications of a scientific frontier.* New York: Simon & Schuster.

Bales, Robert F. 1965. The equilibrium problem in small groups. In *Small groups: Studies in social interaction,* edited by A. Hare, E. Borgatta, and R. Bales. New York: Knopf.

Bennis, Warren, and Patricia Biederman. 1997. *Organizing genius: The secrets of the creative collaboration.* Reading, MA: Addison-Wesley.

Brassand, Michael. 1995. *The team memory jogger: A pocket guide for team members.* Madison, WI: GOAL/QPC and Joiner Associates.

Browne, M. Neil, and Stuart Keeley. 1997. *Striving for excellence in college.* Upper Saddle River, NJ: Prentice Hall.

Cabanis, Jeannette. 1997. Diversity: This means you. *PM Network* 11(10), 29–33.

Cherbeneau, Jeanne. 1997. Hearing every voice: How to maximize the value of diversity on project teams. *PM Network* 11(10), 34–36.

Cohen, Don, and Laurence Prusak. 2001. *In good company: How social capital makes organizations work.* Cambridge, MA: Harvard Business School Press.

Covey, Stephen R. 1989. *The seven habits of highly effective people.* New York: Simon & Schuster.

Edmondson, Amy. 1999. Psychological safety and learning in work teams. *Administrative Science Quarterly* 44 (2).

Edmondson, A. C. 2008. The competitive advantage of learning. *Harvard Business Review* 86 (7/8), 60–67.

———. 2012. *Teaming: How organizations learn, innovate, and compete in the knowledge economy.* San Francisco: Jossey-Bass.

Goleman, Daniel. 1998. *Working with emotional intelligence.* New York: Bantam Books.

Hackman, J. R. 1990. *Groups that work (and those that don't): Creating conditions for effective teamwork.* San Francisco: Jossey-Bass.

———. 2002. *Leading teams: Setting the stage for great performances.* Cambridge, MA: Harvard Business Press.

Hargrove, Robert. 1998. *Mastering the art of creative collaboration.* New York: McGraw-Hill.

Jackson, Phil, and Hugh Delehanty. 1995. *Sacred hoops: Spiritual lessons of a hardwood warrior.* New York: Hyperion.

Johnson, David W., and Frank P. Johnson. 1991. *Joining together: Group theory and group skills,* 4th ed. Englewood Cliffs, NJ: Prentice Hall.

Johnson, David W., and Roger T. Johnson. 2005. New developments in social interdependence theory. *Genetic, social and general psychology monographs,* 131(4), 284–358.

Johnson, David W., Roger T. Johnson, and Karl A. Smith. 1991. *Cooperative learning: Increasing college faculty instructional productivity.* Washington, DC: ASHE-ERIC Reports on Higher Education.

———. 1998a. Cooperative learning returns to college: What evidence is there that it works? *Change* 30(4), 26–35.

———. 1998b. Maximizing instruction through cooperative learning. *ASEE Prism* 7(6), 24–29.

———. 2006. *Active learning: Cooperation in the college classroom,* 3rd ed. Edina, MN: Interaction Book.

———. 2007. The state of cooperative learning in postsecondary and professional settings. *Educational Psychology Review* 19(1), 15–29.

Katzenbach, Jon, and Douglas Smith. 1993. *The wisdom of teams: Creating the high-performance organization.* Cambridge, MA: Harvard Business School Press.

Leifer, Larry. 1997. *A collaborative experience in global product-based learning.* National Technological University Faculty Forum, November 18.

Lewin, Kurt. 1935. *A dynamic theory of personality.* New York: McGraw-Hill.

Marshall, Joseph M. III. 2001. *The Lakota way: Stories and lessons for living.* New York: Penguin.

McGourty, Jack, and Kenneth P. DeMeuse. 2001. *The team developer: An assessment and skill building program.* New York: Wiley.

Medearis, Cheryl, and Albert White Hat, Sr. 1995. *Mitakuye oyasin.* Paper presented at the Collaboration for the Advancement of College Teaching and Learning Faculty Development conference, Minneapolis, MN, November.

Miller, J., and S. E. Page. 2007. *Complex adaptive systems: An introduction to computational models of social life.* Princeton, NJ: Princeton University Press.

Page, S. E. 2009. *Understanding complexity.* The Great Courses. Chantilly, VA: The Teaching Company.

Pelz, Donald. 1976. Environments for creative performance within universities. In *Individuality in learning,* edited by Samuel Messick (pp. 229–247). San Francisco: Jossey-Bass.

Pelz, Donald, and Frank Andrews. 1966. *Scientists in organizations: Productive climates for research and development.* Ann Arbor: Institute for Social Research, University of Michigan.

Perkins, David. 2002. *King Arthur's round table: How collaborative conversations create smart organizations.* New York: Wiley.

Scholtes, Peter R., Brian L. Joiner, and Barbara J. Streibel. 1996. *The team handbook.* Madison, WI: Joiner Associates.

Schrage, Michael. 1991. *Shared minds.* New York: Random House.

———. 1995. *No more teams! Mastering the dynamics of creative collaboration.* New York: Doubleday.

Smith, Karl A. 2011. Cooperative Learning: Lessons and insights from thirty years of championing a research-based innovative practice. *Proceedings 41st ASEE/IEEE Frontiers in Education Conference.* Rapid City, SD, p. 7.

Smith, Karl A., Sheri D. Sheppard, David W. Johnson, and Roger T. Johnson. 2005. Pedagogies of engagement: Classroom based practices (Cooperative learning and problem-based learning). *Journal of Engineering Education* 87(1), 87–101.

Tuckman, Bruce. 1965. Development sequence in small groups. *Psychological Bulletin* 63, 384–399.

Tuckman, Bruce, and M. Jensen. 1977. Stages of small group development revisited. *Groups and Organizational Studies* 2, 419–427.

Wenger, Etienne, Richard McDermott, and William Snyder. 2002. *Cultivating communities of practice.* Cambridge, MA: Harvard Business School Press.

Wulf, William A. 1998. Diversity in engineering. *Bridge* 28(4), 8–13.

Yerkes, R. M., and J. D. Dodson. 1908. The relation of strength of stimulus to rapidity of habit-formation. *Journal of Comparative Neurology and Psychology* 18, 459–482.

CHAPTER 4

Teamwork Skills
and Problem Solving

*I will pay more for the ability to deal with people than any other ability under
the sun.*

JOHN D. ROCKEFELLER

*If you can't operate as a team player, no matter how valuable you've been,
you really don't belong at GE.*

JOHN F. WELCH (1993)

Former CEO, General Electric

 REFLECTION Have you been a member of a team that got the job done
(wrote the report, finished the project, completed the laboratory assignment) but that ended up with the members hating one another so
intensely they never wanted to see each other again? Most students
have, and they have found it very frustrating. Similarly, have you been
a member of a team whose members really enjoyed one another's company and had a great time socially, but in the end didn't finish the
project? Again, most students have, and they also have found this frustrating. Take a moment to recall your experiences with these two
extremes of teamwork.

Importance of Task and Relationship

As noted in Chapter 3, to be most effective, groups need to do two things
very well: accomplish the task and get better at working with one another.
Both of these require leadership—not just from a single person acting as the
leader but from every member contributing to the leadership of the group.
This chapter focuses on teamwork skills using a "distributed actions approach"
to leadership. Distributed actions are specific behaviors that members engage
in to help the team accomplish its task or to improve working relationships.
Napier and Gershenfeld (1973) summarize many of these behaviors (see
Table 4.1). Note the date—1973—which indicates that effective groupwork is
not a new concept.

Table 4.1 Group Task and Maintenance Roles

Group Task Roles	Group Maintenance Roles
Initiating	Encouraging
Seeking information	Expressing feelings
Giving information	Harmonizing
Seeking opinions	Compromising
Giving opinions	Facilitating communications
Clarifying	Setting standards or goals
Elaborating	Testing agreement
Summarizing	Following

Table 4.2 Management Behavior Change Needed for Team Culture

From	To
Directing	Guiding
Competing	Collaborating
Relying on rules	Focusing on the process
Using organizational hierarchy	Using a network
Consistency/sameness	Diversity/flexibility
Secrecy	Openness/sharing
Passivity	Risk taking
Isolated decisions	Involvement of others
People as costs	People as assets
Results thinking	Process thinking

Source: McNeill, Bellamy, and Foster, 1995.

To achieve the benefits of a team culture, some changes in management behavior are needed, as shown in Table 4.2. To learn more about the behaviors listed on the right-hand side of Table 4.2, read on.

Organization—Team Norms

A common way to promote more constructive and productive teamwork is to have the team create a set of guidelines for the team, sometimes called team norms. Take a minute and list some things (attitudes, behaviors, and so on) that you have found (or believe) can help a team be more effective. Then compare your list with the following two lists, both of which are from McNeill, Bellamy, and Foster (1995). The first was adapted from the Boeing Airplane Group's training manual for team members and the second is from the Ford Motor Company.

Code of Cooperation
1. Every member is responsible for the team's progress and success.
2. Attend all team meetings and be on time.
3. Come prepared.
4. Carry out assignments on schedule.
5. Listen to and show respect for the contributions of other members; be an active listener.

6. Constructively criticize ideas, not persons.
7. Resolve conflicts constructively.
8. Pay attention; avoid disruptive behavior.
9. Avoid disruptive side conversations.
10. Only one person speaks at a time.
11. Everyone participates; no one dominates.
12. Be succinct; avoid long anecdotes and examples.
13. No rank in the room.
14. Respect those not present.
15. Ask questions when you do not understand.
16. Attend to your personal comfort needs at any time, but minimize team disruption.
17. Have fun.
18. ?

Ten Commandments: An Effective Code of Cooperation

- Help each other be right, not wrong.
- Look for ways to make new ideas work, not for reasons they won't.
- If in doubt, check it out. Don't make negative assumptions about each other.
- Help each other win, and take pride in each other's victories.
- Speak positively about each other and about your organization at every opportunity.
- Maintain a positive mental attitude no matter what the circumstances.
- Act with initiative and courage, as if it all depends on you.
- Do everything with enthusiasm; it's contagious.
- Whatever you want, give it away.
- Don't lose faith.
- Have fun!

Team norms are common today not only in business and industry, but also in academic and research settings. The nearby box "Tips for Working Successfully in a Team" presents a list developed by Randy Pausch for use in a course he taught at Carnegie Mellon University (Pausch, 2002). (Pausch also had terrific ideas on time and project management, for example, his time management lecture given at the University of Virginia in 2007 is legendary.) Having an agreed-upon, abided-by code of cooperation such as Pausch's will help teams get started toward working effectively. However, if team members haven't developed the requisite communication, trust, loyalty, organization, leadership, decision-making procedures, and conflict management skills, then the team will very likely struggle or at least not perform up to its potential. One way a team can develop such a code is to create a team charter—a sample format for a team charter is given below. Also see Exercise 3 at the end of this chapter.

Team Charter Guidelines

- Team name, membership, and roles
- Team mission statement
- Anticipated results (goals)

- Specific tactical objectives
- Ground rules/guiding principles for team participation
- Shared expectations/aspirations

Team charters typically are created during a team meeting early in the project life cycle. Involvement of all team members in creating the charter helps build commitment of each to the project and to other members. A set of guidelines such as the Team Charter Guidelines often helps the team through this process. An article by Mathieu and Rapp (2009) provides research evidence supporting the use of team charters for successful team performance. They also include a sample charter in the article. Additional team charter examples are available on my website, www.ce.umn.edu/~smith. Follow the Teamwork and Project Management link.

Tips for Working Successfully in a Team

Meet people properly. It all starts with the introduction. Then exchange contact information and make sure you know how to pronounce everyone's names. Exchange phone numbers, and find out when it is acceptable to call.

Find things you have in common. You can almost always find something in common with another person, and starting from that baseline, it's much easier to then address issues where you have differences. This is why cities benefit from professional sports teams, which are socially galvanizing forces that cut across boundaries of race and wealth. If nothing else, you probably have in common things like the weather.

Make meeting conditions good. Have a large surface to write on, make sure the room is quiet and warm enough, and that there aren't lots of distractions. Make sure no one is hungry, cold, or tired. Meet over a meal if you can; food softens a meeting. That's why they "do lunch" in Hollywood.

Let everyone talk. Even if you think what's being said is stupid, don't interrupt. Cutting someone off is rude, and is not worth whatever small time gain you might make. Don't finish people's sentences for them; they can do it for themselves. And remember: talking louder or faster doesn't make your idea any better.

Check your egos at the door. When you discuss ideas, immediately label them and write them down. The labels should be descriptive of the idea, not the originator, e.g., "the troll bridge story," not "Jane's story."

Praise each other. Find something nice to say, even if it's a stretch. Even the worst of ideas has a silver lining inside it, if you just look hard enough. Focus on the good, praise it, and then raise any objections or concerns you have about the rest of it.

Put it in writing. Always write down who is responsible for what, by when. Be concrete. Arrange meetings by e-mail, and establish accountability. Never assume that someone's roommate will deliver a phone message. Also, remember that "politics is when you have more than two people"—with that in mind, always copy any piece of e-mail within the team to all members of the team. This rule should never be violated; don't try to guess what your teammates might or might not want to hear about.

Be open and honest. Talk with your team members if there's a problem, and talk with [the team leader] if you think you need help. The whole point . . . is that it's tough to work across cultures. If we all go into it knowing that's an issue, we should be comfortable discussing problems when they arise. . . . Be forgiving when people make mistakes, but don't be afraid to raise the issues when they come up.

Avoid conflict at all costs. When stress occurs and tempers flare, take a short break. Clear your heads, apologize, and take another stab at it. Apologize for upsetting your peers, even if you think someone else was primarily at fault; the goal is to work together, not start a legal battle over whose transgressions were worse. It takes two to have an argument, so be the peacemaker.

Phrase alternatives as questions. Instead of "I think we should do A, not B," try "What if we did A, instead of B?" That allows people to offer comments, rather than defend one choice.

Source: Randy Pausch, for the Building Virtual Worlds course at Carnegie Mellon, Spring 1998.

Teamwork Skills

What are teamwork skills, and how does one learn them? This is an area we've researched in our study of active and cooperative learning (Johnson, Johnson, and Smith, 1998). We identified the following categories of skills—forming, functioning, formulating, and fermenting—and have suggestions for mastering them.

Cooperative Teamwork Skills

Forming skills—*Initial management skills*
- Move into groups quietly.
- Stay with the group.
- Use quiet voices.
- Take turns.
- Use names, look at the speaker.
- No "put-downs."

Functioning skills—*Group management skills*
- Share ideas and opinions.
- Ask for facts and reasoning.
- Give direction to the group's work (state assignment purpose, provide time limits, offer procedures).
- Encourage everyone to participate.
- Ask for help or clarification.
- Express support and acceptance.
- Offer to explain or clarify.
- Paraphrase others' contributions.
- Energize the group.
- Describe feelings when appropriate.

Formulating skills—*Formal methods for processing materials*
- Summarize out loud completely.
- Seek accuracy by correcting/adding to summaries.
- Help the group find clever ways to remember.
- Check understanding by demanding vocalization.
- Ask others to plan for telling/teaching out loud.

Fermenting skills—*Stimulating cognitive conflict and reasoning*
- Criticize ideas without criticizing people.
- Differentiate the ideas and the reasoning of members.
- Integrate ideas into single positions.
- Ask for justification of conclusions.
- Extend answers.

- Probe by asking in-depth questions.
- Generate further answers.
- Test reality by checking the group's work.

Learning Cooperative Teamwork Skills
1. Observe and reflect to see the *need* to learn the skill.
2. *Learn how* to do it (T-chart—what does it look like? what does it sound like?).
3. *Practice* the skill daily.
4. *Reflect* on, process, and refine use.
5. *Persevere* until skill is automatic.

These cooperative teamwork skills are essential for productive and successful teamwork, and they must be learned and practiced with the same seriousness with which other engineering skills are learned.

Communication

Effective communication—listening, presenting, persuading—is at the heart of effective teamwork. The task and maintenance roles we have listed all involve oral communication. Here are the listening skills emphasized in an Arizona State University's course called Introduction to Engineering Design (McNeill, Bellamy, and Foster, 1995):

Stop talking.
Engage in one conversation at a time.
Empathize with the person speaking.
Ask questions.
Don't interrupt.
Show interest.
Concentrate on what is being said.
Don't jump to conclusions.
Control your anger.
React to ideas, not to the speaker.
Listen for what is not said; ask questions.
Share the responsibility for communication.

Three listening techniques they recommend are these:

Critical listening
- Separate fact from opinion.

Sympathetic listening
- Don't talk—listen.
- Don't give advice—listen.
- Don't judge—listen.

Creative listening
- Exercise an open mind.
- Supplement your ideas with another person's ideas and vice versa.

You may be wondering why so much emphasis is placed on listening. The typical professional spends about half of his or her business hours listening, and project managers may spend an even higher proportion of their time listening. Most people, however, are not 100 percent efficient in their listening. Typical listening efficiencies are only 25 percent (Taylor, 1998). The first list provides suggestions to help the listener truly hear what is being said, and the second highlights the fact that different situations call for different types of listening.

 REFLECTION Take a moment to think about the listening skills and techniques. Do you listen in all three ways listed above? Which are you best at? Which do you need to work on?

David Perkins (2002) writes, "How smart an organization or community is reflects the kinds of conversations that people have with one another, taking conversations in a broad sense to include all sorts of interactions" (p. 14). Perkins writes that for systems to be habitually smart, they have to dramatically increase the number of "progressive interactions" and minimize the amount of "regressive interactions." Progressive interactions maximize quality knowledge and social cohesion. He calls these two aspects "process smart" (good exchange of ideas, good decisions and solutions, far-seeing plans) and "people smart" (interactions that foster cohesiveness and energize people to work together). Regressive interactions don't get at ideas, or do so poorly; plans don't get made, or are not followed if they are made; people are dissatisfied, at loggerheads, or opt out because it is easier to do so.

System or organizational intelligence is very hard to come by, says Perkins (2002), for at least six big reasons:

1. *The five-brain backlash*—too many voices making things unproductively complicated;
2. *Cognitive oversimplification*—the human tendency to oversimplify cognitive processing;
3. *Emotional oversimplification*—the equally human tendency to oversimplify emotions;
4. *Regression in the face of stress;*
5. *The domino effect* in which one person's regressive behavior tips others in the same direction; and
6. *Power advantage*—the fact that power figures sometimes take advantage of regressive interactions.

Regressive interactions are more likely to happen and persist because they are easier to do. Progressive interactions are more sophisticated and complex and therefore are less likely to catch on. The bad news is, *under stressful conditions, individuals and teams are more likely to revert to regressive behaviors.*

I encourage all of you to read David Perkins' *King Arthur's Round Table: How Collaborative Conversations Create Smart Organizations.* More importantly, I encourage all of you to practice *progressive interactions.*

Perkins suggests regularly asking the question, "How round is your table?" The cooperative learning table I set in my classes is round but some people don't seem to perceive it as round, in part, I think, because they lack skills for working cooperatively. I regularly grapple with how to make the learning and design table round and how to give everyone a seat at it.

Leadership

A common notion is that leadership is a trait that some are born with. Another common notion is that a person's leadership ability depends on the situation. There is an enormous body of literature on leadership, so I'll only provide insights that I've found useful. I'll also try to guide you to more reading and resources on the topic.

 INDIVIDUAL AND GROUP REFLECTION What does it mean to lead a team? What does it take? Take a moment to reflect on the characteristics you admire most in a leader. Jot down 8 to 10 of them. Compare your list with your teammates' lists.

Leadership researchers and authors Kouzes and Posner (1987, 1993, 2011) have asked thousands of people to list the characteristics of leaders they admire. Table 4.3 lists the most common responses from their 2002, 2010 studies (Kouzes and Posner, 2011). Many students and workshop participants

Table 4.3 Characteristics of Admired Leaders (percentage of people selecting the characteristic)

Characteristic	2010	2002	1987
Honest	85	88	83
Forward-looking	70	71	62
Inspiring	69	65	58
Competent	64	66	67
Intelligent	42	47	43
Broad-minded	40	40	37
Dependable	37	33	32
Supportive	36	35	32
Fair-minded	35	42	40
Straightforward	31	34	34
Determined	28	23	20
Cooperative	26	28	25
Ambitious	26	17	21
Courageous	21	20	27
Caring	20	20	26
Imaginative	18	23	34
Loyal	18	14	11
Mature	16	21	23
Self-controlled	11	8	13
Independent	6	6	10

Source: Kouzes and Posner, 2011.

express surprise that honesty is listed as number one. They say it's a given. Apparently honesty is not a given for many leaders in business and industry. In 1993, Kouzes and Posner also asked the respondents to list the most desirable characteristics of colleagues. Honesty was number one again, with 82 percent selecting it. Cooperative, dependable, and competent were second, third, and fourth, with slightly more than 70 percent of respondents selecting each. Kouzes and Posner (2011) note the following characteristics based on responses from over 75,000 people around the globe who have completed the "Characteristics of Admired Leaders" survey:

- Integrity (is truthful, is trustworthy, has character, has convictions)
- Competence (is capable, is productive, is efficient)
- Leadership (is inspiring, is decisive, provides directions)

Kouzes and Posner found that when leaders do their best, they challenge, inspire, enable, model, and encourage. They suggest five practices and ten behavioral commitments of leadership:

Challenging the Process
  1. Search for opportunities.
  2. Experiment and take risks.

Inspiring a Shared Vision
  3. Envision the future.
  4. Enlist others.

Enabling Others to Act
  5. Foster collaboration.
  6. Strengthen others.

Modeling the Way
  7. Set the example.
  8. Plan small wins.

Encouraging the Heart
  9. Recognize individual contributions.
  10. Celebrate accomplishments.

Credibility is key according to Kouzes and Posner (2011) and they identify six disciplines for earning and sustaining credibility:

1. Discover your self
2. Appreciate constituents
3. Affirm shared values
4. Develop capacity
5. Serve a purpose
6. Sustain hope

Peter Scholtes, author of the best-selling book *The Team Handbook,* recently published *The Leader's Handbook* (Scholtes, 1998). He offers the following six "New Competencies" for leaders:

1. The ability to think in terms of systems and knowing how to lead systems.
2. The ability to understand the variability of work in planning and problem solving.

3. Understanding how we learn, develop, and improve; leading true learning and improvement.
4. Understanding people and why they behave as they do.
5. Understanding the interaction and interdependence between systems, variability, learning, and human behavior; knowing how each affects the others.
6. Giving vision, meaning, direction, and focus to the organization.

 REFLECTION Take a moment to reflect on what you've learned thus far about the competencies Scholtes emphasizes—systems, thinking, variability, learning and improvement, understanding people, interdependence, and giving vision—and list connections both with your personal experiences and with earlier sections of this book.

The latest breakthrough work on leadership is Jim Collins' concept of Level 5 leadership (Collins, 2001a, 2001b). Collins and his research team studied companies which moved from being good to being great. Their central finding was that the leaders of these companies "build enduring greatness through a paradoxical combination of personal humility plus professional will." Collins' revelation reminds me of a virtue that philosopher Walter Kaufmann said is a cardinal virtue—the fusion of humility and ambition (Kaufmann, 1973). I've tried to live by Kaufmann's cardinal virtue of fusing humility and ambition for the past 25 years. I find it interesting that Collins' work has focused on a similar fusion. There is something significant here, and I suggest that you reflect on it.

Harlan Cleveland (2002) argues in his book *Nobody in Charge* that the world has become so complex that nobody can possibly know enough to be in charge of anything really interesting or important, and therefore lots of us need to take responsibility. Therefore, we need leadership for the management of complexity and he offers the following eight attitudes that he argues are indispensable to the management of complexity:

- A lively intellectual curiosity—because everything is related to everything else.
- A genuine interest in what other people think and why they think that way.
- A feeling of responsibility for envisioning a future that's different from straight-line project of the present.
- A hunch that most risks are there not to be avoided but to be taken.
- A mindset that crises are normal, tensions can be promising, and complexity is fun.
- A realization that paranoia and self-pity are reserved for people who *don't* want to be leaders.
- A sense of *personal* responsibility for the *general* outcome of your efforts.
- A quality of "unwarranted optimism."

In addition to group norms, communication, and leadership, teamwork depends on effective decision making and constructive conflict management, described in the next two sections.

The title of this reflection comes from a story told by Gregory Bateson: "A man wanted to know about mind, not in nature but in his personal, large computer. So he asked it, 'Do you compute you'll ever think like a human being?' The computer set about to analyze its computational habits. Some time later it printed out its results. The man ran to read the results and found the words neatly typed, THAT REMINDS ME OF A STORY."

In 1998 I wrote a *Journal of Engineering Education* Academic Bookshelf column on the Role of Narrative (Story). I was reluctant since I thought the engineering community would think it too far out, too soft. The column, in which I summarized books such as *The Call of Stories* by Robert Coles, *Stories Lives Tell* by Carol Witherell and Nel Noddings, and *Hamlet on the Holodeck: The Future of Narrative in Cyberspace* by Janet H. Murray, received more e-mail and personal responses than any of the other 12 or so columns that I wrote. You can find summaries of several of the books on my website, www.ce.umn.edu/~smith. Follow the Teamwork and Project Management link.

Stories and storytelling are gaining a prominent place in the current leadership and workplace literature. Several prominent business leaders and scholars are making a case for stories. One interesting short book is *Storytelling in Organizations: Why Storytelling Is Transforming 21st Century Organizations and Management* by John Seely Brown, Stephen Denning, Katalina Groh, and Laurence Prusak (2005). In response to the question, "Why does narrative pervade organizations?" they offer 23 reasons. Here's a sampling:

- Stories have salience to the lives of people in organizations.
- Stories help us make sense of organizations.
- Storytelling communicates collaboratively.
- Storytelling communicates context.
- Storytelling flies under the corporate radar.
- Storytelling is memorable.
- Storytelling spurs double-loop learning.
- Storytelling is key to leadership.

Norman R. Augustine, former CEO of Lockheed-Martin, highlights the role of story in his 1997 book, *Augustine's Travels: A World-Class Leader Looks at Life, Business, and What It Takes to Succeed at Both,* in which he documents an around-the-world-in-eight-days, five-country whirlwind trip taken in 1995 with a group of leaders. It is packed with insights, advice, and wisdom, and infused with humor. He seems particularly partial to Yogi Berra and Winnie the Pooh, and writes in the preface, "I want this book to help readers deal with issues, make decisions, and solve problems." As in *Augustine's Laws,* I've used lots of stories to illustrate my points.

Don't get me wrong here. To be successful as an engineer you must have done your homework, that is, developed a sufficient level of analysis skills and technical rigor (the vertical dimension of the T-shaped person). But it's not enough today, because if you're going to persuade others to support your ideas and fund your projects you need to provide a compelling story.

REFLECTION Take a moment to recall stories from your family, friends, teachers, or others that have stayed with you. Think about how you can convey your ideas in a story-like format. One common metaphor for thinking about this is the "elevator speech," or sometimes called "the pitch." The essential idea of the elevator speech is to get your main point across in a minute or less, and of course, in a memorable way. Yes, this is hard work, but you'll surely benefit from the preparation and practice when you have an opportunity to pitch your ideas.

Decision Making

There are several approaches to making decisions in groups. Before exploring them, however, I suggest that you try a group decision-making exercise. Common exercises to assist in the development of teamwork skills—especially communication (sharing knowledge and expertise), leadership, and decision making—are ranking tasks, such as survival tasks, in which a team must decide which items are most important for survival in the desert, on the moon, or in some other difficult place. Ranking tasks is common in organizations that must select among alternative designs, hire personnel, or choose projects or proposals for funding.

My favorite ranking task for helping teams focus on communication, leadership, decision making, and conflict resolution is "The New 'They'll Never Take Us Alive!'" This exercise, which includes both individual and team decision making, is Exercise 1 at the end of this chapter. Do that exercise now.

 TEAM REFLECTION 1: How did your team make the decision? Did you average your individual rankings? Did you vote? Did you discuss your individual high and low rankings and then work from both ends toward the middle? Did you try to reach consensus? Were you convinced by team members who seem to have "expert" knowledge? Did you start with the number of fatalities for one of the activities and work from there?

 TEAM REFLECTION 2: How well did your group work? What went well? What things could you do even better next time?

The method a group uses to make a decision depends on many factors, including how important the decision is and how much time there is to decide. Groups should have a good repertoire of decision-making strategies and a means of choosing the one that is most appropriate for the situation.

Several methods have been described in the literature for making decisions. One of my favorites is from David Johnson and Frank Johnson (1991). The authors list seven methods for making decisions:

1. *Decision by authority without discussion.* The leader makes all the decisions without consulting the group. This method is efficient but does not build team member commitment to the decision.

2. *Expert member*. The most expert member is allowed to decide for the group. The difficulty with this method often lies in deciding who has the most expertise, especially when those with power or status in the group overestimate their expertise.

3. *Average of members' opinions*. The group decision is based on the average of individual group members' opinions.

4. *Decision by authority after discussion*. The designated leader makes the decision after discussion with the group. The effectiveness of this method often depends on the listening skills of the leader.

5. *Minority control*. Two or more members who constitute less than 50 percent of the group often make decisions by acting as (a) an executive committee or (b) a special problem-solving subgroup.

6. *Majority control*. Decision by a majority vote is the method used by the U.S. Congress. Discussion occurs only until at least 51 percent of the members agree on a course of action.

7. *Consensus*. Consensus is probably the most effective method of group decision making in terms of decision quality and gaining members' commitment to the decision, but it also may take the most time. Perfect consensus is achieved when everyone agrees. A lesser degree of consensus is often accepted where everyone has had their say and will commit to the decision, even though not everyone completely agrees with the decision.

David and Frank Johnson (1991) note that the quality of the decision and the time needed vary as a function of the level of involvement of the people involved in the decision-making method, as shown in Figure 4.1.

They also list the following characteristics of effective decisions:

1. The resources of the group members are well used.
2. Time is well used.
3. The decision is correct, or of high quality.

Figure 4.1 Decision Type and Quality

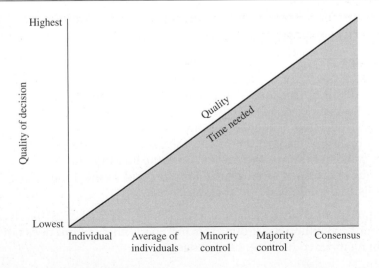

4. The decision is put into effect fully by all the necessary members' commitments.

5. The problem-solving ability of the group is enhanced.

 GROUP REFLECTION How well did your group do on each of these five characteristics of effective decisions?

Typically, novice decision-making groups don't take full advantage of the skills and talents of their members, and they often struggle to get started. Some researchers report a series of stages in team development (e.g., forming, storming, norming, performing) and offer suggestions for working through each stage (Scholtes, Joiner, and Streibel, 1996). Also, if you ask a group to invest time and effort in making a decision, it is very important that the decision or recommendation of the group be implemented (or that very good rationale be provided for why it wasn't implemented). Few things are more frustrating than to be asked to spend a lot of time and effort on work that goes nowhere.

Some of the latest and most interesting work on decision making comes from David Garvin and Michael Roberto (2001). They propose that we view decision making as an inquiry process rather than as an advocacy process, so that decision making is seen as collaborative problem solving rather than as a contest. Key differences between an advocacy approach and an inquiry approach are shown in Table 4.4. Their inquiry approach to decision making is consistent with a constructive academic controversy approach my colleagues and I devised to help students learn about reaching decisions in controversial situations (Johnson, Johnson, and Smith, 2000). Approaching, framing, and working through decisions in this manner can result in far more enlightened and constructive decisions.

Russo and Shoemaker (2002) describe an interesting and straightforward four-step decision-making process:

1. *Frame.* Decide what you are going to decide and what you are not going to decide.

2. *Gather intelligence.* Gather real intelligence, not just information that will support your biases.

Table 4.4 Two Approaches to Decision Making

	Advocacy	**Inquiry**
Concept of decision making	A contest	Collaborative problem solving
Purpose of discussion	Persuasion and lobbying	Testing and evaluation
Participants' role	Spokespeople	Critical thinkers
Pattern of behavior	Strive to persuade others	Present balanced arguments
	Defend your position	Remain open to alternatives
	Downplay weaknesses	Accept constructive criticism
Minority views	Discouraged or dismissed	Cultivated and valued
Outcome	Winners and losers	Collective ownership

Source: Garvin and Roberto, 2001.

3. *Come to conclusions.* Determine how your team will act on the intelligence it gathers.

4. *Learn from experience.*

Russo and Shoemaker's approach helps demystify the process of decision making. Their guidance through each of the steps provides insight into the process and highlights key concepts. They also provide case studies and worksheets to help readers apply the approach to their own decision-making situations.

Making decisions and providing information so that others can make decisions are two of the most important and common activities of practicing engineers.

Conflict Management

Conflict is a routine aspect of every project manager's job. Conflict is a situation in which an action of one person prevents, obstructs, or interferes with the actions of another person. On complex projects and tasks, highly talented and motivated people routinely disagree about the best ways to accomplish tasks and especially about how to deal with trade-offs among priorities. A conflict often is a moment of truth, because its resolution can follow either a constructive or a destructive path.

> *The work life of a project manager is a life of conflict. Although conflict is not necessarily bad, it is an issue that has to be resolved by the project manager. Without excellent negotiation skills, the project manager has little chance for success.*
>
> JAMES TAYLOR
> A Survival Guide for Project Managers

 INDIVIDUAL REFLECTION Write the word *conflict* in the center of a blank piece of paper and draw a circle around it. Quickly jot down all the words and phrases you associate with the word *conflict* by arranging them around your circle.

Review your list of associations and categorize them as positive, negative, or neutral. Count the total number of positive, negative, and neutral associations, and calculate the percentage that are positive. Did you have more than 90 percent positive?

Fewer than 5 percent of the people I've worked with in classes and workshops have had higher than 90 percent positive associations with the word *conflict*. Most, in fact, have had lower than 50 percent positive associations. Many have lower than 10 percent positive.

The predominance of negative associations with conflict is one of the reasons conflict management is so difficult for project managers. Many people prefer to avoid conflict or suppress it when it does arise. They become fearful, anxious, angry, or frustrated; consequently, the conflict takes a destructive path.

The goal of this section is to help you develop a set of skills and procedures for guiding conflict along a more constructive path. I'd like to begin by asking you to complete a questionnaire to assess how you typically act in conflict situations. The "How I Act in Conflict" questionnaire is included as Exercise 2 at the end of this chapter. Take a few minutes now to complete and score the questionnaire. Try to use professional conflicts and not personal conflicts as your point of reference.

Set the questionnaire aside for a few minutes and read Exercise 3, the Ralph Springer case study. Work through the exercise, completing the ranking form at the end.

 GROUP ACTIVITY Share and discuss each member's results from Exercise 2. Discuss each of the possible ways to resolve the conflict.

Then compare your individual responses from Exercise 2 to your rankings in Exercise 3. Note that each of the alternatives listed in Exercise 3 represents one of the strategies listed on the scoring form in Exercise 2. Match the alternatives to the strategies they represent. Discuss similarities and differences in the order in which each team member would have used the strategies and the relative effectiveness of each.

The five conflict strategies shown in Exercise 2—withdrawal, forcing, smoothing, compromise, and confrontation—were formulated into a model for analyzing approaches to conflict by Blake and Mouton (1964). The authors used two axes to represent the conflict strategies: (1) The importance of the goal, and (2) the importance of the relationship. The placement of each of the five strategies according to this framework is shown in Figure 4.2. The five conflict strategies are described as follows:

1. *Withdrawal.* Neither the goal nor the relationship is important—you withdraw from the interaction.
2. *Forcing.* The goal is important but not the relationship—use all your energy to get the task done.
3. *Smoothing.* The relationship is more important than the goal. You want to be liked and accepted.
4. *Compromise.* Both goal and relationship are important, but there is a lack of time—you both gain and lose something.
5. *Confrontation.* Goal and relationship are equally important. You define the conflict as a problem-solving situation and resolve through negotiation.

Each of these strategies is appropriate under certain conditions. For example, if neither the goal nor the relationship is important to you, then often the best thing to do is withdraw. If the relationship is extremely important and the goal is not so important (at the time), then smoothing is appropriate. In many conflict situations, both the goal and the relationship are important. In these situations, the strategy of confronting and negotiating often leads to the best outcomes.

Figure 4.2 Blake and Mouton Conflict Model

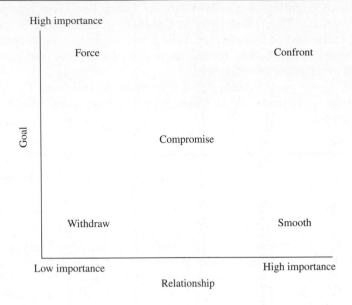

A confrontation is the direct expression of one opponent's view of the conflict, and his or her feelings about it, and an invitation to the other opponent to express his or her views and feelings.

Guidelines for Confrontation
1. Do not "hit-and-run." Confront only when there is time to jointly define the conflict and schedule a negotiating session.
2. Openly communicate your feelings about and perceptions of the issues involved in the conflict, and try to do so in minimally threatening ways.
3. Accurately and fully comprehend the opponent's views and feelings about the conflict.

Negotiation is a conflict resolution process by which people who want to come to an agreement try to work out a settlement.

Steps in Negotiating a Conflict
1. Confront the opposition.
2. Define the conflict mutually.
3. Communicate feelings and positions.
4. Communicate cooperative intentions.
5. Take the other person's perspective.
6. Coordinate the motivation to negotiate.
7. Reach an agreement that is satisfactory to both sides.

Constructively resolving conflicts through a confrontation–negotiation process takes time and practice to perfect, but it's worth it. Conflicts that do not get resolved at a personal level must be resolved at more time-consuming and costly levels—third-party mediation, arbitration, and, if all else fails, litigation.

Finally, here are some heuristics for dealing with conflicts in long-term personal and professional relationships:

1. Do not withdraw from or ignore the conflict.
2. Do not engage in "win–lose" negotiations.
3. Assess for smoothing.
4. Compromise when time is short.
5. Confront to begin problem-solving negotiations.
6. Use your sense of humor.

Remember that heuristics are reasonable and plausible, but not guaranteed. I suggest that you develop your own set of heuristics for dealing with conflict as well as for the other skills needed for effective teamwork. Some of my former students who now work as project managers emphasize during classroom visits that they spend a lot of time resolving conflicts—over meeting specifications, schedules, delivery dates, interpersonal problems among team members—and that they deal with most conflicts informally.

Teamwork Challenges and Problems

 REFLECTION What are some of the most common challenges and problems you've had working in teams? Please reflect for a moment. Make a list. Has a professor ever had you do this in your teams? If so, it's a clear indication that the professor understands the importance of group processing for identifying and solving problems.
What's on your list?

The challenges and problems you listed in the above Reflection may have included the following:

- Members who don't show up for meetings or who show up unprepared.
- Members who dominate the conversation.
- Members who don't participate in the conversation.
- Time wasted by off-task talk.
- Members who want to do the entire project themselves because they don't trust others.
- Team meeting scheduling difficulties.
- No clear focus or goal.
- Lack of clear agenda, or hidden agendas.
- Subgroup excluding or ganging up on one or more members.
- Ineffective or inappropriate decisions and decision-making processes.
- Suppression of conflict or unpleasant flareups among team members.
- Members not doing their fair share of the work.
- Lack of commitment to the team's work by some members.

These problems are commonly encountered by students (and professionals) working in teams. If they are not addressed they can turn a cooperative group into a pseudo group (as described in Chapter 3), where the group performs worse than the individuals would have performed if working alone. If the challenges are addressed in a problem-solving manner, then the team is likely to perform at much higher levels (and the members will have a much more positive experience). The following process is widely used to address team problems.

Step 1: Identify Challenges, Difficulties, and Barriers to Effective Group Work: Develop a List of Challenges, Barriers, and Problems

- Reflect individually for a moment and start a list of challenges, difficulties, and barriers, or problems facing the group. Share the individual lists and create a joint list that includes at least one item from each group member.
- Do not solve (yet).
- Be realistic and specific.
- Work cooperatively.
- If more than one group is involved, list challenges, difficulties, barriers, and problems for all groups on an overhead projector or flip chart.

Step 2: Addressing Barriers, Challenges, and Problems

1. Have each group (or if only one group is involved, each member) select one item from the joint list.
2. Clarify: Make sure you have a common understanding of what the item means or represents.
3. Identify three possible actions that will solve or eliminate the barrier or problem.
4. Prioritize the possible solutions: Plan A, Plan B, Plan C.
5. Focus on what will work; be positive and constructive.
6. Implement the solutions; report back; celebrate and extend the ones that are effective.

Caveat: During implementation of group work, expect some challenges, barriers, and problems in the process. Doing so will help you recognize a roadblock when it appears. When it does appear, apply the appropriate parts of Step 2 above. With one or more colleagues, develop three or more solutions. Implement, evaluate, replan, and retry.

The problem-identification/problem-formulation/problem-solving format described above does not guarantee that your teamwork experiences will be free of troubles. But having a format for getting problems out on the table and then dealing with them in a problem-solving manner usually reduces the frustration and interference of group problems.

Reflection on Teamwork

I've tried to address many of the highlights of effective teamwork and team problem solving, but I've barely scratched the surface. Hundreds of books and articles have been written on effective teamwork, and I've listed a few of my favorites in the reference section (in particular, see Fisher, Rayner, and Belgard, 1995; Goldberg, 1995; Hackman, 1990, 2002; Katzenbach and Smith, 1993a, 1993b). As I mentioned earlier, a widely used teamwork book is Scholtes, Joiner, and Streibel's *The Team Handbook* (1996).

Questions

1. What other skills do you feel are essential for successful teams? How about trust and loyalty, for example? I briefly dealt with trust and loyalty in the section "Organization," but you may want to emphasize them more. Check the references for more (e.g., see Johnson and Johnson, 1991). What other teamwork skills would you like to follow up on?
2. What are some of the strategies for developing a good set of working conditions in a team?
3. What are your reactions to the list of characteristics of effective leaders in Table 4.3? Were you surprised by the high ranking of honesty?
4. Why is conflict central to effective teamwork and project work? What are some strategies for effectively managing conflict?
5. Keep a log of problems you've faced in working on project teams. How do the problems change over the life of the team?
6. The next time a problem occurs in a team, try the problem-solving process outlined in this chapter. Then evaluate how well it worked.

Exercises

1. The New They'll Never Take Us Alive!

Below, in alphabetical order, are listed the top 15 causes of death in the United States in 2003. The data were taken from an annual review of death certificates reported in the *National Vital Statistics Report,* Vol. 53, No. 15, February 28, 2005. Your task is to rank them in the order of the number of deaths each causes each year. Place the number 1 next to the product or activity item that causes the most deaths, the number 2 by the item that causes the second most deaths, and so on. Then, in the last column, write in your estimate of the number of fatalities each product or activity causes annually in the United States.

Product or Activity	Ranking	Number of Fatalities
Accidents		
Alzheimer's disease		
Blood poisoning		
Cancer		
Diabetes		
Heart disease		
Hypertension		
Influenza and pneumonia		
Kidney disease		
Lung disease		
Parkinson's disease		
Pneumonitis		
Stroke		
Suicide		

Team Tasks
- After individuals have filled in their charts, determine one ranking for the team. (Don't worry yet about the estimates for the numbers of fatalities.)
- Every team member must be able to explain the rationale for the team's ranking.
- When your team finishes, and each member has signed the chart, (a) record your estimated annual number of fatalities in the United States for each, and then (b) compare your ranking and estimates with those of another team.

Note: A list of rankings and annual fatalities is available from the author at ksmith@umn.edu.

1a. Variation on Annual Fatalities Ranking
Below, in alphabetical order, are listed the top causes of death in the world in 2003. The data were taken from the World Health Organization (WHO) Report. Your task is to rank them in order. Place the number 1 next to the item that is the most frequent cause of death, the number 2 next to the item that is the second most frequent, and so on. Then, in the last column, write in your estimate of the number of deaths per year.

World Mortality Causes

Product or Activity	Ranking	Number of Fatalities
Cancer		
Childhood diseases		
Chronic obstructive pulmonary disease		
Cirrhosis of the liver		
Diarrheal diseases		
Heart disease		
HIV/AIDS		
Hypertensive heart disease		
Lower respiratory infections		
Malaria		
Measles		
Nephritis/nephrosis		
Other unintentional injuries		
Road traffic accidents		
Self-inflicted		
Stroke		
Tuberculosis		

Group Members: TASKS
- Individually determine the ranking.
- Determine one ranking for the group.
- Every group member must be able to explain the rationale for the group's ranking.
- When your group finishes (each member has signed), (a) record your estimated number of fatalities in the world for each, and then (b) compare your ranking with that of another group.

1b. Variation on Ranking

Motor vehicle accidents are a major cause of death in the United States; in fact they are the leading cause of death for people age 4 to age 34. In 2002, motor vehicle deaths were ranked eighth overall as a cause of death. What are the most common types of motor vehicle accidents? What can be done from an engineering perspective to minimize the frequency and severity of motor vehicle accidents?

Below, in alphabetical order, are listed the top 9 types of motor vehicle crashes in 2004. The data were taken from the Minnesota Motor Vehicle Crash Facts, 2004. Your task is to rank them in order. Place the number 1 next to the item that is the most frequent type of crash, the number 2 next to the item that is the second most frequent, and so on. Then, in the last column, write in your estimate of the number of crashes in Minnesota.

Minnesota Motor Vehicle Crash Frequency

Crash Type	Ranking	Number of Crashes
Head On		
Left Turn – Oncoming Traffic		
Ran Off Road – Left		
Ran Off Road – Right		
Rear End		
Right Angle		
Right Turn – Cross Street Traffic		
Sideswipe Opposing		
Sideswipe Passing		

Group Members: TASKS
- Individually determine the ranking.
- Determine one ranking for the group.
- Every group member must be able to explain the rationale for the group's ranking.
- When your group finishes (each member has signed), (a) record your estimated number of crashes, and then (b) compare your ranking with that of another group.

2. How I Act in Conflict

The proverbs listed below can be thought of as descriptions of some of the different strategies for resolving conflicts. Proverbs state conventional wisdom, and the ones listed here reflect traditional wisdom for resolving conflicts. Read each carefully. Using the scale provided, indicate how typically each proverb describes your actions in a conflict. Then score your responses on the chart at the end of the exercise. The higher the total score in each conflict strategy, the more frequently you tend to use that strategy. The lower the total score for each conflict strategy, the less frequently you tend to use that strategy.

5 = Very typical of the way I act in a conflict
4 = Frequently typical of the way I act in a conflict
3 = Sometimes typical of the way I act in a conflict
2 = Seldom typical of the way I act in a conflict
1 = Never typical of the way I act in a conflict

_____ **1.** It is easier to refrain from quarreling than to retreat from a quarrel.

_____ **2.** If you cannot make a person think as you do, make him or her do as you think.

_____ **3.** Soft words win hard hearts.

_____ **4.** You scratch my back, I'll scratch yours.

_____ **5.** Come now and let us reason together.

_____ **6.** When two quarrel, the person who keeps silent first is the most praiseworthy.

_____ **7.** Might overcomes right.

_____ **8.** Smooth words make smooth ways.

_____ **9.** Better half a loaf than no bread at all.

_____ **10.** Truth lies in knowledge, not in majority opinion.

_____ **11.** He who fights and runs away lives to fight another day.

_____ **12.** He hath conquered well that hath made his enemies flee.

_____ **13.** Kill your enemies with kindness.

_____ **14.** A fair exchange brings no quarrel.

_____ **15.** No person has the final answer but every person has a piece to contribute.

_____ **16.** Stay away from people who disagree with you.

_____ **17.** Fields are won by those who believe in winning.

_____ **18.** Kind words are worth much and cost little.

_____ **19.** Tit for tat is fair play.

_____ **20.** Only the person who is willing to give up his or her monopoly on truth can ever profit from the truths that others hold.

_____ **21.** Avoid quarrelsome people as they will only make your life miserable.

_____ **22.** A person who will not flee will make others flee.

_____ **23.** Soft words ensure harmony.

_____ **24.** One gift for another makes good friends.

_____ **25.** Bring your conflicts into the open and face them directly; only then will the best solution be discovered.

_____ **26.** The best way of handling conflicts is to avoid them.

_____ **27.** Put your foot down where you mean to stand.

_____ **28.** Gentleness will triumph over anger.

_____ **29.** Getting part of what you want is better than not getting anything at all.

_____ **30.** Frankness, honesty, and trust will move mountains.

_____ **31.** There is nothing so important that you have to fight for it.

_____ **32.** There are two kinds of people in the world, the winners and the losers.

_____ **33.** When someone hits you with a stone, hit back with a piece of cotton.

_____ **34.** When both people give in halfway, a fair settlement is achieved.

_____ **35.** By digging and digging, the truth is discovered.

Withdrawal	Forcing	Smoothing	Compromise	Confrontation
1.	2.	3.	4.	5.
6.	7.	8.	9.	10.
11.	12.	13.	14.	15.
16.	17.	18.	19.	20.
21.	22.	23.	24.	25.
26.	27.	28.	29.	30.
31.	32.	33.	34.	35.
Total	Total	Total	Total	Total

Source: David Johnson and Frank Johnson, 1991.

3. Case Study—Ralph Springer

The following case gives you a chance to apply the Blake and Mouton (1964) conflict model to a hypothetical situation. Read the case carefully and then label each of the possible actions from most to least effective and from most to least likely.

You have been working as a project manager in a large company for some time. You are friends with most of the other project managers and, you think, you are respected by all of them. A couple of months ago, Ralph Springer was hired as a supervisor. He is getting to know the other project managers and you. One of the project managers in the company, who is a friend of yours, confided in you that Ralph has been saying rather nasty things about your looks, the way you dress, and your personal character. For some reason you do not understand, Ralph has taken a dislike to you. He seems to be trying to get other project managers to dislike you also. From what you hear, there is nothing too nasty for him to say about you. Your are worried that some people might be influenced by him and that some of your co-project managers are also beginning to talk about you behind your back. You are terribly upset and angry at Ralph. You have a good job record and are quite skilled in project management, so it would be rather easy for you to get another job.

Rank each of the following five courses of action from 1 (most effective, most likely) to 5 (least effective, least likely). Use each number only once. Be realistic.

Effective   Likely

_____ _____ I lay it on the line. I tell Ralph I am fed up with the gossip. I tell him that he'd better stop talking about me behind my back, because I won't stand for it. Whether he likes it or not, he is going to keep his mouth shut about me or else he'll regret it.

_____ _____ I try to bargain with him. I tell him that if he will stop gossiping about me I will help him get started and include him in the things other project managers and I do together. I tell him that others are angry about the gossiping and that it is in his best interest to stop. I try to persuade him to stop gossiping in return for something I can do.

_____ _____ I try to avoid Ralph. I am silent whenever we are together. Whenever we speak, I show a lack of interest, look over his shoulder, and get away as soon as possible. I want nothing to do with him for now. I try to cool down and ignore the whole thing. I intend to avoid him completely if possible.

_____ _____ I call attention to the conflict between us. I describe how I see his actions and how it makes me feel. I try to begin a discussion in which we can look for a way for him to stop making me the target of his conversation and a way to deal with my anger. I try to see things from his viewpoint and seek a solution that will suit us both. I ask him how he feels about my giving him this feedback and what his point of view is.

_____ _____ I bite my tongue and keep my feelings to myself. I hope he will find out that the behavior is wrong without my saying anything. I try to be extra nice and show him that he's off base. I hide my anger. If I tried to tell him how I feel, it would only make things worse.

4. Group Ground Rules Contract Form

Project groups are an effective aid to learning, but to work best they require that all group members clearly understand their responsibilities to one another. These project group ground rules describe the general responsibilities of every member to the group. You can adopt additional ground rules if your group believes they are needed. Your signature on this contract form signifies your commitment to adhere to these rules and expectations.

All team members agree to:

1. Come to class and team meetings on time.
2. Come to class and team meetings with assignments and other necessary preparations done.

Additional ground rules:

1.

2.

If a member of the project team repeatedly fails to meet these ground rules, other members of the group are expected to take the following actions:

    Step 1: (fill in this step with your team)
           If not resolved:
    Step 2: Bring the issue to the attention of the teaching team.
           If not resolved:
    Step 3: Meet as a team with the teaching team.

The teaching team reserves the right to make the final decisions to resolve difficulties that arise within the teams. Before this becomes necessary, the team should try to find a fair and equitable solution to the problem.

Members' Signatures: Team Number:_____

1. _____   2. _____

3. _____   4. _____

Source: Adapted from a form developed by Dr. Deborah Allen, University of Delaware.

References

Augustine, Norman R. 1997. *Augustine's travels: A world-class leader looks at life, business, and what it takes to succeed at both.* AMACOM.

Blake, R. R., and J. S. Mouton. 1964. *The managerial grid.* Houston: Gulf.

Brown, John Seely, Stephen Denning, Katalina Groh, and Laurence Prusak. 2005. *Storytelling in organizations: Why storytelling is transforming 21st century organizations and management.* Burlington, MA: Elsevier Butterworth-Heinemann.

Cleveland, Harlan. 2002. *Nobody in charge: Essays on the future of leadership.* San Francisco: Jossey-Bass.

Collins, Jim. 2001a. *Good to great: Why some companies make the leap . . . and others don't.* New York: Harper Business.

———. 2001b. Level 5 leadership: The triumph of humility and fierce resolve. *Harvard Business Review* 67–76.

Edmondson, A. C. 2012. *Teaming: How organizations learn, innovate, and compete in the knowledge economy.* San Francisco: Jossey-Bass.

Fisher, Kimball, Steven Rayner, and William Belgard. 1995. *Tips for teams: A ready reference for solving common team problems.* New York: McGraw-Hill.

Garvin, David, and Michael Roberto. 2001. What you don't know about making decisions. *Harvard Business Review* 79(8), 108–116.

Goldberg, David E. 1995. *Life skills and leadership for engineers.* New York: McGraw-Hill.

Hackman, J. R. 1990. *Groups that work (and those that don't): Creating conditions for effective teamwork.* San Francisco: Jossey-Bass.

———. 2002. *Leading teams: Setting the stage for great performances.* Cambridge, MA: Harvard Business Press.

Johnson, David W., and Frank Johnson. 1991. *Joining together: Group theory and group skills.* Upper Saddle River, NJ: Prentice Hall.

Johnson, David W., Roger T. Johnson, and Karl A. Smith. 1998. *Active learning: Cooperation in the college classroom,* 2nd ed. Edina, MN: Interaction Book Company.

Johnson, David W., Roger T. Johnson, and Karl A. Smith. 2000. Constructive controversy: The power of intellectual conflict. *Change* 32(1), 28–37.

Katzenbach, Jon R., and Douglas K. Smith. 1993a. The discipline of teams. *Harvard Business Review* 71(2), 111–120.

———. 1993b. *The wisdom of teams: Creating the high-performance organization.* Cambridge, MA: Harvard Business School Press.

Kaufmann, Walter. 1973. *Without guilt and justice: From decidophobia to autonomy.* New York: Peter H. Wyden.

Kouzes, J. M., and B. Z. Posner. 1987. *The leadership challenge: How to get extraordinary things done in organizations.* San Francisco: Jossey-Bass.

———. 1993. *Credibility: How leaders gain and lose it, why people demand it.* San Francisco: Jossey-Bass.

———. 2011. *Credibility: How leaders gain and lose it and why people demand it – All new and revised.* San Francisco: Jossey-Bass.

Mathieu, John E., and Tammy L. Rapp. 2009. Laying the foundation for successful team performance trajectories: The role of team charters and performance strategies. *Journal of Applied Psychology* 94(1), 90–103.

McNeill, Barry, Lynn Bellamy, and Sallie Foster. 1995. *Introduction to engineering design.* Tempe: Arizona State University.

Napier, Rodney W., and Matti K. Gershenfeld. 1973. *Groups: Theory and experience.* Boston: Houghton Mifflin.

Pausch, Randy. 2002. Tips for working successfully in a group. http://wonderland. hcii.cs. cmu.edu/Randy/teams.htm (accessed 1/4/03).

Perkins, David. 2002. *King Arthur's round table: How collaborative conversations create smart organizations.* New York: Wiley.

Russo, J. Edward, and Paul J. H. Shoemaker. 2002. *Winning decisions.* New York: Currency Doubleday.

Scholtes, Peter R. 1998. *The leader's handbook: Making things happen, getting things done.* New York: McGraw-Hill.

Scholtes, Peter R., Brian L. Joiner, and Barbara J. Streibel. 1996. *The team handbook,* 2nd ed. Madison, WI: Joiner Associates.

Schrage, Michael. 1991. *Shared minds.* New York: Random House.

———. 1995. *No more teams! Mastering the dynamics of creative collaboration.* New York: Doubleday.

Taylor, James. 1998. *A survival guide for project managers.* New York: AMACOM.

Effective Interpersonal Communication Skills for Teamwork and Project Management*

Practical Methods and Tools for Multiple Settings and Tasks

Teamwork is fundamental to project work. Yet the reality is that at any stage of teamwork and project management it is possible to lose technical clarity and professional intentionality due to ineffective communication. If your team progress gets stalled due to a communication issue between your teammates, if you are struggling with a teammate who won't respond to requests to contribute to the project work, if you need to confront your teammates and resolve an existing conflict, what do you do?

First, ask yourself the following questions.

- Where in the teamwork or project management communication landscape are you being blocked from forward movement? Are you stuck in areas that are primarily interpersonal, primarily technical, or a mix of both?
- How do you navigate this landscape more successfully once you have identified the roadblocks in technical and interpersonal communication that are inhibiting smooth flows of project management practice?

The knowledge, skills, and tools presented here enable you to learn how to answer the questions that arise when teamwork and project management goals are lost in communication roadblocks. Learning to use these skills and tools makes you an effective project manager, allowing you not only to navigate the communication landscape of projects and teaming but also to shape that landscape for the benefit of your own and your team's success.

Communication Contexts

Teamwork and project management communications are not just abstract ideas. They are *in vivo* processes that occur among people sharing primary resources. Here are two key context principles of these processes to keep in mind:

---

*By Cliff and Leslie Whitcomb.

85

Chapter 5:
Effective
Interpersonal
Communication
Skills for Teamwork
and Project
Management

First, remember that shared primary life resources, such as the salary that provides you with food, shelter and socioeconomic stability, are always part of the professional communication context. So communications that occur in teaming and project settings may be technical, but they impact primary resources (salary, promotion, long-term career stability) of the professionals involved. Perhaps even more important, they are communications that will impact public resources (safe bridges, functional products or services) of project outcome consumers.

Shared social resources generate shared social dynamics so communications happening in shared social contexts of teaming and project management involve both interpersonal dynamics and technical concepts. This key context principle of your communication as a professional means that a single focus on interpersonal dynamics *or* technical analyses won't fix team and project problems. What *will* get you closer to solutions is behavioral integration of effective technical and interpersonal communication skills.

Second, remember that teamwork and project management occur in a *system*. Systems of teamwork and project management are impacted by effective and/or ineffective technical and interpersonal communication by three important dynamics of systems.

- **You are an integral part of your system.** "In order to be part of a system, you must be in communication with that system" (Cohen, 2007, p. 52).
- **Information holds the system together.** "Many of the interconnections in systems operate through a flow of information. Information holds systems together and plays a great role in determining how they operate" (Meadows, 2008, p. 14).
- **Systems move from an unlikely state of order to a likely state of disorder.** Boltzmann and Capra, a molecular scientist and a systems theorist, established that "movement of order to disorder in any system is a movement from an unlikely state to a likely state" (Capra, 1997, p. 188).

We are going to give you some very pragmatic steps to take in order to move this wisdom into your professional and teaming communications. In order to use these steps proficiently, it will be helpful if you understand that

- You are part of a holistic social system (not just a technical or business-based social system) as a project manager, so you need to be in holistic communication with that system, using both technical and interpersonal modes of communication effectively.
- Your technical and interpersonal communications will fundamentally shape the flow of your teamwork and project operations.
- Your communications are more likely to *not* be understood by your teammates, colleagues, and clients than they are *to be* understood by your teammates, colleagues and clients.

 REFLECTION How do you know your team is a system? What are the interconnections among the participants of your team system? How does information flow through your team system?

Understanding the above communication contexts will not happen as a thought process. It will happen as a behavior and response pattern. In order to begin translating your ideas about communication into skills for communication, we offer you the following analogy.

When you get in your car and program your GPS, it works because the GPS unit knows where you are, you know where you want to go, and you can simply program the device to get you from where you are to where you want to be. The GPS gives you cues to help you along your way. Our Communication Microskills Model acts as your communication GPS. You provide the input to the controls process to guide yourself to your desired destination by using your communication navigation knowledge and skills to realize desired forward momentum.

Components of Your Communication Navigation System

Components of your Communication Navigation System are adapted for this chapter from the Communication Microskills Model in *Effective Interpersonal and Team Communication Skills*, Whitcomb and Whitcomb, 2013.

The **Space, Face and Place Spectrum** tells you how a specific professional context impacts a teamwork or project management communication exchange. This is important because you can't get where you are going unless you know your starting location.

Appropriate **I, You and Team Statements** tell your teammates where you want to go with your communication exchange.

The **Attending Behaviors** of **SOLER** and **RECAP** allow you to program, and if necessary reprogram, your communication exchange so it gets you to your desired communication destination—a balanced and clear interpersonal and technical exchange of information that moves tasks and projects forward.

The use of **Open and Closed Questions** allows you to keep your dialogue on course if it gets side-tracked by interpersonal roadblocks or technical potholes.

The **Six Step Cycle** for problem solving provides the navigation and control process that allows you to successfully find your way through the teamwork and project management landscape even when you have become hopelessly lost in interpersonal issues or technical glitches.

We have just described your communication navigation tool set and put you on the road to experiencing communication rather than just thinking about it. We will now provide you skills that will help you use this tool set with precision as you take data input from your communication landscape to fine-tune tool usage and response.

Basics of Shared Communication Systems Exchanges

The shared space of all team and project management communications happens in a system. The system components include

- The physical space within and directly around you.
- The physical space within and directly around others.

87

*Chapter 5:
Effective
Interpersonal
Communication
Skills for Teamwork
and Project
Management*

- This shared space includes the patterns of hearing, seeing, speaking and posturing exchanged whenever two or more people speak to each other.
- This shared space is present in all technical and nontechnical communication exchanges that happen in project management.

Every successful communication exchange you will engage in as a team member or project manager will begin with the basics of managing this shared physical space and these shared patterns of speaking and listening in social contexts of project management.

We call this shared context the *Space, Face and Place Spectrum.*

Space refers to the shared social and/or professional context that exists among or between the people who are communicating.

Face refers to whom you are talking, a peer, a supervisor, or a technical group, for example.

Place refers to where the communication is happening—in a team meeting room, a conference venue, a video teleconference, a boardroom, or a coffee shop, for example.

These spectrum components interface with each other on a spectrum ranging from primarily social to purely technical/professional.

Technical and Interpersonal Space, Face, and Place Spectrum

Range One: Primarily Social Team formation, job interviews, project startups, client interviews, conference meet and greets, professional networking make up Range One.

On this part of the spectrum

- Your conversation choices are general: weather, common interests, sports scores.
- Your goal is to keep yourself comfortable and make others comfortable.

Range Two: A Balance of Social and Technical Team meetings, project report sessions, client presentations, or conference presentations make up Range Two.

On this part of the spectrum

- Your conversations and presentations are about a specific topic, goal, design or operation.
- Your delivery holds both technical and interpersonal content because you are communicating concepts that must attend to both technical aspects and interpersonal dynamics.

The shared space holds clues about patterns of hearing, seeing, speaking and posturing of yourself and those around you that would indicate signs of confusion, misunderstanding, emotional reactions or technical disagreements.

Range Three: Purely Technical Class lectures, team design meetings, individual project design meetings, presentations to teammates, lab workouts, data sharing, design analyses are Range Three.

At this point on the spectrum you are

- Focusing on conveying accurate technical detail to peers, supervisors and clients.
- Ensuring your details are accurately understood.
- Listening carefully to take in the technical details others are conveying to you.
- Receiving detailed feedback in a way that allows the speakers to fully explain their position.

The Space, Face, and Place Spectrum helps you deal with colleagues who want to overwhelm you with technical details about a project on your coffee break, and then expect you to remember those details in a meeting. The spectrum helps you deal with teammates who can't focus for more than a few minutes at a meeting without diverging into discussions on work-mates, supervisors, budgeting or the latest "new thing" that just came out this morning.

During these types of challenging or disorganized team and project management interchanges you can keep in mind the space around you and others, the face you present, and the place for each exchange. This will give you a functional communication anchor to hold to as you learn how to engage in effective communication exchanges.

I, You and the Team

Effective communication exchanges consist of "I" statements, "You" statements and "Team" (or Global) statements.

"I" is the Center from Which You Communicate

Using "I" statements says that you take responsibility for what you are saying, seeing, feeling and doing. Actions taken based on "I" statements help meet expectations for getting things done, since everyone has stated what they have agreed to do in their own terms, and in the presence of other team members. "I" statements can be seen as the engine of not only coordinated team communication but also coordinated team action.

Learning the use of "I" statements might seem like an almost kindergarten-level of basic communication. It is. However, the fundamental nature of these statements gives them the power to either drive task fulfillment or inhibit progress, because "I"-centered statements are so basic to human communication. Their effective usage can transform illogical responses and functional errors into clear thinking and pro-active task completion.

- To better understand the fundamental nature of "I" statements, try to think about any communication exchange you had over the past 24 hours.
- Your exchanges most likely included situations where "I" statements were necessary.
- When greeting a friend, coworker, or colleague, you might have said, "Sorry I'm late" or "I'll be right with you" or "Sorry I missed yesterday's meeting; can you please fill me in?"

89

*Chapter 5:
Effective
Interpersonal
Communication
Skills for Teamwork
and Project
Management*

Notice that in each of these statements, you are taking responsibility for what you know about yourself, what you are requesting and what shared actions can go forward from the exchange.

Even better, "I" statements allow you to provide your teammates with information about your intended content and your perspective on a given situation at the same time. The following "I" statement from a team meeting illustrates this concept.

> "I understand the analysis results in this discussion, but I don't see how the dialogue is moving us forward."

By using this statement you are not only expressing that you are engaged in the meeting, but you are expressing something only you can know (that you understand the technical content) and focusing attention on the specific concern you have (that the dialogue is not moving the project forward). You are expressing YOUR concern that the discussion is not going to move the project ahead. This leaves room for your team members to respond knowing that you need to be convinced that they are headed in the right direction, or that you might be correct, and everyone needs to reconsider the context for the discussion. In engineering terms, this is similar to an elegant solution—a seemingly simple solution that meets multiple needs simultaneously.

You use these methods and tools to stay interpersonally stable and technically accurate when you encounter imbalances in teammate communications and project needs/resources. You use them to reorient your communication exchanges and thus your technical design and project work flows when you get lost in road-blocked landscapes along the way.

 REFLECTION Karina is in a team meeting. The team has been stuck on a point of discussion for twice the allotted time on the agenda. She wants to help her team stay on task and accomplish their goals for the meeting.

Should she say, "We've been stuck on this point for too long, so we'd better move on"?

Or should she say, "I want to see resolution on this so we don't lose our other agenda items; how can we do this?"?

Which of these statements presents a critical, closed-door approach and which of these statements creates a firm starting point for collaboration and proactive solutions? This is the power of "I" statements.

Because these statements are powerful, their misuse can really alter the flow of team communications toward negative outcomes. Misuse of "I" statements is called making Opaque "I" statements.

The following are examples of opaque "I" statements made in a team meeting.

Opaque "I" Statements: Examples

"Your numbers make sense but you're not dealing with them correctly."

"This discussion is getting us nowhere."

These express the same communication as the example given above in the "I" statement section, but do so with roadblocks and confusion rather than an invitation to move forward in team task fulfillment.

Opaque "I" Statements Defined Opaque "I" statements are those that replace the "I" with a "You" or "We" (in the context of the team or perhaps more generally in a global sense like the "royal We"). These we call "misplaced You and Team" statements. They are opaque because they hide your perspective behind the facade of another's.

When "I" statements are substituted with misplaced "You" and "Team" statements, then communication effectiveness is compromised. Your team members now do not have a grounded context within which to understand what you might really be saying. They have to guess at what you mean. Is something wrong with what is being discussed? Is there an unspoken problem? Is one of them individually messing up? Or is it that the team is not functioning well? Using an "I" statement makes the intention of your communication clear and concise, and avoids having everyone fill in the blanks, with possible bad assumptions that divert creative energy into discussion rather than task drive.

Using an opaque "I" statement, wrapping your intent and perspective in "You" and Global statements, obscures your meaning. Worse, it focuses the implied initiative for action or change *on your peers only* or *the group as a whole*, leaving *you and your perspective* out of the dynamic, when it is you that desire the action or change or have a need to contribute your perspective.

Using a self-grounded "I" statement makes the intention of your communication clear and concise, and avoids having everyone fill in the blanks, with possible bad assumptions that divert creative energy into discussion rather than task drive. This can happen when "You" and Global statements are used in the following ways.

Misplaced "You" Statements: Examples

- You always
- You never
- You think
- You don't care
- You can't
- You won't

Misplaced "You" Statements Defined Misplaced "You" or Global statements are those that

- Focus what you don't know on the supposed thoughts, feelings and actions of others.
- Ask the other person(s) to act or change.
- Can feel like blaming.

You as an individual person cannot know what another person is thinking or feeling. So using misplaced "You" statements to express how *you* yourself are experiencing a situation is not effective communication.

Furthermore, asking another person to act or change as a way of express-ing your own experience or needs is also not effective communication. Another person's behavior can never really be an accurate reflection of your internal feelings and perceptions. So expressing yourself and your perspective through "You" statements can feel directive and nonnegotiable to the person receiving your information.

Finally, when you communicate by using "You" statements instead of expressing your own thoughts, feelings or actions, then your unexpressed emotions or thoughts and frustrated actions can add an edge to your com-munication that might feel like blaming and criticism to others. These state-ments are more easily received as a closed-door, noninvitational position.

Misplaced "You" statements can cause situations where the people you are communicating with might feel a need to spend time and energy defend-ing their own thoughts, feelings and actions rather than putting their energy into working together on the tasks at hand. Misplaced "You" statements are often made even more complicated by being delivered right along with mis-placed "Team" statements.

Misplaced "Team" Statements

- "We're missing the point."
- "They never get anything done on time."
- "We never get anywhere in these team meetings."

Misplaced "Team" Statements Defined Misplaced "Team" Statements

- Make general descriptors of group and team realities that might not be shared by all.
- Are stated as if they are inarguable facts.
- Can sound as if things cannot be changed or negotiated.

When you don't actually want to individually criticize or blame but you still are attempting to express your own experience without making "I" state-ments, it is easy to fall into making misplaced "Team" statements.

These are statements that make a general description of a situation but don't really address your place, needs, actions or perception of the situation. This mis-placement invites forms of expression that are globally based "Team" statements.

Because they are floating around out there in the ether of shared com-munication, they are not grounded in what you can definitely know, that is, your own thoughts, feelings and perspective. Nor are they grounded in a consensus-based group choice about a perspective. You may end up claiming facts, norms, or "everybody does it this way" positions in order to anchor your own thoughts, feelings and experience.

When your misplaced "Team" statements are ungrounded and thus need to be explained by using more global, blanket statements, they often can sound nonnegotiable or resistant to change.

Because you communicate in groups as well as communicating as an indi-vidual, misplaced "You" and "Team" statements cannot always be remedied by using appropriate "I" statements. You need to also know how to make constructive "You" and "We" statements to make your communications clear and proactive.

91

Chapter 5:
Effective
Interpersonal
Communication
Skills for Teamwork
and Project
Management

REFLECTION Impacts of deficits in clear communication proficiencies were starkly demonstrated in the space shuttle *Challenger* disaster. Top-level decision makers had not been accurately informed of problems with O-ring seals and external sheath joints on the shuttle, even as the countdown to launch commenced. Concerns about the impact on these elements due to the cold weather and servicing delays on the morning of launch were neither communicated adequately by professionals on the project, nor given full attention by NASA project management officials immediately prior to launch.

Communication that could have prevented tragedy was not expressed or received with enough accuracy to make a difference. The shuttle was engulfed in flames soon after launch, killing all on board, due to an O-ring failure. Investigations after the event supported the conclusion that flawed team and project management communication were significant factors in a social and technical endeavor gone terribly wrong (McDonald and Hansen, 2009).

Your own and your teammates' clear "I," "You," and "Team" statements can make the difference between products and projects that succeed and serve adequately or those that create systemic breakdowns leading to unintended social or technical consequences.

You and We Complete the Exchange "You" statements clarify your communication exchanges when you task peers and teammates, give information about the performance or roles of co-workers and peers, request information from advisors and supervisors and elicit needs of stakeholders and consumers.

Good Communication: "You" Statement Examples

- "Anna, can you please give me that analysis before the meeting winds down."
- "You can create the customer surveys."
- "Would you mind repeating the tasks you assigned to me?"

Appropriate "You" Statements Defined "You" statements clarify your communication exchanges when you task peers and teammates, give information about the performance or roles of co-workers and peers, request information from advisors and supervisors and elicit needs of stakeholders and consumers.

Because teams communicate through individual team members talking to each other and also as a cohesive set of individuals with a shared understanding that their statements are expressed based on a unified consensus, appropriate "We" statements are also a necessary component of effective engineering communication.

Good Communication: "We" Statement Examples

- "We did it!"
- "We can schedule the next meeting before we break up."
- "We have seven days left until the prototype demonstration."

93

*Chapter 5:
Effective
Interpersonal
Communication
Skills for Teamwork
and Project
Management*

Appropriate "We" Statements Defined An appropriate "We" takes the place of "I" in team communication statements, showing that the team takes responsibility for the communication. We call these statements "Team" statements, statements that you use to clarify your communication exchanges when you are interacting from a team context.

In real-life situations "I," "You," and "Team" statements are used interchangeably and fluently within even very brief communication exchanges. Putting it all together makes the exchange a balanced, effective communication.

 REFLECTION For each of the following situations, prepare an "I," "You" or "Team" statement that is appropriate for the context and intent of the communication.

1. You are in a design meeting and the team has strayed from the agenda and nothing is being accomplished.
2. You are the team leader and you have to assign roles for initial design responsibilities.
3. You are asked to report on individual task completion of all team members in a project cycle. Two team members have not handed in work and they are making the whole team run off schedule with their delays.
4. You and a teammate are tasked with fixing a programming glitch that is delaying delivery of a product demonstration to a supervisor. You are preparing to go to a check-in meeting and tell the supervisor you cannot fix the problem and will need some input from outside the team.
5. You want to tell your team that it appears they don't care if there is success on this project or not, based on evident lack of progress and lack of enthusiasm. How do you find appropriate "You" and "We" statements to express this observation?
6. You did not complete the action items that you signed up for at the previous meeting.
7. You and some other teammates agree that another team member takes over the whole conversation in the meetings.

Note: These are actual scenarios in the book *Effective Interpersonal and Team Communication Skills,* Whitcomb and Whitcomb, 2013. If you would like to see these scenarios resolved please access this resource.

Attending Behaviors

You might think communication is just the words, but it is more than that. The words come wrapped up in a nonverbal package. *Attending behaviors* address both the nonverbal package and the words in the package. They allow you to get the whole package out of the "I," "You" and "Team" statements made between you and your coworkers.

It is important to get the whole communication package between you and your coworkers because communication is understood by using 87 percent nonverbal message comprehension (Mehrabian, 2007; Knapp and Hall, 2009; Birdwhistell, 1970) in technical and nontechnical communications. In any given exchange between yourself and peers or yourself and a group, your communication of technical or information-based knowledge is *transmitted and received through a field* of voice tone, body posture, visual cues, and sensory feelings.

Attending behaviors help you navigate this *atmospheric field* of transmission. They do so both when you are transmitting information and receiving information. *Attending behaviors* allow you to accurately understand what others are saying and they allow you to monitor how your words are impacting your listeners. We'll discuss both verbal and nonverbal aspects of communication so you learn skills from the whole package.

Verbal Communication *Listening* is a foundation of attending behavior that encompasses both verbal and nonverbal behavior. You need to be able to let peers and teammates tell their perspective and you need to be able to hear and observe how your words and intentions and nonverbal cues are impacting your listeners. Therefore, first, we will tell you how to listen using attending behaviors, giving you examples of listening skills that support this attending behavior.

Next, we will tell you how you can be aware of how others receive your communication by using attending behaviors, giving you examples of information transmission skills that support these behaviors. Finally we will put both the transmitting and receiving of communication in an active practice of attending behaviors to clarify how simple it actually is to optimize communication by using these skills. We will give a listening/speaking sequence that is easy to remember and practice in the use of attending behaviors across a range of communication exchanges.

When You Are the Listener When you are the listener you are receiving your teammates' communications to you. You use *attending behaviors* to track both nonverbal and verbal communication. You do this by tracking voice tone, body posture, visual cues, feelings and technical information.

When You Are the Speaker When you are the speaker you are monitoring your own transmission to make sure your verbal and nonverbal communication is giving the message you intend.

You use *attending behaviors* to track voice tone, body posture, visual cues, feelings and technical content of your teammates. You take in this feedback to make sure you have both nonverbal and verbal understanding of what people are saying to you.

You use *attending behaviors* to monitor your own voice tone, body posture, visual cues, feelings and your teammates reception of your technical content so that you know your communication delivery is complete.

Learning to track your own nonverbal cues and learning to read the nonverbal cues of others allows you to practice complete communication reception. Complete communication reception is accurate communication reception. Accurate communication allows technical information to be related, understood and acted upon for maximum clarity in design and implementation fulfillment.

Nonverbal Communication Even without knowing it, you exhibit nonverbal communication aspects as a natural function of even your most simple communication exchanges. What we are helping you do in this section is to *attend* to those aspects. Attending to these aspects means keeping nonverbal impacts in mind while you are speaking and listening.

Just as with the appropriate use of "I" statements, attending to nonverbal aspects of speaking/listening gives you the power to shape your communication rather than having your communication miscues shape how your information content is given and received.

Nonverbal Communication for the Speaker: SOLER Nonverbal aspects are simply how to posture and compose yourself while you communicate, from your face and your eyes to your whole body, including breathing and muscle tension. Their foundation can be followed in these behaviors.

- **Squarely** face your teammate. Let the person you are speaking to know you are fully engaged in the dialogue by directly facing them.
- **Open** your body posture. Arms across your chest can be perceived as a closed door or a body half turned away can be perceived as a lack of attention.
- **Lean** slightly into the conversation to direct your attention toward fully receiving the person you are listening to.
- **Eye** contact. Maintain regular and appropriate eye contact.
- **Relax**. Your own presence and attention are enough to move communication forward. Also, when you are relaxed you take in more information.

These basic, nonverbal attending behaviors can be recalled by thinking SOLER.

It is important to note Attending Behaviors as practiced through SOLER are discussed in this section from a context that follows practices primarily based in Western cultural communication norms. *To be respectful of colleagues and teammates who live/work in other cultural settings, a different approach to attending behaviors may be necessary.*

The steps of SOLER allow you to intentionally receive *all* the information that peers and teammates are sending, including nonverbal, sense/feeling–based *and* technical/nontechnical cues and words.

 REFLECTION SOLER can't be learned through reading. It is a sensory-based, physiological process. To better integrate this skill, try to remember a situation in which you knew that you had gotten your point across, or that your suggestions were being heard and understood clearly and positively received by teammates. What were the expressions on the faces of your teammates? What was their body posture and their voice tone? What were the cues you received from them that allowed you to have a sense of being heard and understood?

This reflection leads you into the question of how you attend to the nonverbal reception in others while you are talking. This is important because the nonverbal field of transmission of voice tone, body posture, eye contact and gestural expression includes both the listener and the speaker.

Nonverbal Communication for the Listener: RECAP Just as with the appropriate use of "I" statements, attending to how your verbal statements and nonverbal behaviors are being received by others in the room gives you the

95

*Chapter 5:
Effective
Interpersonal
Communication
Skills for Teamwork
and Project
Management*

power to shape the effectiveness of your communication. Attending to the impact of your nonverbal and verbal information is simple and can become an automatic skill.

- **Relax** into your own body posture. Notice how the chair feels beneath you or how it feels to be standing as you speak, your feet on the floor, your spine supporting your posture.
- **Earmark** your voice tone, as you speak. Do you hear your voice as convincing? As quiet and measured? As assertive?
- **Catch** your impact. How do the people around you who are receiving your communication look to you? Bored and distracted? Engaged? Ready to fire right back at you with a new piece of information?
- **Ask** questions. Check into your listening partner. Simple questions, such as, "How does that sound?" or "Am I making sense to you?" can diffuse resistance to your content and engage the listener very quickly.
- **Pick up** flying cues. What cues is your listener sending that seem random, unrelated, out there, or that give you a feeling you are really being heard?

RECAP allows you to intentionally monitor your own presence in the communication, the nonverbal cues that your voice, eyes, senses/feelings and posture convey while you are receiving technical and nontechnical information from peers and teammates.

It is important to note Attending Behaviors as practiced through RECAP are discussed in this section from a context that follows practices primarily based in Western cultural communication norms. *To be respectful of colleagues and teammates who live/work in other cultural settings, a different approach to attending behaviors may be necessary.*

Complete communication reception can be accomplished through SOLER and RECAP practice of attending behaviors. When these skills are integrated into your communication exchanges you are able to practice attending behaviors that move peer-to-peer and team discussions forward with a minimum of time-sapping misunderstandings and a maximum of successful task fulfillment.

 REFLECTION When you are listening to others, how do you show them that they have your full attention? How do you let them know you have understood their communication even before you use words to do so? This is important to know about yourself because 87 percent of your listening and speaking content is understood by your teammates through nonverbal cues. No matter how brilliant or technically correct your words and logic are, if your content is delivered with nonverbal static due to lack of self-awareness or missed cues from your listener, your communications will not be clearly received and excellent content will be lost.

Attending behaviors are nebulous and take practice to track. While you are gaining proficiency in assessing the landscape of your communication you can use the road markers of Open and Closed Questions to help you keep your bearings.

Open and Closed Questions

97

Chapter 5:
Effective
Interpersonal
Communication
Skills for Teamwork
and Project
Management

We have established a foundation for interpersonal communication using "I" statements and Attending Behaviors. We'll now expand into how to pose two specific types of questions, open and closed. We then show how these are used to form attentive communication (including nonverbal and verbal aspects), develop more accurate information, and control the dynamic flow of the dialogue and resulting actions.

Open and closed questions extend attentive behavior by asking questions that can control the flow of interpersonal and technical information in a communication exchange.

Open questions ask for general information, and ask you to think and reflect in order to form an answer. They are open in that they seek answers that are synthetic, inviting someone (or a group) to collaborate with you to put information together into a full and meaningful answer, one that includes the participant's knowledge and feelings.

Closed questions ask for specific information, and can typically be answered in just a word or two. They are closed in that they seek answers that are more analytic, inviting specific points of reference to give you information to address a direct need.

Open and closed questions operate through asking for general information (open), or through asking for specific information (closed). They are open in inviting answers that include both interpersonal content and technical data. They are closed in inviting answers that offer specific points of reference that are both interpersonal and technical. Open and closed questions are dynamic, allowing you to control or hand control of the communication exchange over to your listeners.

Open questions can shape the flow of information toward including more interpersonal content. Closed questions can shape the flow of information toward including more technical and behavioral actions that follow on the conclusions drawn from using open questions.

Open questions also draw out sensory responses, emotions, role confusion or role responsibility taking. Open questions are very powerful. When you ask an open question, and listen to the answer with SOLER attending behaviors, the response may end up giving you a wealth of the invisible, nonverbal and interpersonal dynamics that are the filter through which all technical information is conveyed.

Closed questions help take this information and funnel the energy generated by open questions into behaviors, operations and actions that move task fulfillment forward. Closed questions are also very powerful when you ask them using SOLER, in a focus that is grounded in both interpersonal and technical understandings of any given situation.

Without the benefits of the information gathered through open-ended questions you are working blindly, similar to trying to drive at night without your lights on. Without the benefits of the dynamic energy gathered through closed questions you can get mired in interpersonal *cul de sacs* that inhibit action and task fulfillment, similar to gunning a car engine without engaging the transmission.

REFLECTION Which are easier to construct in a dialogue, the closed or the open questions? You may have noticed how easy it would be to answer the closed questions with a single word answer. You may also have noticed that in answering the closed questions with a single word answer, your answer would have been less than complete in response to the actual question.

Can you think of an open-ended question? Can you structure a question to ask a partner about the weather, or what they had for lunch that invites them to give you detail, a sense of their perspective and experience? That would be an open question.

Can you structure a question to ask a partner about what they had for lunch that gives you a specific, single word response that allows you to choose, or to choose not, to eat lunch where they ate? That would be a closed question. Working with constructing the questions themselves is the best way to learn the skill of both asking and answering open and closed questions.

One extremely important use of Open and Closed Questions is to help you assess nonverbal and verbal cues you receive by usage of Attending Behaviors. Another highly important usage of these types of questions is in the following the *Six Step Cycle* for solving interpersonal and technical issues in team meetings and project management evolutions. This structure helps you regain footing, find a missed turn, or lead teammates back to a clearly mapped route while making team choices and accomplishing team tasks.

Six Step Cycle for Problem Solving

The value in this cycle is that it implements a basic problem-solving approach and it can be iterated or repeated as needed over the full course of a design development or project execution. When used with proficiency, the skills in this cycle answer the question, "What can I do when I get lost in the landscape of teaming and project management as interpersonal issues and technical challenges arise?"

You can:

1. **Identify Context**. Establish rapport and understand the area of the Space, Face, and Place spectrum in which you have lost your bearings.
2. **Define the Problem.** What concerns and issues are there? Define what to talk about—primarily technical, a balance of technical and interpersonal, or primarily interpersonal. This is like telling the story that describes the situation.
3. **Define the Goals**. Know what you want to happen from the communication.
4. **Generate Alternatives**. Explore alternatives of more effective communication and behavior to create intentionality in the situation. This is like retelling the story in Step 2, only this time changing some parts along the lines of what you need to have happen.

5. **Take Action**. Choose an action and follow through.
6. **Iterate**. Repeat any and all of the steps as necessary if initial solutions meet resistance while being translated into sustainable actions.

99

*Chapter 5:
Effective
Interpersonal
Communication
Skills for Teamwork
and Project
Management*

Seeing this cycle in action is the best way to understand its value. We'll do this through an annotated dialogue among team members in a project scenario after we define each step in more detail here.

Step One: Identify Context On the Space, Face and Place spectrum your interaction may be happening in a coffee shop off campus to discuss team issues with a friend (primarily interpersonal), it may be happening in the design lab with a few teammates to work out bugs in a design program (primarily technical), or it may be happening in a team meeting where crucial costs/customer requirement needs are being assessed in context of design functions (balance of interpersonal and technical). Understanding context helps you know what cues and details to listen for and what interpersonal and technical responses you can contribute to move the communication toward a successful conclusion.

Step Two: Define the Problem The person defining the problem typically *gets stuck in the concrete details* of problem definition. An important skill to master while intentionally driving the flow is in getting yourself and/or the person you are dealing with to *move on* to steps 3, 4, 5 and 6.

In other words . . .

> *"If you can't tell me what you'd like to be happening . . . you don't have a problem yet. You're just complaining. A problem only exists if there is a difference between what is actually happening and what you desire to be happening."*
>
> KENNETH BLANCHARD

Encourage the use of appropriate "I," "You" and "Team" statements and effective use of Open and Closed Questions with perceptive Attending Behaviors to move from concrete problem definition into metacognitive problem comprehension and insight toward resolution.

Step Three: Define the Goals You can shape the flow of communication toward action and pro-active choices in an exchange even when team members are frustrated with each other and edging toward unproductive communication exchanges. Use Open and Closed Questions and "I" statements to generate shared goals and choices.

Step Four: Generate Alternatives Now that a goal has been potentially defined, it needs to be accomplished in such a way that all team members can agree on the way forward. To do this, you need to let the team generate a set of possibilities in order to find the best way for everyone to move along. Use Attending Behaviors and Open and Closed Questions and appropriate "I," "You" and "Team" statements to gather inclusive team perspectives and choices based in consensus.

Step Five: Take Action Through implementation of all the skills, you have just shaped communication flows. The crucial step now is to take action, and to follow up. Taking action will be doable for all teammates because the choices agreed upon and goals generated include all perspectives.

Step Six: Iterate Sometimes taking actions generates new solutions or shows roadblocks for potential solutions. You then iterate, or repeat, the six-step cycle to filter through and deal with new developments.

 REFLECTION When you can move through a Six Step Cycle of problem resolution repeatedly and get pro-active results you have reached a high level of proficiency in effective interpersonal and team communication skills. You have demonstrated the best of interpersonal communication effectiveness, the rapport, insight, team loyalty creation, and professional ethics that are possible when teams communicate fully and effectively.

This process is clarified in a quote from Druskat and Wolff in an article in the *Harvard Business Review* based on their research about building the emotional intelligence of teams. This quote is important because it takes the complex idea of team systems functioning and translates multimodal interpersonal and technical dynamic processes into relational behaviors.

"To be most effective, the team needs to create emotionally intelligent norms—the attitudes and behaviors that eventually become habit—that support behaviors for building trust, group identity, and group efficacy. The outcome is complete engagement in tasks." (Druskat and Wolff, 2008)

Easy to say and quick to read, but what does this mean and how do you do it? The following project scenario and team dialogue provide a model for one approach to reaching the functional norm identified by Druskat and Wolff and practiced using the skills we have given you above.

Project Scenario and Dialogue

The following scenario and dialogue address issues in teamwork and task completion for a project. The dialogue includes highlighted, effective usage of practical communication tools and communication skills. Brief instances of the interpersonal communication skills are highlighted and an analysis of their usage follows the dialogue. A user-friendly rubric highlights key capabilities and behaviors opened for you by usage of these tools and skills. You can practice these proficiencies in a variety of settings to become a more effective communicator on teams and as a project manager.

Project Scenario The team in this project is working on a senior capstone design project that involves delivering affordable, sustainable bio-medical products to rural clinics that are attempting to meet the medical life needs of severely underserved populations. The organization sponsoring the project has networks of cross-cultural customer/design team interfaces, design component supply sources and product delivery in place. Each team must create a design solution that works within this network. Each team has a challenge that is based in technical requirements, i.e. a long-lasting hinge elbow joint for a prosthetic arm for children injured in civil war conflicts on the African continent. The design and implementation of this prosthetic joint is challenging because the single plane motion of the elbow hinge must also allow for articulation that mimics the natural motion of a human wrist. Each team is tasked with understanding customer needs, design materials and supply chain constraints impacting their designs. Teamwork means coordinating individual tasks and team goals within these constraints and still designing and producing a usable product that works well and in long-term product life cycles for the population served. Project management involves coordinating not only the project as a whole but also the likely project disruptions created by the complexity generated when a project team and the population being served live in two daily realities that are so completely diverse from each other.

Alyssa, the project manager, has requested a meeting with team members tasked for materials analysis and customer requirements. There are four members involved in this aspect of the project. The materials analysis teammates keep coming up with materials that will be applicable to a variety of prosthetic devices and uses and will be long lasting. The glitch is that these materials are expensive and not consistently available for future production. The team as a whole is getting frustrated by this obstacle in both task completion and interpersonal balance. They are losing their place in project timelines and are overdue for two deliverables. The meeting that unfolds below has been called to deal with a central tension starting to take over the project.

Alyssa has done preliminary data gathering and found that the core of the problem involves the fact that the team members responsible for customer requirements had the privilege of joining a departmental trip to the village being served by the project. Their ideas about customer needs and the real impacts of delivering an affordable, usable product in this environment got transformed by this visit; they came home both overwhelmed by the constraints and really inspired to overcome them. Team members with other tasks are glad to have a first-hand perspective on customer needs. But the team as a whole has been unable to generate a solution to the discrepancy between design ideas and customer needs/available resources. They have struggled with the materials cost/customer need issue for three unproductive, somewhat contentious team meetings. There have been no design or process breakthroughs in between meetings.

The current meeting is intended to deal with this issue that is now obstructing a smooth flow of task completion. The central obstruction is that the materials team is not able to engineer designs with affordable materials that can also handle the stress the joint will take over the lifetime of a prosthetic device. And the customer requirements team keeps indulging in a "we were there so we are the experts" form of conveying customer needs. Alyssa's challenge in this meeting is to facilitate a solution that transforms a communication roadblock into an opportunity for collaboration.

She is going to use her own very effective GPS of communications skills mapping to do this. Her teammates are going to both resist her and collaborate with her in the usage of these skills, almost driving the meeting off course in several individual exchanges.

101

*Chapter 5:
Effective
Interpersonal
Communication
Skills for Teamwork
and Project
Management*

(Dialogue statements are italicized. Microskills are analyzed in text between dialogue statements.)

Dialogue Subteams are in the labs and design rooms provided for the project. They are all doing a three-hour lab on the project. Todd and Alex are the team members responsible for customer requirements. By lottery selection they were the members chosen to take the trip with faculty members to the village served by the project. Devanni and Simon are the team members responsible for materials analysis. They are struggling with finding materials that are affordable and that meet customer requirements.

Alyssa:
"Todd and Alex, and Devanni and Simon, can you please come with me into the meeting room? You don't need to bring anything. I have your reports with me."

REFLECTION Space, Face and Place Spectrum: Alyssa is programming her GPS to drive the meeting in a direction that will help her reach her goal. She takes her teammates into an environment that creates a primary focus that is both interpersonal and technical. If they stayed in a lab or design room, the focus of the dialogue could keep shifting toward computers and spreadsheets. Additionally, she is providing data, keeping her teammates from shifting focus to their own smartphones and laptops, so that the focus stays on a holistic group solution focus.

Todd (looking up from his console):
"We should meet out here, Alyssa. There's more info on customer regions' impact on requirements available in the lab. We should focus on that."

REFLECTION Misplaced "Team" statement. Generalizing team solutions from a preferred personal perspective.

Alyssa (heading toward the meeting room):
"I appreciate your idea on that Todd, but I need the 'no interruption' factor we get in the meeting room. I need to focus on the complexity we're stuck with. Maybe after we reach a few goals in the meeting we can move out here."

REFLECTION Alyssa is using her GPS to let her teammates know she is driving the communication vehicle right now. They are welcome to create input, but the direction is set. She is using *appropriate "I" statements* to do this. Stating personal preference and need while still respecting a teammate's opinion and perspective.

Alex:
"I'm coming along, Alyssa. You want me to bring anything?"

Devanni:
"Are you sure you want to meet now? We're only half way through this lab."

Simon:
"I've got a new design material here, Alyssa. You want that to add to your info?"

 REFLECTION Attempting to reprogram Alyssa's GPS by shifting the Space, Face or Place Spectrum toward purely technical rather than balanced between interpersonal and technical, but using appropriate "I" statements and appropriate "You" statements. Moving communication exchange forward while adding a personal perspective.

103

Chapter 5:
*Effective
Interpersonal
Communication
Skills for Teamwork
and Project
Management*

Alyssa (turning and facing each team member, smiling, but squaring her shoulders and speaking firmly):
"Devanni, we have to meet now or the team can't make progress to plan the next lab. They are waiting on us. Simon and Alex. No thanks on the extra info. I'm good. Like I said. I've got everything I need."

 REFLECTION Alyssa is letting her teammates know, through use of SOLER and RECAP—self-monitoring of voice tone impact on the listener and attention to personal, nonverbal posturing—and through use of appropriate "I," "You" and "Team" statements, that the GPS is programmed, they have a direction, and they all need to take a ride together in that direction.

Devanni, Simon, Alex and Todd grab their gear and head toward the meeting room. Once inside the room they pull their chairs in a circle. Alyssa hands around a few pages of a customer requirements analysis and a materials costing analysis.
Alyssa:
"Here we go. You can see I added a number into each analysis that shows the unworkable gap between materials costs for each alternative Devanni and Simon have designed and the customer requirements Todd and Alex drew up. For this project, customer requirements include keeping the budget for parts replacement over our program's three-year sponsorship cycle. Devanni and Simon have great ideas and Alex and Todd are showing a realistic assessment of the customer requirements that goes far beyond anything we could get by just reading the customer needs description online. So how come you four haven't found a solution to this issue yet?"

 REFLECTION Alyssa's voice tone is neutral and positive, even though she is asking a loaded question. Her posture is welcoming and stable. She used SOLER and RECAP to keep her GPS programming on track, showing her teammates through her own self-monitoring and communication choices how they can stay on track. This is the place where these teammates usually get lost, so this is a key place for Alyssa to drive the exchange but also leave airspace for input that leads to solutions. She is using her own communication skills to open dialogue in a way that addresses discrepancies in technical needs and outcomes, but she is staying balanced interpersonally and technically on the Space, Face and Place Spectrum.

Todd (placing his papers on the floor beneath his seat and sighing heavily, sitting up and crossing his arms over his chest and speaking sternly and curtly):
"We're not starting from the right place here, Alyssa. I've said this in all three meetings before this one that there is no way you guys can really get this unless you've been there. And that we shouldn't start at costs, requirements or technical needs, but at the real life deficits we're working with over there."

 REFLECTION Inappropriate use of "You" and "Team" statements. Using critical "You" and blaming "Team" statements to block further dialogue and advance personal positions rather than invite input and listen or state positions in positive frames that leave alternate positions open.

Alex (looking at the sheets and then at Todd and Alyssa, nodding his head vigorously, hunched over his knees with his elbows supporting his torso, making no eye contact with Devanni or Simon):
"You got it Todd. I hear you, buddy. People who didn't see this straight up just shouldn't be trying to throw solutions at it that cost so much money."

 REFLECTION Inappropriate use of "You" and "Team" statements.

Devanni rolls her eyes and crosses her arms and taps her foot on the floor. Simon shifts in his chair so that he is facing more toward the window than the group. He puts his head down and grimaces.

 REFLECTION Alex and Todd are attempting to shift the GPS direction into more interpersonal territory, from costing and requirements to a push-pull over who gets to drive decisions. This would shift the setting of the Space, Face and Place Spectrum that Alyssa set for the meeting. Their lack of SOLER—attention to the impact of their words on teammates—and inability to RECAP—monitor their own nonverbal and verbal reactions—are working against communication flows rather than in support of them. Their use of inappropriate "You" and "Team" statements is increasing communication roadblocks, not transforming them.

Alyssa (slumps in her chair, crosses her arms behind her head and closes her eyes; she takes a breath and says in a relaxed and easy voice):
"Don't mind me you all. I have so much confidence that you can work this out, because you are all showing me how firm you are in your own position on the solutions, that I am just going to take a nap and let you handle it."

105

Chapter 5:
*Effective
Interpersonal
Communication
Skills for Teamwork
and Project
Management*

 REFLECTION Alyssa is using SOLER and RECAP to keep her GPS on track even in the midst of an escalating conflict. Her self-monitoring, her RECAP skills, have alerted her that if she doesn't take a breath and relax, she'll lose it on Alex and Todd. As the discussion moved forward, she could feel her shoulders tighten, her feet flex against the floor and her breath get shallow. She knows this is how she reacts right before she turns into a drill sergeant and orders people around. But she's learned that doesn't work over the long-term cycle of a project, because people lose authorship if she takes over and then their productivity goes way down.

So she uses her SOLER, her ability to attend to the nonverbal cues of everybody in the room, to clarify her sense that all four teammates are not able to move forward. Her ability to read Devanni's and Simon's body language, and hear the stress underlying Alex's and Todd's seemingly assertive statements, lets her know that her teammates are lost in the landscape of the needs/cost/design discrepancy. They are having imbalanced interpersonal reactions to technical constraints. And she needs to try something really new to rescramble the dynamic.

By completely neutralizing her own body posture and withdrawing her attention from the group, she is doing a transformative communication programming on her GPS. By going under the radar, and taking it down a notch, she is continuing to drive the direction of the communication away from conflict and toward open dialogue.

 REFLECTION The rest of the dialogue shows how this transforms a roadblock into an opportunity for creative thinking and teamwork. The following section is not highlighted with GPS factors. Read it as a whole unit and try to find at least two examples of each from the microskills of (1) balance on the Space, Face and Place Spectrum, (2) appropriate "I," "You" and "Team" statements, (3) proactive use of Open and Closed Questions, and (4) Attending Behaviors.

Silence ensued after Alyssa's last statement.
Todd and Alex look at each other, surprised.
Devanni leans over and starts searching in her backpack.
Simon turns toward the group. He glances at Devanni.
Devanni looks back at him.

Devanni:
"Simon, did you get the e-mail from Sarah about that other project in Central America that is like what we are doing here?"

Simon (clearing his throat and swallowing hard):
"Yup. I got it last week."

Devanni:
"Why didn't you do anything with it or send it on to me?"
Alyssa sits up slowly and quietly. Todd starts to talk, but she puts her hand on his shoulder.

Simon:
"Well I'm not good with making those, you know, 'cultural translations'" (he smirks with embarrassment, then shrugs his shoulders).

Alex:
"I'll say you're not. I've been trying to get that through to you for a month."

Alyssa (sitting back again and putting her arms behind her head, speaking clearly and quietly):
"Alex, we're getting momentum here for the first time in three meetings. If I have to send you out of the room to keep it going, I will. For real. Please just take a breath and listen here. I think Devanni is onto something because I got that e-mail too."

Alex turns red, shrugs his shoulders, glances at Todd, who shakes his head in a "no" motion. Alex sits back.

Devanni:
"Well I am good at the culture thing, Simon, and you know that. Remember, I did a double major in undergrad with Anthropology and Engineering. I love that stuff—mixing it up with the people and the engineering. I told you 'bout that last semester, bro. What are you doin' keeping that e-mail from me? I didn't see til Alyssa sent it on to me."

Simon sits back and laughs, unexpectedly.

Simon:
"Oh, man. I'm in trouble now. You start talking to me like I don't got your back, and I know you're gonna prove me wrong and show me up right in front of everybody. I've seen you do it."

Devanni laughs in a friendly way at Simon, then smiles at Alyssa.

Devanni:
"Yeah, but that's only to people I feel good with, Simon. You know that. We're cool, it's okay. I'll wait til later to bring you down."

Alyssa sits forward and takes in the whole group with her glance. She nods encouragingly at Todd and Alex. She smiles at Devanni and Simon.

Alyssa:
"Okay, Devanni and Simon, good recovery. Now Devanni I'm on the edge of my seat to hear more on your thoughts about this. Bring it up."

Devanni glances at Todd and Alex and opens her posture, sits back, relaxes her shoulders:
"Well, I don't know if you two got the e-mail from Sarah about that project. But it had one good point in it that I think you been drivin' into the ground but I get it. The project in Central America solved a materials cost issue by cutting back prosthetic fitting hours. They brought in a Physician's Assistant Intern who trained local folks how to help with fitting visits. He didn't cost anything because it was his internship and he was supervised by Doctors Without Borders. Then, the money they saved on the fitting hours with the paid Doc, which was like, thousands of dollars, they were able to spend instead by making socket covers that were nylon instead of wool. That way people didn't sweat as much and the joints didn't corrode as quickly. So then they were able to use the cheaper material for their socket joints."

Alex nods his head and smiles and leans forward. Todd smiles too.

Alex:
"That's right, Devanni. That's all we were trying to say. Find local resources. Don't keep looking at materials that maybe make sense here but not over there."

Alyssa:
"Well the way you said it, guys, didn't sound like that to me. I kept feeling like I didn't know anything because I wasn't there. I didn't hear any solutions in that."
Devanni and Simon nod their heads.
Todd clears his throat.

Todd:
"Sorry guys. I got carried away."

Alex:
"Yeah, sorry. It didn't sound that way to me when I said it. Then nobody seemed to listen and I was worried the team wouldn't do okay and I just kept pushing on it."

Alyssa:
"All right, thanks for taking accountability for that. That's really important. Now, let's use that Six Step Cycle they gave us for problem solving and finish this thing off."
Alex slumps down in his chair.

Alex:
"Geez, Alyssa. Too much talking. I'm toast. Can't we just go out and generate some alternatives and then e-mail 'em around and make a choice?"

Simon:
"That already didn't work that well for us, Alex. Let's just give this a shot even though it feels like kindergarten Kumbaya and a sing-song. I just want to get this done for the rest of the team today, okay?"

Alyssa:
"Thank you, Simon. I agree with that. Can you live through it Alex?"

Alex:
"Yup. I'm in."

Alyssa:
"Great, thank you. Everybody try to keep it real to the point and short, since I think Alex is right, this has been a lot of interpersonal to get through. Here's the six stages. I'll put them on the white board: Identify Context, Define the Problem, Define the Goal, Generate Alternative Solutions, Take Action, Iterate. We don't have to tackle the whole solution right now. But let's come up with some steps to take a move forward on it. Todd, you define the context of the problem, don't tell us the story—just outline the technical and then interpersonal. Alex, you define the problem. Briefly. Devanni, you define the goal. Simon, you mention alternative solutions. And we'll all decide on actions and possible iterations together. Todd, are you ready?"

Todd:
"Well, um, let's see. The context is we went there and we got to see what it really means that the budget can't go over so, uh."

107

Chapter 5:
Effective
Interpersonal
Communication
Skills for Teamwork
and Project
Management

Alyssa:
"Not the story, Todd. The context."

Todd:
"Sorry. Okay, we have a need for high quality ball joint material but if we choose the best we have, we'll use up our whole budget on just that and our customer has no backup budget. So the context is the customer needs vs. technical considerations vs. costs and me and Alex and Devanni and Simon working as a whole unit on that."

Alyssa, Devanni and Simon:
"Thanks! Perfect! I'm with you."

Alyssa:
"Let's keep moving. Alex, your turn."

Alex:
"The problem is we can't find materials that solve the problem."

Devanni:
"I think the problem is supposed to be more openly defined than that, Alex."

Alex:
"Oh, man. All right. We haven't done an adequate resources analysis. We've only done an investigation of obvious resources like money and materials. There might be resources we don't see yet."

Simon:
"Uh oh, Alex is going Group Hug on us."

Alyssa smiles and looks with a friendly grin at Simon:
"Shut up, Simon. That was brilliant and you know it. You wish you said it."
Simon and the group laugh.

Simon:
"Devanni, say your piece quick, so I can bring it home and show you guys up for real."

Devanni, laughing:
"So the goal is that we find a material that fits customer requirements and the product setting constraints, including budgeted long term usage needs. And the goal is that we begin to find a way to do that that includes investigating resources we aren't used to accessing."

Alyssa:
"Nice, Devanni. Alex and Todd, any objections?" (No one objects, everyone gives a go forward nod or smile.) "Simon, go."

Simon:
"Okay, I read that e-mail and then went to the website and read the story of the project. Our customer needs are different. The materials need isn't so much around the corrosion of the joint. It's more around the need to have a joint that doesn't keep costing max dollars in initial materials and replacement costs. Those wear out first. So not only are the materials expensive, the replacement costs could break the whole thing. So we need a joint that has materials that can be affordable at outset, but where the replacement costs don't also send the ship down. So how about we look at some stuff like training the people to check the joints every three months so we don't

109

*Chapter 5:
Effective
Interpersonal
Communication
Skills for Teamwork
and Project
Management*

have early wearouts? And how about we look at some stuff like a study of occupation-based repetitive movement stress on a joint? And then maybe look at different tiers of materials quality?"

Todd:
"I'll do the writeup for the resources in the village social structures and access to regional materials we might not be aware of. That's the thing I've wanted to do since I got home."

Alex:
"I'll help with that."

Devanni:
"I'll look at occupational repetitive stress stats across cultures and climate zones."

Simon:
"I'll look at materials analysis studies in conjunction with occupational repetitive stress motion stats. The DOD has a lot of that from their amputees in new job training."

Alyssa:
"Wow guys. Super. We have a goal and alternative solutions and actions to take. Unfortunately, we're pressed for time. So I'll ask each of you to do this ASAP and send each other and the group progress updates over the next four days. We'll take it from there. And please, if you get stuck, ask for feedback. That's my job and I'd much rather do preventive maintenance than play referee again. (Alyssa looks around the room at each teammate for emphasis.) Thanks everybody!"

 REFLECTION Identify several statements made by one of the team members in the dialogue that let you know they were now functioning as an individual member interactive with the flow of information happening for the team as a whole unit, rather than as an individual member attempting to have their position or needs made primary by the team.

Bringing It All Together

You now have the methods and tools to take the complex ideas of team systems functioning and translate their multimodal interpersonal and technical dynamic processes into relational behaviors. You now have skills available that enable you to be in communication with the social system of which you are a member as a project manager, both interpersonally and technically. You will be able to use these skills not only to make yourself clearly understood and understand others in this social context but also to fundamentally shape the flow of your teamwork and project operations. Using skills and modeling presented here you will be able to anticipate the fact that you are more likely to be misunderstood than to be understood by teammates and project partners. You have the tools to ensure that obstacles and missed turns generated by this reality of human communication do not become project cycle roadblocks and team conflicts. You have the skills to drive your team and project management communications to desired goals and outcomes.

REFLECTION The knowledge, skills and tools presented here enable you to work through and even prevent communication roadblocks in meeting teamwork and project management technical and programmatic goals. Use the Interpersonal Skills Rubric to check your progress toward development of effective interpersonal communication skills.

Interpersonal Skills Rubric

	1 = Not Attained	3 = Satisfactory	5 = Outstanding
Space, Face and Place Spectrum	Content and/or delivery does not match social and/or professional context, who is being addressed, or place where the communication is happening.	Content and delivery adequately matches social and professional context, who is being addressed and place where the communication is happening. Maintaining flows of constructive communication and influencing outcomes is not yet present.	Content and delivery match social and professional context, who is being addressed and place where the communication is happening. Constructive flows of communication are maintained and outcomes are effectively influenced.
I, You and Team Statements	Communication exchanges include criticism and/or blame. Personal responsibility is not articulated for opinions and feelings expressed.	Personal responsibility is expressed. Articulates balanced interpersonal and technical content. Capacity to reorient communication flows toward productive outcomes is not yet exhibited.	Personal responsibility is expressed. Articulates balanced interpersonal and technical content. Reoriented communication flows toward productive outcomes.
Attending Behaviors	Is not receiving or transmitting accurate interpersonal and technical content. Is missing visual and audio cues transmitted by self and others during communication exchanges.	Receives and transmits accurate interpersonal and technical content. Catches visual and audio cues transmitted by self and others during communication exchanges. Clarity in communication flows is not yet present.	Anticipates the impact of verbal and nonverbal missed cues on communication exchanges. Maintains clear and accurate interpersonal and content flow.

Interpersonal Skills Rubric

111

*Chapter 5:
Effective
Interpersonal
Communication
Skills for Teamwork
and Project
Management*

	1 = Not Attained	3 = Satisfactory	5 = Outstanding
Open and Closed Questions	Inadequate usage of open or closed questions to elicit necessary information that furthers interpersonal and/or technical communication flows.	Uses open and closed questions to elicit necessary information to further interpersonal and technical communication flows. Ability to shape the flow of communication not yet present.	Uses open and closed questions to elicit necessary interpersonal and technical communication flows that shape productive outcomes.
Six Step Cycle for Problem Solving	Does not create workable problem-solving context. Does not define goals to adequately address problem. Does not explore alternatives. Does not choose an action for follow-through.	Establishes rapport and understanding. Defines concerns and issues while accepting personal responsibility. Defines desired outcomes. Explores alternatives. Chooses actions and follows through. Iterates as needed.	Establishes rapport and understanding that actively engages others and invites collaboration. Reflects the big picture of concerns and issues. Elicits and defines desired outcomes. Creates intentionality in exploring alternatives. Obtains consensus on potential actions that empower everyone to follow through.

Becoming a successful and proficient team member and project manager will not happen solely as a thought process. It will happen as you practice and apply the skills in authentic teaming and project management situations. You will develop proficiency in the form of effective behaviors and response patterns that will enable you to create solutions and manage conflict with robust fluency in a diversity of professional settings.

Questions

1. How would you define interpersonal skills? As abstract ideas? As interactive processes?
2. Do you feel they are a necessary component of teamwork? Why? Or why not?
3. Describe a situation in which you used interpersonal skills to influence outcomes.

Exercises

Please first read B. Oakley, R. M. Felder, R. Brent, and I. Elhajj, "Turning Student Groups into Effective Teams," *Journal of Student Centered Learning* 2, no. 1 (2004).

1. How could you modify a team member evaluation and peer rating forms as referenced in Oakley et al. to include consideration of microskills of communication to address assessment areas that need attention?
2. Read the section of the Oakley paper on coping with Hitchhikers and Couch Potatoes on teams. Apply any of the microskills defined in this chapter in a scenario in which you are stuck on a team with a hitchhiker or a couch potato and a team task deadline is looming.

References

We gave you brief definitions of skills and tools in the chapter. For more in-depth information on effective interpersonal and technical communication, cueing relevant response skills in communication, and communication in systems theory, you can access the following.

Bateson, G. 1979. *Mind and nature: A necessary unity (advances in systems theory, complexity, and the human sciences)*. London: Hampton Press.

Birdwhistell, R. 1970. *Kinesics and context*. Philadelphia: University of Pennsylvania Press.

Bundy, A., S. Lane, and E. Murray. 2002. *Sensory integration: Theory and practice*. F. A. Davis Company.

Capra, F. 1997. *The web of life: A new scientific understanding of living systems*. New York: Random House.

Cohen, M. 2007. *Reconnecting with nature*. Lakeville, MN: Green Press.

Druskat, V. U., and S. B. Wolff. 2008. Building the emotional intelligence of groups. *Harvard Business Review* 79(3), 81–90.

Greenspan, S. 1988. The development of the ego: Insights from clinical work with infants and young children. *Journal of the American Psychoanalytic Association* 36 (S), 33–55.

Knapp, M., and J. Hall. 2009. *Nonverbal communication in human interaction*. Kentucky: Wadsworth Publishing.

Meadows, D. 2008. *Thinking in systems: A primer*. White River Junction, VT: Chelsea Green Publishing.

McDonald, A., and J. Hansen. 2009. *Truth, lies, and o-rings: Inside the space shuttle Challenger disaster*. Gainesville: University Press of Florida.

Oakley, B., R. M. Felder, R. Brent, and I. Elhajj. 2004. Turning student groups into effective teams. *Journal of Student Centered Learning* 2(1).

Whitcomb, C., and L. Whitcomb. 2013. *Effective interpersonal and team communication skills for engineers*. Hoboken: Wiley, IEEE Series on Communications.

CHAPTER 6

Joining Existing Teams, Projects, and Organizations*

Getting On-board: Learning the Ropes of Working in Teams

Jamie was really excited and a little nervous. Tomorrow was the start of her first "real" job after graduating with a degree in Civil Engineering. She had her choice among several job offers, but chose to work for a government agency that specialized in building and maintaining the transportation infrastructure for her home state. She spent much of her life traveling on the roads and crossing the bridges that she was about to help design, build, and maintain. That was the exciting part.

Wondering what it would be like working as an employee instead of studying day and night as a student made her a little nervous. Sure, she had talked several times to the HR recruiters and met with her new boss in the last few weeks. Still there was a little apprehension about walking in the door that first day and sitting down at her desk.

Edgard, one of her friends from school, who majored in mechanical engineering, was starting his new job with one of the big vehicle manufacturers in a couple of days. Although you might not have guessed it, he was also excited and a little nervous. He chose this job because it promised to be exciting work. He was joining a team of engineers responsible for testing and validating some of the latest automotive technology—technology that was still a few years from hitting the market—and he would help get it ready for customers. That was the exciting part.

Both graduates were joining a team of engineers in their respective organizations. What would that be like? That was the part that made both of them a little nervous. A few of the questions that raced through their minds were similar. Would they learn fast enough to earn the respect of their manager? Would they make too many mistakes the first few days or weeks? Would they look foolish at first? How should they ask for help if they didn't know the answer? These were not big anxieties; after all they had just finished one of the most grueling programs of study at the university. Still, leaving school and starting out in the "real world" seemed a little stressful—no matter who you were.

Fast-forward a few weeks on the job. Jamie was having a great time, working hard, learning many new things about engineering roads and bridges, as well as all the planning and decision making that goes on behind the scenes. Edgard was slightly disappointed and more worried now. So far, he had only

---

*By Russell Korte.

been assigned simple tasks (entering data in spreadsheets) and he spent more time than he'd care to admit trying to look busy. Despite their accomplishments in school, the workplace was a different experience. Their experiences differed largely because of differences in the nature of their work teams.

When joining existing teams, newcomers begin a process of learning to integrate into the social structure of the group. Learning how the teams work and getting accepted by the members of the team is an important process for newcomers. This involves learning how work is done and why it is done that way, as well as learning the norms or unwritten rules that govern the interactions of team members. Newcomers must "learn the ropes" as they attempt to become valued members of the team. This integration process is typically called *socialization* or *on-boarding* and is the topic of this chapter. What happens during socialization and why are explored in the following sections.

 REFLECT ON YOUR EXPERIENCES Take a minute to think back to your first day of school at the university or other institution—or your first day on a new job or internship. Answer the following brief questions as specifically as possible:

- What did you expect your first day would be like?
- What did you hope would happen?
- What did happen?
- What surprised you (positively and negatively)?
- Were you excited or disappointed?
- What else did you feel that first day?
- Did anything happen that gave you an indication about the way things are done?
- Did someone step up to help you get through the first few days or weeks?

Research indicates that the first impressions of a new school or job are hard to overcome. And they go both ways: that is, the impressions you have of the organization and the impressions others have of you. Rather than leaving these impressions to chance, think about how you can position yourself for greater success regardless of what you experience. Knowing how important the first few weeks are can help you to make the most of it because the transition into a new group is too important to leave to chance.

What's This All About? Background Research on Socialization

The sketch above about Jamie and Edgard starting their new jobs came from recent research I conducted about the experiences of newly hired engineers starting new jobs in large corporations. In all cases, these newcomers joined small teams of 8–20 other engineers organized as teams or work groups assigned to different processes in the overall workflow of their companies. Their experiences clearly showed that, even though each of them officially joined a large multinational corporation, they really joined a small team of people engaged in a complex social system focused (mostly) on working to achieve the goals of their particular work group. Each group also varied in their preferences for the way work was done and how the members interacted with each other (Korte, 2009, 2010).

Based on the results of the study, it was apparent that each of these teams had developed different subcultures within the company—including slightly different norms and expectations for their members and for newcomers. The best teams were exciting places to work—full of activity and challenging work. The worst were dull and lonely places. Most of the newcomers' experiences fell somewhere between these extremes with various combinations of rewarding and frustrating work.

In these studies, we found a wide range of experiences that depended on the efforts of the newcomer to learn to fit in *and* on the efforts of the current team members to help the newcomer learn to fit in. Newcomers that received help, in the form of guidance and mentoring, from their manager and coworkers generally had the best experiences. They learned quickly, not only how to do the tasks of the job, but also the important norms of the group—those unwritten rules that govern how things are done in this work group. Unfortunately, some new engineers joined teams where the guidance was inadequate and no mentors could be found (Korte, 2009, 2010). You can imagine how frustrating it might be to get little help as you tried to figure out what to do on your new job.

Successfully joining a new team requires an enormous amount of learning and relationship building as quickly as you can. In many cases, new hires get a short "honeymoon" period, although as the pace of business increases, the honeymoon period is getting shorter or disappearing altogether. Current results from a longitudinal study of employer expectations for newly hired engineers show that the honeymoon period has gone. New hires are expected to "hit the ground running" and any honeymoon period is expected to occur before they are hired, at the university and through the internships that students experienced (Hanneman and Gardner, 2011).

There is a lot to learn quickly. Past research of the socialization process in organizations found several different domains that newcomers had to learn and master during the early phase of their employment (Chao et al., 1994). Obviously, newcomers had to learn their job tasks and how to work with other people on their team and outside of their team. They also had to learn the specialized language of the group (often full of acronyms, codes, and slang). They had to learn the formal and informal work relationships and power structures of their team and other teams with whom they interacted. They also had to learn the explicit and implicit norms, values, and beliefs of their team and the larger organization, as well as the historical backgrounds of the people and the culture of their work group. This is a lot to learn, even with the best guidance and mentoring. With limited or little help, it is a formidable task based in large part on trial-and-error.

When I asked new engineers what was the hardest part of starting their work, nearly all of them told me it was learning what were the appropriate ways to work with others. It was learning the unwritten rules for interacting in the social and political systems of the workplace that caused the most frustration for newcomers. I also asked these new engineers what they wished they had learned in school to help them better transition into their jobs. Most reported that they wished they had learned much more about the social and political processes in the workplace. One guy said it best when he told me,

"I wish someone had taught me how to play the political game here." It was surprising to most of these engineers how much the social and political processes influenced their work and the work of others.

"First, Get to Know Them": Beginning the Socialization Process

After careful analysis of all the interviews with newly hired engineers, it became apparent that the most important driver of success for newcomers was the quality of relationship building between them and their coworkers and manager. The work relationships that developed between newcomers and their coworkers mediated the quality of their learning and work. If you had good (high quality) relationships with your coworkers you got more and better information and instruction, and you learned more about your work. You learned more—not only the basic job tasks, but also why things were done the way they were and not some other way. You learned more about the unwritten rules that governed the decisions and interactions of the team. As a result, your performance was better, you got up to speed faster, you were valued more as a member of the team, and best of all, you were more satisfied with your job. For those struggling to build good work relationships, their learning, performance, integration, and satisfaction suffered accordingly.

The importance of work relationships for success was corroborated by a study of employers' expectations done by the Collegiate Employment Research Institute at Michigan State University (Hanneman and Gardner, 2011). Based on the data they reported, the number one attribute that employers consistently looked for in job applicants was the ability to develop and maintain effective work relationships. Many new employees, including myself, mistakenly thought that doing excellent work (defined as the technical job tasks) was the key to success in the workplace. Doing good work is expected, but it is surprising to many of us to find out that building high-quality working relationships is a key requirement of work success.

One of the important pieces of advice given to new engineers by managers was, "First, get to know them." This advice was given to a new engineer that had recently joined a team of validation engineers. Their work was to test (validate) many of the functional parts of vehicles before the vehicle went into full production. The new engineer in this team described his discussion with his manager regarding how to get work done in the test lab with the technicians that set up and conducted all the testing for the validation engineers. The manager said that before you ask others to do something or to help you, you must first get to know them as people—not just as technicians or coworkers. Get to know what they do outside of work, what their hobbies and interests are, and what they think about different things outside of the workplace. Also share your interests with others as a way to build good work relationships.

In these teams, the work is complicated and the work systems are complex. What makes them so complex is that, in addition to the technical work, these systems include a variety of social and political norms. Professional work is a complex mix of historical processes and relationships, cultural norms, power structures, and personalities. Effectively getting work done requires an awareness of the interdependent social systems in which the work and the team is embedded—and most importantly, the ability to effectively work in these systems as a team. Establishing effective work relationships is the key to avoiding, or at least lessening, the misunderstandings and conflicts that can make work less effective or efficient. Appreciating the complexity of teamwork and the value of effective work relationships are important drivers of success in team environments.

 REFLECTION ON BUILDING EFFECTIVE WORK RELATIONSHIPS
Getting to know people beyond their roles as coworkers, colleagues, staff, managers, supervisors, or suppliers is critical to forming the good relationships that are essential to becoming successful on a new team—a new job. In some cases this can be tricky, as you need to sense how others might perceive you. If people sense that you are only interested in getting to know them because it will help you get ahead, you will run into resistance and resentment.

Research shows that even the most technical or work-focused conversations have some relational element that affects the relationship between the speaker and the receiver (Keyton and Beck, 2009). Studies also show that people have a keen sense of knowing when someone is sincere and when they are not. For example, Verbeke and Wuyts (2007) found that people were more accepting of others if their intentions were communal (intended to build a sense of camaraderie) rather than instrumental (intended to get something done for oneself). Thus, a request or action by a newcomer can be accepted or rejected by the others in the group based on the perceived intentions of the newcomer (Verbeke and Wuyts, 2007). It can be tricky because others do not always perceive your messages and actions in the way you intended. People often filter what they hear and see based on their past experiences, expectations, and personalities (Bandura, 2001).

Sincerely taking an interest in people beyond the work tasks and workplace helps build the camaraderie and community that improve the work and working conditions. Becoming good at your job entails more than getting good at technical job tasks; it is getting good at building relationships and building community. The team or work group you join is a small community or social system. Therefore the tasks of your job must include the social aspects of your team, as well as the technical or procedural aspects of the job.

Everyone knows that some people are more socially oriented than others. However, even those that are less comfortable or adept at small talk and social interaction can learn to get better. Taking a sincere interest in others is the first step. It helps to recognize that work is not just about solving technical problems, it is about building a community of people that solve problems and accomplish great work. Being curious and asking questions are two means of getting to know others and building community. I know someone that is truly an expert at getting to know strangers. When I asked her how she did it, she said she thinks about the idea of "20 questions." When she met someone she asked him or her several questions about what they did, what they thought, what they liked, where they lived, and so on. After 20 questions (plus or minus) they were on their way to becoming well acquainted. Good sales people, interviewers, journalists, and detectives are examples of people whose roles are based on getting to know others well. You can pick up more "tricks of the trade" from these people and adapt them to your needs.

Getting Beyond the "New Guy" Label: Becoming an Experienced and Valued Member of the Team

Social psychologists have studied the process by which newcomers join teams or work groups. While many of the practices in organizations for helping newcomers "learn the ropes" place most of the responsibility on newcomers, there is strong evidence that the process is reciprocal. That is, both the current members of the team and the newcomer have an important part to play in the success of the newcomer joining a team (Moreland and Levine, 1982, 2001).

Being the "new kid on the block" isn't easy. Many of the expectations others have for you are not readily apparent, other expectations are open for negotiation, and others are simply the deeply held assumptions people have about the way things work. Trying to learn what these assumptions are and how to meet or exceed them is difficult because people take these things for granted and they are rarely discussed openly—until something goes wrong. For example, many of the newly hired engineers I interviewed assumed that doing good work and solving problems was what they were expected to do—and if they did these things well they would succeed. Little did they realize that there were additional assumptions and expectations about what defined good work and appropriate ways of solving problems. These seemingly objective expectations of what the job required were open to interpretation and sometimes meant different things to different people. It was important to come to a clear agreement about what was needed or expected for a project to be considered a success. It was important to clarify your role and understand the others' roles in the project—in other words, what did others expect you to do, and not to do? And do they know what you expect of them and the job?

As stated earlier, learning the ropes was helped by receiving good advice and mentoring—and the prerequisite of getting good advice and mentoring was the need for building good relationships with others, in other words, getting to know them as people. One of the critical things that newcomers learned was that many of the work processes were far more complicated than expected. For example, several of the newly hired engineers I interviewed were amazed at the paper trail needed to get even the simplest tasks done. One person described to me his understanding of the complexity of organizational procedures and the need to have detailed procedures to guard against mistakes and misunderstandings. He also described how experienced people in the group knew short-cuts or work-arounds that were more efficient. However, newcomers were expected to follow procedures "by the book" until they were more experienced and earned the right to take short-cuts.

Another newcomer described how he learned to provide his advice in different ways to different people. For example, he quickly learned that some people did not want him telling them what he thought should be done—instead, he had to make suggestions and let them decide. Other people did not want to make the decisions and expected him to tell them what to do. Of course, none of this is written down and he needed to carefully figure this out as he got to know the others with whom he worked. It all sounds like common sense, and in many ways it is, but understanding that learning how to interact is more important than getting the work tasks done is sometimes surprising. An important thing to remember is that work is a social affair, not just a technical task. Thus, getting beyond the "new guy" label requires close attention to the social dynamics of the team—especially the hidden rules that form the culture of the team.

Realizing the Real Work of Teams and Getting Ahead

You might notice that much of the process of starting a new job or joining a team has little to do with what is usually considered to be the "real work" of the team or the job. Jeffrey Pfeffer (2010) of the Stanford Business School conducted extensive research on the relation between intelligence, job performance, and power in the workplace. His conclusion was that intelligence explained only about 20 percent of individuals' job performance, and explained far less of their success (as measured by income). Pfeffer identified three personal qualities and four skills that help people get ahead in the workplace. The personal qualities are ambition, energy, and focus, and the skills are self-reflection for self-knowledge, confidence and self-assurance, empathy, and a high tolerance for conflict. The lessons from these studies, and the experiences of countless people, indicate that it is the social and political systems in which individuals work that govern their success. Technical expertise is taken for granted. Hundreds of thousands of people have technical expertise in some form or another, thus it is those who are skilled at using their technical expertise in the context of working with people that are most likely to succeed.

The strength and quality of good relations among team members is not often recognized as such an essential factor in teamwork—especially in technical and project-oriented teams. However, there is strong evidence that the relational structure of the team drives the performance of the group toward accomplishing its tasks or projects. Think of the relational structure of the group as the structure that supports or impedes the work of the group, similar to the way a building supports or impedes the activity of the people working within it.

Relationships among members form over time and constitute the deep structure of the group that facilitates or impedes the surface structure of task coordination and decision making. Problems arising from relational concerns have greater impact than problems arising from task concerns. The relational system includes inputs (messages having relational components—including primarily task messages); processes (group/relationship development and development of shared meaning); and outcomes (norms, cohesiveness, satisfaction, groupthink, stress, climate).

In studies of the communication processes in small groups (or teams), Keyton and Beck (2009) described two types of communications among members: task-oriented and relations-oriented. The two are tightly intertwined such that even explicitly task-oriented messages also have subtle, or not so subtle, relational messages. Many of the relational components of team communications are nonverbal and serve to establish the nature of the relationship between the sender and receiver of a message. The existence of mixed messages in the communications among people is a commonly recognized phenomenon in professional as well as social settings. The mix-up is usually because the task and relational components of a message are saying different things. For example, I interviewed a team leader during one of my consulting projects and he stated how important he believed it was for team leaders to take charge of their projects and run them as if they were CEOs of a small company; however, before they made any decisions, they needed to get his approval first. Requiring approval certainly contradicts his wish for team leaders to take charge of their work in an executive manner. These kinds of mixed messages are common and hamper the performance of teams.

It is important to attend to the relational structure among the members of teams. It is the relational structure that drives the task or project structure. The importance of relationships cannot be overemphasized, if only because people resist the notion that relations are part of the real work of teams. I have heard students and engineers say that they went into engineering to minimize their need to attend to the social and political relationships of the workplace. They thought that engineering was primarily about technical expertise and had little use for politics or social interactions that they considered to be interference with their real work. Yet, to a large degree, the underlying relational, social, and political structures in the team and in the organization govern what gets done and how it gets done. One of my colleagues described it this way: He studied numerous "technical visionaries" in high-tech companies and found that those who were most successful at innovating new technologies were those that saw the ability to navigate the social and political environments of the workplace as more important than technical expertise to achieving success with their innovative efforts (Vojac, Griffin, Price, and Perlov, 2006). It would be foolish and incompetent to underestimate the crucial properties of materials in buildings or the electrical components in your work. It is just as foolish to underestimate the crucial properties of the social and political environment. The real work of teams is relational, as well as task oriented.

Achieving Membership: Do You Identify with Your Team?

Member identification is an important attribute of teams because it affects how members engage with others and the tasks of the team. People develop various levels of identification, which tends to affect the level of the team's performance. Fostering high engagement among team members helps develop a high-performance team.

Social psychologists study how people identify with various groups in which they participate. Social identity is the notion that people identify themselves with certain groups and behave in ways that are influenced by the groups to which they belong (Jenkins, 2004). Think about your identity as a student, professional, researcher, friend, neighbor, sibling, child, parent, football fan, soccer player, manager, employee, and so on. All of us have our personal identities, and more importantly, we have our social identities. We belong to many groups that elicit and promote specific attributes that form our social identities. One of the primary objectives for newcomers joining a new team is to identify with the team or group. Turner and his colleagues (1987, 1999) described this process of identification as Self-Categorization Theory. The essential components of this theory say that groups or teams have an idea of what is a typical member of the team—what researchers call a prototype of the team. The closer one is to the prototypical characteristics of the team, the more one can identify with the team and the more other members of the team see one as a core member. Conversely, the less one identifies with prototypical characteristics of the team, the more marginalized and isolated one becomes. Identification with the team is a major factor affecting one's integration, relationships, and performance in the team. Thus, it is critical for newcomers to figure out what is the identity or prototypical characteristics of the team and work to affiliate with the team. Of course, this doesn't mean you need to give up everything to be a member, but it is a critical factor in your success on a team. You decide how far you want to go, and knowing the consequences of identification is important to your engagement with and success at joining a team.

Sink or Swim, the Trial by Fire, and Other Challenges for Newcomers

While most of the preceding discussion focused on the newcomer, keep in mind that the socialization process is a two-way process. It is also the responsibility of the team and the organization to help newcomers fit in. The common beliefs held by human resource managers in organizations and in the literature written about socialization (starting a new job) generally assume that it is the responsibility of the new person to learn to fit in. I listened to HR managers in a couple of the organizations I studied as they told me about their rigorous selection and hiring processes. A couple of them said things supporting the belief that they tried very hard to hire the best—the ones believed to be able to swim when thrown into the deep end, or survive when thrown into the fire. The research says otherwise. Of course the newcomer must be strong enough to take initiative and learn to fit in; however, it is also the responsibility of the work team to help the newcomer get on board.

Nearly all of the new engineers I interviewed were extremely savvy individuals—very smart, competent, engaging, motivated, and outgoing. Realizing that indeed they were hired because they were the best of the best, it was surprising to see some of them struggle to fit in. The best explanation we had was that the team made it difficult for newcomers to join and do good work.

Social psychologists have studied group dynamics and propose that the process of joining a team follows a general pattern (Moreland and Levine, 1982, 2001). First there is a period of evaluation, then commitments develop, and then roles change from newcomer to full member of the team. During the evaluation period, the group assesses the newcomer and decides how well he or she lives up to the group's expectations and matches the prototypical characteristics of a valued member. Usually these expectations are not explicit or written down and many newcomers reported that they learned about these expectations by trial-and-error. For many newcomers, this was one of the most difficult processes of starting a new job. In the best situations, newcomers learned from their coworkers and managers what was expected of them. In other situations, newcomers had little information and feedback to go on.

In a similar manner, the group must learn what the newcomer needs and expects (Moreland and Levine, 1982, 2001). How well the two parties make the effort to learn about each other and help each other determines the success of the experience. This might seem obvious in hindsight, but in the process of starting a new job the mutual obligations and interactions that the newcomer and the group have for each other often get lost as each side focuses on its own immediate needs, projects, deadlines, and goals. Yet, it is critical for both parties to constantly be aware of and effectively develop the social systems within which all members work—especially when newcomers join a team.

After the evaluation stage there develops a sense of commitment between the newcomer and others in the team. Psychologists measure different levels and dimensions of commitment; however, the general idea is that people (newcomers and teammates alike) develop commitments to each other based on past and present experiences, and future expectations. Some research measures commitment as the consequence of an evaluation of value. In other words, how much the relationship will contribute or detract from the work experience (Moreland and Levine, 1982, 2001). As with evaluation, commitment is a two-way process. Newcomers develop a level of commitment to the group just as the group must develop a level of commitment to the individual. Research shows that this mutual interaction rarely correlates very well. That means that newcomers and their groups often perceive the evaluation and commitment in different ways. So, working through these different perceptions is a key part of the socialization process. You might think you are doing the team a favor with your ideas, questions, and challenges; however, others on the team might not perceive your actions as favorably as you intended. The social process of joining a team is like a dance between initial strangers that must learn how to get acquainted and coordinate their ideas, values, and behaviors toward the mutual benefits of working as effective members of a team.

A next step in the process of joining a team is the transition to a new role in the team, such as from the role of newcomer to becoming a full member (Moreland and Levine, 1982, 2001). Again, this transition is a mutual process that is often not explicitly apparent to the newcomer and other members of the group. Many of the new hires I interviewed couldn't wait to move beyond the role of being the "new guy." They worked very hard to become a valued and regular member of the team. And the most successful ones had the early support of their coworkers and managers during their transition. Newcomers experiencing less support from their coworkers made the process of becoming a full member of the team more difficult. With good guidance and feedback, the transition from newcomer to full member was significantly improved. From my research and the research of others, the primary driver of successful transitions into the role of a full member was dependent on the quality of relationships between the newcomer and other members of the team.

What Makes for a High-Performing Team Culture?

Ideally, what are the prototypical characteristics of a high-performing team? An important characteristic of teams is the ability of members to adapt to changing conditions, recognize emerging problems, learn new ways of solving problems, acquire or learn new knowledge, and take action (Edmondson, 1999). Because teams are so important to getting work done in current organizations, continuously improving team performance is a critical objective for all team members—new and old. Many of the newcomers I interviewed talked about their personal objectives to become valued members of the team and contribute to the organization. Helping the team improve performance is one of the benefits of team learning.

There is a growing field of research on team learning and several factors have been identified that foster greater learning in teams. Similar to individuals, different teams have different abilities to learn. Researchers of team learning found that the teams that learn best are teams that have cultures that appreciate and foster interaction and the sharing of knowledge among members; in other words, these teams recognize and appreciate the importance of effective working relationships among members. As important as the tasks of the work are to the team, these teams also value the input of individual members and provide a safe environment for experimenting and failing. These factors are not built into every team, but those teams that excel and perform at high levels have a high regard for learning as well as for team members and the relationships that structure team interactions. At the risk of repeating myself, it is the relationships among team members that drive learning and performance. This further supports the evidence reported by many successful newcomers that their primary objective in joining a team was to develop high-quality work relationships with their new coworkers and manager.

Building good relationships is a two-way process and is not always easy or even possible with some people. So, what can go wrong? Sometimes, the pressures on team members to conform and save face make it difficult for individual members to identify mistakes or bring up information that might be controversial. Members are more likely to bring up negative information if they believe they are safe from recrimination or blame. Social and organizational psychologists have studied the relative safety of the team environment and its effects on learning and performance. They call this characteristic of teams the *psychological safety* of the team (Edmondson, 1999). How safe team members believe they are has an effect on their openness to take risks and bring up potentially negative information—both of which are necessary for high-performance teams to increase their creativity, innovation, and performance.

Assessing the relative psychological safety of a team is one of the first tasks of newcomers as they begin to build relationships with coworkers.

The range of experiences reported by the newcomers I interviewed showed that some teams were extremely open and friendly to newcomers, others were closed and unsociable—and everything in between. After talking with over 100 newly hired engineers, I concluded that all but two or three had extremely competent skills at social interaction (otherwise they probably wouldn't have been hired in the first place). Despite their social skills not all of them were successfully integrating into their assigned teams. This was because the other members of the team or the culture of the team was not open to new members, and was not oriented toward high performance or learning. Sometimes you find yourself in a difficult situation and you have to make the best of it. Again, relationship building goes a long way to overcoming such difficulties.

When I present this research, students often ask me what should they do if they find themselves in a team that is not open or friendly or functioning well. My answer comes from those newcomers that figured out how to deal with these same conditions. Some adapted and changed their expectations to better fit with the existing team culture and some made the best of it until they could find a different team. The point is to understand that the relational structure of a team is very important to its success and the well-being of team members. Whether you are a newcomer or an old-timer in a team, attending to the relational structure of your team is critical. It is one of the primary drivers of successful socialization into a team.

So, What Can You Do to Be More Successful Joining a Team?

Throughout all the thousands of pages of interviews with newcomers I analyzed, there emerged several factors that seemed to indicate whether a newcomer would have a successful experience or not. Three of these factors are the responsibility of the newcomer and four of these factors are the responsibility of the team. Have a look at these factors for success in the table below.

Criteria for Individual Success	Description of Criteria and Sample Statement
Collaboration efforts	Does the newcomer regularly consult or collaborate with others about work tasks or projects? *"After informing people what I thought was going to happen, I kind of got nods and—okay."*
Developing nonwork relationships	Does the newcomer share nonwork-related information and try to know others outside of work situations? *"We're always chatting. Always, I mean a lot of it's work related, but let's say like 30 to 40 percent of our conversation is just about personal life and going out and doing things."*
Extra-role behavior	Does the newcomer contribute effort to the group beyond expected responsibilities? *"And at that time, it was just, I volunteered to take this on because I was new to the organization."*

Criteria for Work Group Success	Description of Criteria and Sample Statement
Local mentoring	Does a coworker in the group provide regular, ongoing direction and instruction to the newcomer? *"And so I feel like the one main guy who I have been working with, he's been very helpful in straightening things out."*
Group inclusion	Does one or more coworkers invite the newcomer to lunch or after-work social activities? *"So pretty much almost every day we'd go out to lunch. I mean a lot of times it would just be kind of me, the steering guy, and this other guy."*
Interaction with manager	Does the newcomer have frequent and regular contact or interaction with the manager? *"But he'll also stop over and ask how I'm doing, how the weekend was. Very personal."*
Meaningful assignment	Does the newcomer have a meaningful, responsible project or assignment soon after entry into the organization? *"My manager will give you a certain car program or a truck program, and you will follow it through from start to finish."*

Source: Based on Korte (2009).

References

Bandura, A. 2001. Social cognitive theory: An agentic perspective. *Annual Review of Psychology* 52, 1–26.

Chao, G. T., A. M. O'Leary-Kelly, S. Wolf, H. J. Klein, and P. D. Gardner. 1994. Organizational socialization: Its content and consequences. *Journal of Applied Psychology* 79 (5), 730–743.

Edmondson, A. 1999. Psychological safety and learning behavior in work teams. *Administrative Science Quarterly* 44, 350–383.

Hanneman, L. F., and P. D. Gardner. 2011. *Changing employer expectations: Under the economic turmoil a skills gap simmers.* Distinguished Lecture of the American Society for Engineering Education Annual Conference and Exposition, 2011, Vancouver, B.C.

Jenkins, R. 2004. *Social identity*, 2nd ed. London: Routledge.

Keyton, J., and S. J. Beck. 2009. The influential role of relational messages in group interaction. *Group Dynamics: Theory, Research, and Practice* 13 (1), 14–30.

Korte, R. 2010. First, get to know them: A relational view of organizational socialization. *Human Resource Development International* 13 (1), 27–43.

Korte, R. F. 2009. How newcomers learn the social norms of an organization: A case study of the socialization of newly hired engineers. *Human Resource Development Quarterly* 20 (3), 285–306.

Moreland, R. L., and J. M. Levine. 1982. Socialization in small groups: Temporal changes in individual-group relations. In L. Berkowitz (ed.), *Advances in experimental social psychology*, vol. 15, 137–192.

———. 2001. Socialization in organizations and work groups. In M. E. Turner (ed.), *Groups at work: Theory and research*, 69–112. Mahwah, NJ: Lawrence Erlbaum Associates.

Pfeffer, J. 2010. *Power: Why some people have it—and others don't.* New York: HarperCollins.

Turner, John C., Michael A. Hogg, Penelope J. Oakes, Stephen D. Reicher, and
Margaret S. Wetherell. 1987. *Rediscovering the social group: A self-categorization
theory.* Oxford: Basil Blackwell.

Turner, John C., and R. S. Onorato. 1999. Social identity, personality, and the self-
concept: A self-categorization perspective. In Tom R. Tyler, Roderick M. Kramer,
and Oliver P. John (eds.), *The psychology of the social self,* 11–46. Mahwah, NJ:
Lawrence Erlbaum Associates.

Verbeke, W., and S. Wuyts. 2007. Moving in social circles: Social circle membership
and performance implications. *Journal of Organizational Behavior* 28, 357–379.

Vojac, B. A., A. Griffin, R. L. Price, and K. Perlov. 2006. Characteristics of technical
visionaries as perceived by American and British industrial physicists. *R&D
Management* 36 (1), 17–26.

CHAPTER 7

Innovation in a Team Environment*

What Is Innovation?

If you were to ask 100 people to define "innovation," you would likely hear a diverse array of interpretations. So, before we discuss what innovation is, take some time to reflect on your own definition.

 REFLECTION Write your definition of innovation below or on a piece of paper. Share your definition with others. Discuss the commonalities of these definitions and aspects of innovation these may not have addressed.
- Innovation is
  _____
- The key indicators of true innovation include:
  _____
  _____
- _____ by itself is not enough to call something or some process an innovation.

When you compared your definition of innovation with those of others, did you notice any differences? The term *innovation* is often given a variety of meanings which extend far beyond its actual scope. Many use innovation to refer to the latest consumer technology. Figure 7.1 is another example we found on a roadside advertisement. This advertisement tries to grab people's attention by presenting something new and different. While newness and novelty are two of the indicators of innovation, by themselves they are not sufficient for true innovation.

---

*By Şenay Purzer and Nicholas D. Fila.

Acknowledgment: Some of the materials presented in this chapter are driven from work supported by the National Science Foundation CAREER grant 1150874. Any opinions, findings, and conclusions or recommendations expressed in this material are those of the author(s) and do not necessarily reflect the views of the National Science Foundation.

Figure 7.1 A Roadside Advertisement

Photo courtesy of Şenay Purzer.

Similar to everyday life where we see the term innovation used in diverse ways, contexts, and meanings, the academic literature also demonstrates diverse definitions of innovation. Scholars continue to debate the boundaries and meanings of this construct. Some view innovation as effective design or problem solving; others view innovation as invention or creating new things such as processes and business models. In addition, other terms such as creativity and entrepreneurship intersect with the definitions of innovation in the literature (Carlson and Wilmot, 2006; Ferguson and Ohland, 2012; Ferrari, Cachia, and Punie, 2009). While it is easy to get lost while trying to define innovation, establishing a definition is helpful and even necessary in developing a common understanding.

Definitions of Innovation

When you read further in this chapter, you will notice that we have chosen a specific definition of innovation. This decision will help us pursue and nurture discussions on what innovation is. First, let's start with a note on what innovation is *not*. According to IDEO, a leading product design firm (Kelley and Littman, 2001), having a good idea by itself is not enough for innovation. They argue that ideas must be accompanied by action and implementation. Inventors are not innovators—especially if we define inventors as those who hold patents—unless the invention reaches a broad market. Innovation is also not just about starting a new business, which we call entrepreneurship. And you do not need to be a billionaire who runs a Fortune 500 company to be called an innovator.

Then, what are the indicators of innovation? According to Carlson and Wilmot (2006) one critical aspect of innovation is "creating and delivering new customer value in the marketplace" (Carlson and Wilmot, 2006, p. 6). As stated in their definition, a key criterion for innovation is whether customers find significant positive change and usefulness in the new idea or approach.

This means that novelty alone is not sufficient unless the idea, process, or product is brought to market and found useful by the customers. Another definition, used by IDEO, complements and expands Carlson and Wilmot's definition by specifying the variables that would affect customer value. According to IDEO, innovation is placed at the intersection between feasibility, desirability, and viability (IDEO, 2012).

We have asked both first-year engineering students and engineering or design educators we meet at conferences how they define innovation. Undergraduate engineering students include many key aspects of innovation in their definitions such as creating solutions that appeal to mass audiences and solving important problems relating to the Engineering Grand Challenges (National Academy of Engineering, 2012). As shown in Figure 7.2, however, students emphasize creativity (or novelty) and usefulness more frequently than other aspects such as viability and feasibility.

While it is surprising to see the small emphasis placed on technical feasibility, especially by engineering students, their responses align with some of the literature on creativity (Amabile, 1983). Such definitions, however, are limiting in the context of engineering design where the quality of a solution is important along with its novelty (Shah, Smith, and Vargas-Hernandez, 2003). Shah and colleagues emphasize both performance measures (usefulness) *and* technical feasibility when describing the quality of engineering solutions. Like IDEO, educators often acknowledge that business-related aspects such as economic viability and potential for market acceptance and diffusion, indicated by desirability, are also essential criteria for innovative solutions.

- *Feasibility* refers to the design's technical practicality such as manufacturability.
- *Desirability* requires that the design sufficiently addresses an important need.
- *Viability* implies the cost of the design is comparable with the current alternatives and competitors.

Figure 7.2 First-year Engineering Students' Definitions of Innovation

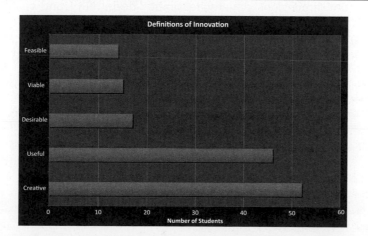

Innovation as a Process

We define innovation as a process comprised of stages during which ideas are created, tested, developed, and then widely disseminated. Ford, Koutsky, and Spiwak (2007) define these stages as: invention, trial production, imitation, and diffusion (see Figure 7.3).

Building on this definition of innovation, we have identified three key phases and three questions we should ask as we judge the innovative potential or value of an idea.

- *Phase I. Potential for Innovation:* Is the idea novel, feasible, desirable, and viable?
- *Phase II. Customer Value:* Is there at least one happy user of the idea?
- *Phase III. Dissemination:* Is the idea widely used by a large number of customers?

Phase I refers to the early stages of innovation, focusing on invention and initiation of trial production. We can investigate this during the initial development of ideas or when evaluating student solutions. Phase II goes one step beyond Phase I and questions whether a trial production is successful. Is the trial production being used by someone and is this imitation found useful? Such innovation can occur within a company where an engineer notices inefficiency in a daily task and develops a new and more efficient way of doing the task. The user can merely be the designer himself or herself. Phase III addresses a more common view of innovation where a given idea finds a place in the marketplace and is widely used by many customers beyond the designer and his or her colleagues.

Phase I: Potential for Innovation

Early in the innovation process we cannot measure the innovation quality of an idea. The idea has not yet been realized and diffused. We can, however, measure an idea's *potential for innovation.* Shah and colleagues (2003) emphasize the importance of quality in the development of any metric and state that robust measures of engineering design creativity, what we refer to as *potential for innovation,* would focus on both novelty and quality. Quality is a multifaceted measure which requires a balance between feasibility, desirability, and viability. Given these criteria, we can quantify and evaluate characteristics of an idea in four dimensions: novelty, feasibility, desirability, and viability. Ideas that are strong along each of these four dimensions have high potential for innovation and should be further developed in Phase II. Your team can practice creating potentially innovative ideas with the nearby Team Activity.

Figure 7.3 Four Components of Innovation

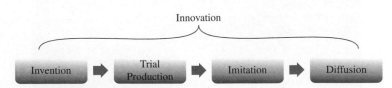

Figure created by Purzer based on Ford et al., 2007.

TEAM REFLECTION—The Innovation Jigsaw

- Form teams of four and select one advocate for each of the following team dimensions: novelty, feasibility, desirability, and viability.
- As a team, select an everyday device or process that can be improved in some way.
- Each person should take a clean piece of paper and individually draw a picture of how that device/process might be improved. (5 minutes)
- Now your team has four different ideas you can improve upon. On top of each drawing write your goal, which is "making a better (or more efficient, more effective, etc.) _____."
- Exchange these drawings with your team members. (5 minutes)
  - *Novelty Advocate:* Your job is to generate a novel, unique, or a surprising idea that is different than currently available solutions. Ask: What similar solutions already exist?
  - *Desirability Advocate:* Your job is to improve the idea to meet user needs. Make sure the solutions you produce would be appealing and useful. Consider a broad range of individuals. What might people not like about it?
  - *Viability Advocate:* Your job is to identify the cost of the idea and make design improvements that will make it competitive in the market.
  - *Feasibility Advocate:* Your job is to evaluate the technical feasibility of the idea and make improvements to increase its feasibility. Ask: Could this solution be implemented?
- Rotate each drawing after five minutes and repeat the process until you have a chance to review and improve on each solution.
- As a team, evaluate the overall "innovation potential" of each solution.

Innovation creates change, though this change can occur in different ways. In the nearby box Kathryn Jablokow, an expert in engineering innovation education, discusses two types of change, and clarifies how change created through innovation can be incremental or evolutionary.

Phase II: Customer Value

Many scholars agree that there is a strong link between creativity and innovation (Charyton, Jagacinski, Merrill, Clifton, and Dedios, 2011; Ferrari et al., 2009). For example, innovation is often considered an outcome of creative thinking, as something that is simply "new." Carlson and Wilmot (2006), however, criticize the focus on creativity, stating, "Focusing just on creativity can lead to misplaced resources and frustration." They argue for the importance of creating *new customer value*, i.e., creating a product, process, or system that improves upon all existing solutions from the perspective of the customer.

Understanding the needs of the customer is essential towards developing new customer value. An innovator must understand those needs before he or she can develop a product, process, or system that meets them. Developing such solutions is difficult and often requires creativity on the part of the innovator. For example, innovative executives are often skilled at associating, which is closely related to creativity (Dyer, Gregersen, and Christensen, 2009). They successfully translate ideas from one domain into valuable solutions in another. Other skills, such as questioning, observing, experimenting, and networking—which are common among innovators (Dyer et al., 2009)—are also necessary in creating customer value (see Table 7.1). By employing these skills, you can develop solutions with potential for innovation that also create new customer value.

Table 7.1 Description of skills used by innovators

	Description	Examples
Associating	Building relationships between prior experiences, events, designs, etc. and the new issues. Being able to apply a solution that works in a previous context to a new context.	One example of association, biomimicry, allows engineers to design products based on examples from nature. For example, Georges de Mestral, the inventor of Velcro, based his idea on the burrs that stuck to his dog's coat after a walk (Budde, 1995). Another type of association is NASA spinoffs such as memory foam mattresses and freeze-dried foods. These commercially available products are adapted from technologies developed by and for NASA (NASA, 2012).

Questioning	Explicit questions, statements or prompts addressing what you need to learn or do next. These questions challenge assumptions and lead to inquiry activities and deeper understanding of underlying issues, needs and concepts.	Asking questions is critical at all stages of innovation. Questions can be asked to users or potential customers to develop deeper understanding of their needs or gaps: What is the most expensive part of this process or approach you use? What other solutions did you consider? Questions can be asked about the current solutions: What are commonalities about current solutions? What if these solutions didn't exist? What problems do current solutions address? What problems do they not address?
Observing	Carefully watching the activities and behaviors of people, products, processes or their interactions.	A person interested in improving effectiveness of health care equipment can observe how the devices operate and how medical personnel, such as nurses, use equipment. Observations can lead to improvements of the current equipment or even be translated to designs in a different domain through association.
Networking	Communicating, developing new or deeper relationships with others, reaching out to those with complementary knowledge and skills.	An electrical engineer can collaborate with a cognitive psychologist and a music teacher to develop a guitar that gives immediate feedback on playing technique and accuracy of notes and chords.
Experimenting	Testing and evaluating prototype designs or new functions for feasibility, viability or desirability. These activities help designers visualize or elaborate upon ideas and predict or test performance.	Sample activities include building models or rapid prototypes, cost or performance calculations, and computer simulations. For example, building primitive functional models allows quick user feedback. More advanced computer-aided design and simulations provide information on performance and technical aspects of a design.

Try the nearby Team Activity on Creating Customer Value.

 TEAM REFLECTION—Creating Customer Value

- Form teams of three or four (make sure you are working with a new group of people).
- First individually think about an everyday activity you engage in at work, at school, at home, etc. (e.g., entering data into spreadsheet, listening to a lecture, flossing your teeth). Identify one that bothers you because you feel there must be a "better way" this task can be done. Note: Make sure you select one you have control over. For example, you may not be able to change how someone teaches a lecture but you can change how you listen to the lecture, how you enter data, or how you floss your teeth. (5 minutes)
- As a team, select one of these ideas that you all think is a critical need. Write your problem statement on a piece of paper. (5 minutes)

- Exchange "your problem" sheet with another team. The other team will be solving this problem and you will act as a customer or user and vice versa.
- Now, each team's goal is to determine what their customers or users value. You should interview the users and find out as much information as possible. You should also research current alternatives and the users' perspectives of these alternatives. (15 + 15 minutes for interviewing and being interviewed.) Ask them to discuss the most labor intensive, expensive, or difficult part of their job. Learn about the details of their job and how they deal with this specific issue.
- As a team, create a list of criteria necessary to satisfy the customer. (10 minutes)

Note: If there is extra time you can repeat the previous team activity and work on solving these problems.

Phase III: Dissemination

Dissemination is the stage when an idea reaches its full potential. Most of the things we use in our everyday life are innovations that have benefited a large number of customers: microwave ovens that cook food without combustion;

 TEAM REFLECTION—Innovators Among Us

- Individually, think about an idea you, your team, or your friends or colleagues had and further developed. Focus on solutions that have been used by at least five people (e.g., a website that is visited by more than 50 people in a month, an Excel macro that is used by a half dozen colleagues at work). (10 minutes)
- Share these examples with your teammates. Discuss whether these ideas can be defined as innovations and you or your friends can be called innovators.
- Based on these examples and the people you know, make a list of characteristics of innovators.

_____   _____
_____   _____
_____   _____
_____   _____

There are five commonly recognized characteristics of innovators (Cooper, 2005; Egan, 2005; Keller and Holland, 1983):

- persistence
- positive self-perception
- risk taking and openness to experience
- strong communication and networking skills
- comfort with ambiguity and low need for clarity

Do these characteristics of innovators match with the list you developed as a team?

Gore-Tex fabric that is waterproof but also breathable (GORE-TEX, 2012); allergy medicines that work without making you drowsy. The list continues to grow!

It is also possible that many of us have reached some sort of dissemination at a much smaller scale. The nearby Team Activity will ask you to reflect on such experiences. If you cannot think of any, listen to other people's examples and think about how you can have one in the future.

Read the nearby box by Eric Berkowitz, who has an engineering degree in Mechanical and Aeronautical engineering. He worked as a new products development engineer for the Cummins Engine Company before completing his MBA. He describes three innovation companies that produce products and services for low-income communities while remaining profitable.

Innovation in Low-Income Communities

You can't give people what you think they need; you need to give people what they want and what they are willing to pay for.

At Bamboo Finance, we are a private equity fund that invests in commercial enterprises that serve low-income communities. We support innovative companies that provide access to basic needs such as education, healthcare, housing, clean water, and energy.

We support different types of innovations. Some are revolutionary innovations which involve complex redesign. Others are innovations in execution and distribution. The latter is more typical of the projects we support. These are evolutionary innovations (as compared to revolutionary innovations). However, in all these innovations the common goal is to provide high quality and affordable solutions that improve the lives of low income communities.

One aspect people generally ignore is that low income communities are already paying for services such as healthcare and energy but receiving inferior services. Hence there is a large underserved market. From historical experience we know that philanthropic projects are not sustainable. It is important that the companies we are supporting are successful (i.e., self-sustaining and making profit) so they can scale and truly make an impact. We recently have funded 14 different companies globally in Latin America, Africa and Asia; more information on our portfolio can be found at www.bamboofinance.com

Case #1. Vortex Engineering in India. http:// vortexindia.co.in
Vortex is an example of innovation with complex re-design. Vortex has developed a new type of ATM with much lower operating costs than current ATMs. This allows the system to operate in rural areas where people do not currently have bank accounts. Its low cost makes it very viable for banks to buy and deploy since the number and size of the transactions is very low. In addition, solar powered designs make it work consistently in rural areas where the delivery of electricity is not reliable. Vortex has deployed 600 ATMs with the State Bank of India and about half of them are solar-powered.

Case #2. Husk Power Systems. http://www. huskpowersystems.com
Husk Power has initially focused their electrical power project in Bihar, one of the most poorly served states in India. Sixty percent of households in India do not have access to grid electricity and many must use kerosene for lighting. Kerosene is expensive and also creates health issues and increased greenhouse emissions. This company uses biogasification, converting rice husks and other biomass waste to supply electricity. Today, they are one of the largest off-grid electricity distributors. They are also the winner of the Ashden Award for off-grid power supply in 2011. You can find their full case study, pictures, and videos at http://www.ashden.org/winners/husk11

A key innovation of Husk Power is their creation of an operational ecosystem that provides affordable and reliable power to the poorer rural areas in India. Today, this company has grown to over 70 plants in India and planning to expand to East Africa. They have also developed a number of so called frugal innovations, where the cost and complexity of a product or process are reduced and the reliability and durability are increased. Components of the Husk Power ecosystem include: (1) Low cost smart meters that cut off energy delivery to individual households when they exceed their limit. (2) An affordable pre-paid model which, for $2/month, allows a household to power two light bulbs. Users can upgrade to power other needs such as charging mobile phones or small appliances. (3) Husk Power University, which trains mechanics and operators for the plants. (4) Performance management system which monitors the distribution of electricity across all their plants.

Case #3. Vaatsalya Healthcare. http://www.vaatsalya.com

Most organized health care systems in India focus on tertiary care for significant illnesses by specialists and are centered around urban locations. A neglected market is people who live in semi-rural or rural areas who are in need of primary and secondary care such as outpatient consultations, minor surgeries, and child birth. This company established small health care clinics with 50–75 beds and has expanded to 17 clinics across two states.

The innovation model of this company is their delivery of high quality services that are also affordable to the low income. In other words, what they do is not rocket science; it is innovation in execution and delivery. They serve traditionally ignored populations who need these resources, employ creative ways to attract high quality doctors, develop standardized procedures that reduce cost and time, and rent facilities, rather than purchasing land or buildings, that help them serve in commercially viable ways.

These are 3 examples of companies we support. For me, there is also personal gratification in what I do. I wanted to have an impact that combines my finance and business skills with my engineering skills. My engineering degree makes me think in an analytical way and helps me appreciate the innovations developed by the technical companies we have invested in. Innovative solutions are not always rocket science and technological breakthroughs. Evolutionary innovations can create huge impacts. We need more engineers who can innovate and solve these problems.

Eric Berkowitz
Chief Investment Officer
Bamboo Finance

Team Diversity and Innovation

In your previous team activities, you may have noticed that some teams worked really well and others may not have been as effective. It is likely that the diversity in these teams had a positive or a negative influence in your team processes. Research studies that compared the innovative outcomes of teams based on their diversity have shown some interesting and surprising results. While it is often believed that more diverse teams produce more innovative solutions, diversity by itself is not sufficient in promoting innovation. Our motto when teaching or working in teams is that "All teams face problems." Good teams can recognize and resolve these problems.

In a study we conducted involving 159 engineering students working in 40 three- to four-person teams, we investigated the differences between teams that were identified as heterogeneous or homogenous based on their gender composition (Purzer and Fila, under review). We compared the innovation potential in these teams' design projects and variety in their solutions. The quantitative results indicated that gender heterogeneous teams were no more innovative than gender homogenous teams. There were also no differences in the variety of potential design solutions these teams generated. However, an in-depth examination of the student reports indicated that, regardless of gender composition, noninnovative teams employed poorer decision-making processes. Further, gender heterogeneous teams were able to make better use of more various sets of potential design solutions.

Other studies of diverse teams show positive differences in performance (Bray, Kerr, and Atkin, 1978; Eagly and Karau, 1991; Sashkin and Maier, 1971; Wood, 1987). However, some show contrary results where diverse teams experience more conflict than homogenous teams (Jehn, Northcraft, and Neale, 1999; Pelled, 1996). One explanation is that conflict may reduce team cohesion and distract team members from the task. Conflict, however, can also allow members to consider alternative ideas or strengthen their reasoning and

---

 TEAM REFLECTION—How Diverse Are We?

- Consider at least three ways your team is diverse (e.g., race, age, gender, work function, discipline, personality type, etc.).
- Calculate how diverse your team is along these dimensions using the following equation:

$$H = - \sum_{i=1}^{S} P_i (\ln P_i)$$

(from Cady, 1999; Teachman, 1980)

H: heterogeneity measure along a single dimension (e.g., work function)
P_i: proportion of team members in category i of a dimension (e.g., proportion of team members with work function as design)
S: number of categories possible in the dimension (e.g., S = 2 for gender)

For a team of 4 members:
Job functions: 2 marketing, 1 design, 1 manufacturing
Gender: 3 male, 1 female

$$H(work\ function) = - \left(\tfrac{2}{4} \ln(\tfrac{2}{4}) + \tfrac{1}{4} \ln(\tfrac{1}{4}) + \tfrac{1}{4} \ln(\tfrac{1}{4}) \right)$$

$$= 1.04$$

$$H(gender) = - \left(\tfrac{3}{4} \ln(\tfrac{3}{4}) + \tfrac{1}{4} \ln(\tfrac{1}{4}) \right) = 0.56$$

Note: Larger H values indicate greater diversity. Maximum H values increase as team size and possible categories increase. Zero is the lowest possible value, indicating homogeneity.

- Discuss how diverse your team is (i.e., did you score close to or above 1 on any of the heterogeneity measurements?) and write ways you can take advantage of this diversity.

- _____
- _____
- _____
- _____

Table 7.2 Tips for Managing Diversity

Watch Out for . . .	Tips for Managing Diversity
Frequent relationship conflict	Relationship conflict can develop from personal differences or frequent task conflict and can result in hostility and irritation toward or between team members. It is harmful to the team and innovation process because it distracts the team from their task. It is important to be cognizant of times when your team is having relationship conflict so that you can take action. We find that developing joint goals and shared understanding of the project early on can prevent later relationship conflict. You can also resolve emergent relationship conflict by identifying ways each member contributes to the team and focusing on these contributions.
Frequent task conflict or no task conflict	Task conflict occurs when there are disagreements about the task and differences in viewpoints related to the task. Task conflict can stimulate creativity and thoughtful decision making (Kurtzberg and Amabile, 2001), but it is also likely to interfere with team performance (De Dreu and Weingart, 2003). A moderate amount of task conflict is beneficial if achieved by scrutinizing team decisions and allowing all team members to contribute to team decisions.
Contributions by the majority	Some teams, although initially set up with equitable responsibilities, can be led by a single person or a majority subgroup that makes most of the decisions. This limits participation by other team members and their potential to foster creativity. In such situations it is important to remember that a critical characteristic of an effective leader is the ability to involve others in team discussions and support collaborative and creative thinking.
Too much cohesion, little discussion and argumentation	While too much argumentation can distract the team and result in time management issues, too much cohesion prevents a team from developing innovative solutions. It is important for team members to value diversity of ideas and allocate time to discuss these ideas in a productive way. To create some argumentation in a cohesive team, you can assign someone to play devil's advocate or encourage team members to suggest off-the-wall or unpopular solutions.
Quick decisions and unquestioned reliance on the work of individuals	Many teams, especially when faced with strict time constraints, divide tasks among individual team members. This often creates unquestioned reliance on individuals' work and quick decision making. Teams should allocate time to check each other's work, such as calculations, before accepting them as facts. In addition, it is important to monitor team decision-making processes and ensure that you are making decisions based on evidence and that these decisions meet the criteria you established early on.

decision-making skills, especially if participation of those with alternative views is high (De Dreu and West, 2001). So, it is critical for innovative teams to reduce relationship conflict while maintaining an open mind about the tasks.

Despite the differences in research findings, researchers agree that diverse teams have a higher potential for innovation. The key is establishing and managing team processes and interactions that will bring about and help diverse viewpoints thrive. Table 7.2 presents some tips for working through problem areas.

Conclusions

Innovation is a critical product of engineering work and, therefore, future engineers are expected to demonstrate innovative thought and processes. Many attribute the need for innovation as contributing to economic prosperity at both global and national levels (Radcliffe, 2005). Others recognize the individual, societal, and global needs engineers must address now and in the future (National Academy of Engineering, 2005). Innovative engineers not only develop solutions to these needs, they contribute to future innovations. The technology and processes they develop form the foundation upon which future innovations will be built. Their success will also inspire and enable future innovators. Innovation is truly cyclical; and it can begin with you!

It is important to remember that innovation is not just iPhones and the Internet. While innovation seems to come in large leaps, it is often created by many smaller advances. Automobiles are a prime example of an innovation built upon other innovations. Modern automobiles resulted from the convergence of prior innovations such as internal combustion engines, rubber and metal manufacture and manipulation, and one of the earliest innovations of all, the wheel. But automobiles also required supportive innovations to achieve mass acceptance and diffusion. The low cost and mass production of the Ford Model T was made possible by innovations in machine shop practices, machine shop technology (such as gravity belts), and the introduction of the moving assembly line (Williams, Haslam, Williams, Adcroft, and Johal, 1993). Think back to your favorite innovation example from the "Innovators Among Us" team activity on page 134. How might this innovation contribute to or be developed into a larger innovation?

Even if your innovation is not universally adopted, it can have profound effects locally and individually. Local innovations can improve efficiency, comfort, or overlooked aspects of professional, academic, and personal life. Further, contributing to an innovation, large or small, can lead you to develop nontraditional engineering and professional skills, confidence, and motivation, not to mention the satisfaction of having contributed to a project of global or local importance. Research on innovation gives us insight into skills and attitudes that help individuals contribute to innovative projects.

Some of the most critical skills, as noted earlier in Table 7.1, include questioning, observing, and networking (Dyer et al., 2009). Innovations are often the result of interdisciplinary collaboration (Bucciarelli, 1994), or associating ideas from one domain to another (Kelley and Littman, 2001). MIT Building

20 is an example of great ideas arising from even informal discussions between individuals from previously unrelated fields (Lehrer, 2012). Thus the ability and propensity to communicate with individuals with diverse skill sets and content expertise is vital for innovators. Innovators must also think critically, reflect on past decisions, and identify needs where none are obvious. Only then can they push past common solutions to those that are truly innovative. Sometimes, such solutions are transported from unrelated concepts. Kelley and Littman (2001) provide colorful examples of innovations that were inspired by nature, cultural practices, and art. Thus, innovators must observe the world around them and recognize opportunities to incorporate their observations into engineering designs.

In this chapter we discussed literature on engineering and the innovation process but also aimed to inspire you to explore your own innovative potential by introducing our three phases of innovation and team activities. By remaining open to communication with diverse individuals, observing unfamiliar sights or viewing familiar sights in new ways, taking risks, questioning the suitability of current and potential solutions, and building networks and connections between previously unconnected domains, you too can innovate at small and large scales.

Questions

1. Innovation occurs in diverse fields. What differentiates engineering innovation from innovation in other fields? Give two examples.
2. Identify three different ways of creating customer value. Give examples for each.
3. What are three phases of innovation described in this chapter?

Exercises

1. The following two concepts are generated to improve transportation on a college campus: (1) shared bike rental system and (2) mobile phone applications that help track bus schedules and routes.
   a. What problem is each concept solving?
   b. Calculate and evaluate the innovation potential for each concept.
   c. According to the innovation potential evaluation, are these solutions innovative? How could they be improved?
   d. Develop your own solution for a campus transportation problem and evaluate it on the same rubric.

Use the accompanying tables.

Shared Bike System	1 = lowest score 10 = highest score	Explanation and Justification of the Given Score
Novelty (1–10)	N score	
Feasibility (1–10)	F score	
Desirability (1–10)	D score	
Viability (1–10)	V score	
Overall Innovation Potential (1–10)	$\sqrt[4]{N * F * D * V}$	

Mobile Phone Application	1 = lowest score 10 = highest score	Explanation and Justification of the Given Score
Novelty (1–10)	N score	
Feasibility (1–10)	F score	
Desirability (1–10)	D score	
Viability (1–10)	V score	
Overall Innovation Potential (1–10)	$\sqrt[4]{N*F*D*V}$	

2. Develop a personal strategy (e.g., a set of guidelines) that you can use when working in a diverse team. Focus on strategies that support innovation and clearly identify strategies for dealing with issues such as personal conflict, too much cohesion, and lack of contributions from all team members. Please note that these strategies should be specific and clarify actions *you* would take. They should not refer to behaviors or actions you would expect from others.

References

Amabile, T. M. 1983. The social psychology of creativity: A componential conceptualization. *Journal of Personality and Social Psychology* 45 (2), 357–376.

Bray, R. M., N. L. Kerr, and R. S. Atkin. 1978. Effects of group size, problem difficulty, and sex on group performance and member reactions. *Journal of Personality and Social Psychology* 36 (11), 1224–1240.

Bucciarelli, Louis L. 1994. *Designing engineers*. Cambridge, MA: MIT Press.

Budde, R. 1995. The story of velcro. *Physics World* 8, 22–23.

Cady, S. H., and J. Valentine. 1999. Team innovation and perceptions of consideration: What difference does diversity make? *Small Group Research* 30 (6), 730–750. doi: 10.1177/104649649903000604.

Carlson, C. R., and W. W. Wilmot. 2006. *Innovation: The five disciplines for creating what customers want*. New York: Crown.

Charyton, Christine, Richard J. Jagacinski, John A. Merrill, William Clifton, and Samantha Dedios. 2011. Assessing creativity specific to engineering with the revised Creative Engineering Design Assessment. *Journal of Engineering Education* 100 (4), 778–799.

Cooper, P. 2005. A study of innovators' experience of new product innovation in organisations. *R&D Management* 35(5), 525–533.

De Dreu, C. K. W., and L. R. Weingart. 2003. Task versus relationship conflict, team performance, and team member satisfaction: A meta-analysis. *Journal of Applied Psychology* 88 (4), 741–749.

De Dreu, Carsten K. W., and Michael A. West. 2001. Minority dissent and team innovation: The importance of participation in decision making. *Journal of Applied Psychology* 86 (6), 1191–1201.

Dyer, J. H., H. B. Gregersen, and C. M. Christensen. 2009. The innovator's DNA. *Harvard Business Review* 87 (12), 60–67.

Eagly, A. H., and S. J. Karau. 1991. Gender and the emergence of leaders: A meta-analysis. *Journal of Personality and Social Psychology* 60 (5), 685–710.

Egan, K. 2005. An imaginative approach to teaching. San Francisco, CA: Jossey-Bass.

Ferguson, Daniel M., and Matt W. Ohland. 2012. What is engineering innovativeness? *International Journal of Engineering Education* 28 (2), 253–262.

Ferrari, A., R. Cachia, and Y. Punie. 2009. *Innovation and creativity in eduaction and training in the EU member states: Fostering creative learning and suppporting innovative teaching.* European Commission Joint Research Centre.

Fila, N. D., W. P. Myers, and S. Purzer. 2012. *Work in Progress: How Engineering Students Define Innovation.* Paper presented at the 42nd ASEE/IEEE Frontiers in Education Conference (FIE 2012), October 3–6, 2012, Seattle, WA.

Ford, G. S., T. M. Koutsky, and L. J. Spiwak. 2007. *A valley of death in the innovation sequence: An economic investigation.* Commerce Department, Technology Administration.

GORE-TEX. 2012. Waterproof and breathable GORE-TEX® Outerwear--GORE-TEX® Products. http://www.gore-tex.com/remote/Satellite/home (retrieved 6/19/2012).

IDEO. 2012. *About IDEO.* http://www.ideo.com/about (retrieved 6/5/2012).

Jehn, K. A., G. B. Northcraft, and M. A. Neale. 1999. Why differences make a difference: A field study of diversity, conflict and performance in workgroups. *Administrative Science Quarterly* 44 (4), 741–763.

Keller, R. T., and W. E. Holland. 1983. Communicators and innovators in research and development organizations. *The Academy of Management Journal* 26 (4), 742–749.

Kelley, T., and J. Littman. 2001. *The art of innovation: Lessons in creativity from IDEO, America's leading design firm* (vol. 10). New York: Crown Business.

Kurtzberg, T. R., and T. M. Amabile. 2001. From Guilford to creative synergy: Opening the black box of team-level creativity. *Creativity Research Journal* 13 (3–4), 285–294.

Lehrer, Jonah. 2012. Groupthink. *The New Yorker* 87(46), 22–27.

NASA. 2012. *Spinoff frequently asked questions.* http://spinoff.nasa.gov/spinfaq. htm#spinfaq (retrieved 6/25/2012).

National Academy of Engineering. 2005. *Educating the engineer of 2020: Adapting engineering education to the new century.* Washington, DC: National Academies Press.

National Academy of Engineering. 2012. Introduction to the grand challenges for engineering: Engineering challenges. http://www.engineeringchallenges.org/cms/8996/9221.aspx (retrieved 6/1/2012).

Pelled, L. H. 1996. Demographic diversity, conflict, and work group outcomes: An intervening process theory. *Organization Science* 7 (6), 615–631.

Purzer, S., and N. Fila (under review). The relationship between team gender diversity, idea variety, and potential for design innovation. *Journal of Engineering Education.*

Radcliffe, D. F. 2005. Innovation as a meta attribute for graduate engineers. *International Journal of Engineering Education* 21 (2), 194–199.

Sashkin, M., and N. R. F. Maier. 1971. Sex effects in delegation. *Personnel Psychology* 24 (3), 471–476.

Shah, J. J., S. M. Smith, and N. Vargas-Hernandez. 2003. Metrics for measuring ideation effectiveness. *Design Studies* 24 (2), 111–134.

Teachman, J. D. 1980. Analysis of population diversity. *Sociological Methods and Research* 8 (3), 341–362.

Williams, K., C. Haslam, J. Williams, A. Adcroft, and S. Johal. 1993. The myth of the line: Ford's production of the Model T at Highland Park, 1909–16. *Business History* 35 (3), 66–87.

Wood, W. 1987. Meta-analytic review of sex differences in group performance. *Psychological Bulletin* 102 (1), 53–71.

CHAPTER 8

Agile Teams and Projects*

The Nature of Change

People, like mules, will do what they have a mind to do. Command-and-control directives, top-down plans, and top-down change rarely endure. Wide-ranging change comes from convening and engaging like minds to rally around a cause. Many antibodies to change threaten the viability of change. Long-living change fights the antibodies to spread like a virus.

Malcolm Gladwell (2000) believes change is sparked in a sudden and often unexpected manner. Gladwell likens social and organizational movements to the behavior of epidemics. Social movements rapidly spread or quickly die out, yet require the minutest of perturbations to initiate.

The Agile movement in software was born from a desire for lightweight process.

The Agile Manifesto

Seventeen software developers convened in February 2001 in Snowbird, Utah, to discuss lightweight software development methods. One motivation of the conferees was to find alternatives to the document-driven and process-ladened software development that characterized many organizations.

Software development had become a ponderous and costly proposition. Software projects were traditionally run using a predictive approach of estimating, designing, and implementing. The Agile approach is more adaptive than predictive.

Many of the Snowbird conferees fancied themselves *organizational anarchists* poised to change the status quo. Out of the Snowbird meeting came the *Manifesto for Agile Software Development* (2001) the most influential software movement in the first decade of the new millennium. See Appendix A at end of this chapter for a list of the principles.

> *The manifesto is a rallying cry: it says what we stand for and also what we are opposed to.*
>
> MARTIN FOWLER

---

*By Robert MacNeal.

Agile Principles

The signees of the Agile Manifesto publically declared that they valued:

- Individuals and interactions over processes and tools.
- Working software over comprehensive documentation.
- Customer collaboration over contract negotiation.
- Responding to change over following a plan.

Individuals and Interactions over Processes and Tools. One of the core principles expressed in the manifesto is to build products around motivated individuals, providing them with the environment they need to succeed. Many Agile teams use open plan lab space configurations so it is convenient for team members to work together brainstorming, problem solving, and pair programming. In the physical space and the intrapersonal space, the emphasis is on breaking down barriers between team members, stakeholders, and product users.

Successful Agile teams are pragmatic about the level of process. Over a decade of Agile practice has shown that there is no one size fits all. It is helpful if the level of process is regularly evaluated (i.e., pragmatic rather than prescriptive).

Don't serve the process. Make the process serve you.

 INDIVIDUAL REFLECTION The success of command-and-control directives in the military is a counter-example to the assertion that top-down change rarely endures. How is the military different from nonmilitary organizations? How willing are people inside and outside the military to act on dubious orders?

Working Software over Comprehensive Documentation. Most Agile products have minimal documentation. Rather, most of the team's productivity is aimed at working software.

Customer Collaboration over Contract Negotiation. Trust is at the core of Agility. Team members can build trust by striving to be humble, honest, and forthright. The team can build trust with the customer by being responsive to needs and forthright about impediments.

Delivering a working product at regular intervals creates transparency to the state of the product. Transparency leads to trust.

Responding to Change over Following a Plan. Perhaps the cornerstone principle of Agile is "responding to change over following a plan," since the word Agile is an adjective meaning *quick and well-coordinated in movement.* Jim Highsmith (2004), a signee of the Agile Manifesto, has written that the manifesto value of "responding to change over following a plan" means to embrace an *Envision-Explore* approach over a *Plan-Do* approach.

The core of an Agile approach is to adapt to change when it occurs, rather than planning for anticipated change.

Everyone has a plan 'til they get punched in the mouth.

MIKE TYSON
Former boxer and heavyweight champion

INDIVIDUAL REFLECTION Were you ever engaged in making something others would use but focused too much on the tools and processes of the "making" at the expense of discovering the end-user's preferences and values through conversation?

Think of situations where you meticulously followed a plan rather than adapting and responding to changing conditions. Did the changes make the original plan obsolete?

Characteristics of Agile Projects

Scrum

Scrum is an Agile framework for completing projects. The *Scrum Method* was first introduced in a paper jointly presented in 1995 by Jeff Sutherland and Ken Schwaber. While originally formalized for software development, Scrum is a simple framework applicable to projects of all sizes and complexity across nearly all problem domains.

Scrum Terminology

- **Sprint** – a defined period of time where planned work is completed.
- **Sprint Team** – a cross-functional group of people responsible for delivering increments of Product at the end of every Sprint.
- **Sprint Burn Down** – a chart of daily progress.
- **Daily Scrum** – a time for teammates to share impactful information or report impediments.
- **Product Backlog** – an ordered list of "requirements" maintained and groomed.
- **Sprint Backlog** – the list of work the team will address in the next sprint.
- **Scrum Master** – person responsible for the Scrum process.
- **Product Owner** – person who maintains the Product Backlog and represents the interests of the stakeholders.

Most Agile projects, particularly those using Scrum, include the following activities:

- Team Manifesto
- Planning and Prioritizing
- Iteration (or Sprint)
- Daily Standup (or Scrum)
- Product Demonstration
- Retrospective

Team Manifesto A team manifesto is a means to articulate the team's definition of craftsmanship, to establish technical standards, and to declare interpersonal behavioral policies. A team manifesto is an agreement among team members.

Three items to consider for a Team Manifesto are:

1. **Craftsmanship Contract:** *How do we define quality?*
   A craftsmanship contract taps into the team's professional pride. Successful craftsmanship contracts will be self-enforcing. Since the craftsmanship contract is a mutual agreement, team members are likely to strive to meet its standards and to encourage teammates to do the same.
2. **Behavioral Contract:** *What's acceptable behavior?*
   Establishing a list of behavioral do's and don'ts enables a team to head off many conflicts. The list might include a policy for paired collaboration, a policy for acceptable and unacceptable interruptions, the definition of personal spaces, a policy for lateness, plans to cover absences, etc.
3. **Organizational Minutiae:** *What time is our stand-up meeting?*
   Organizational minutiae might include guidance for meeting times, locations, and frequency, as well as the length of the iteration and a proposed schedule.

How do we keep the Team Manifesto relevant? Consider the following:

- **Visibility** Is the Team Manifesto prominently displayed rather than buried in a document?
- **Revisited** Is the Team Manifesto periodically revisited at retrospectives?
- **Amendable** Is the Team Manifesto considered a living, amendable constitution: *by the team, for the team*?

Planning and Prioritizing The planning period is where work for an upcoming Sprint (or Iteration) is articulated by stakeholders. The key to Agile planning is to break down the vision of the work product into bite-sized chunks called *User Stories*.

User Stories Ward Cunningham, an American programmer who developed the first Wiki, coined the term *User Story*. By Ward's definition, a User Story is "a story about how the system is supposed to solve a problem or support a business process. Each user story is written on a story card, and represents a chunk of functionality that is coherent in some way to the customer."

Iteration (or Sprint) An iteration is a defined period of time where planned work is completed. Some teams prefer short iterations (e.g., one week) while others find long iterations more suitable (e.g., one month or longer). While length is variable, it depends on the project context, organizational dependencies, team preferences, and the nature of the work to be completed, and it is important to allow a team to develop a cadence of productive work.

Daily Standup (or Scrum) Each day during an iteration, a Daily Standup meeting is held for teammates to briefly share information that impacts the project team or to report impediments. The term *Standup* indicates that everyone is standing rather than sitting for the sake of brevity. The term *Scrum* is often used interchangeably with Daily Standup.

The Daily Standup is *not* a status meeting. Generally the team is assembled in a circle. Each person is given an opportunity to speak or pass. Team members are encouraged to share impactful information.

Most Daily Standup Meetings share one or more of the following guidelines:

- Daily Standup starts on time. Those present are not obligated to update latecomers.
- All members are standing rather than sitting.
- All members of the project team are welcome, but normally only the core roles speak.
- The duration of Daily Standup is time-boxed to 15 minutes.
- Daily Standup occurs at the same time and location every day.
- New groups, and groups not yet accustomed to the importance and brevity of *impactful* information, tend to fall back on the less informative *status update* by using the following three-question template:

  - What have you done since yesterday?
  - What are you planning to do today? and
  - Any impediments?

Note: Caution is advised when using the three-question template. Sometimes the three-question template is okay to smoke out meaningful information from a tight-lipped group. However, following the three-question template day after day smacks of gratuitous ceremony. The spirit of the Daily Standup is impactful information over ceremony.

It is the responsibility of the Scrum Master to resolve impediments and to keep the Daily Standup under 15 minutes.

Often a Daily Burn Down Chart (Figure 8.1) will be viewed during the Daily Standup to get a sense of the hours of work remaining over the course of the iteration.

Demo Regular interaction with the customer, client, or stakeholders is at the core of Agile. The following core principles in the Agile Manifesto focus on regular customer interactions through frequent product delivery:

Figure 8.1 Burn Down Chart

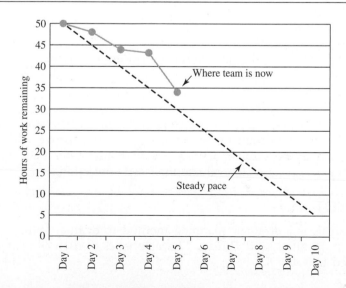

Figure 8.2 Retrospective Ledger

What Went Well?	What Didn't Go Well	Action
Daily Standups succinct.	-	Remind team they can "pass" if they have nothing "wildly informative."
Work completed early. Completed additional story.	-	-
	Not enough feedback from the stakeholders.	Inform the stakeholders the team needs more feedback at next demo.
	Team struggled while Dave was on vacation.	Have Dave pair program with Bob.

1. Our highest priority is to satisfy the customer through early and continuous delivery of valuable software.
2. Deliver working software frequently, from a couple of weeks to a couple of months, with a preference to the shorter timescale.
3. Working software is the primary measure of progress.

The primary form of customer interaction occurs in the *Demo*. The demo is a meeting where the team presents a demonstration of the product to the customer, client, or stakeholders. The objectives are to get feedback and to provide transparency into the direction and progress of the project.

The team uses feedback to adjust or maintain course. Feedback from the customer, client, or stakeholders can also help to queue up future backlog items and to get a sense of ever-changing priorities.

Retrospective Another core principle in the Agile Manifesto states:

At regular intervals, the team reflects on how to become more effective, then tunes and adjusts its behavior accordingly.

The principle of regular reflection most commonly occurs in the *Retrospective*. The Retrospective is an Iteration (or Sprint) ending meeting. During the retrospective, the team gives an honest account of *what went well?* and *what didn't go well?* (See Figure 8.2.)

The keys to successful retrospectives are fostering trust and encouraging candor. It is also important to list actions to fix or improve what didn't go well and then execute those actions. Many teams refer back to previous retrospective action items to evaluate their self-correction.

Agile SWOT

SWOT analysis is a strategic planning method to evaluate Strengths, Weaknesses, Opportunities, and Threats. Characteristics of each as related to Agile are outlined in Table 8.1.

Strengths	• Is product-centric.
	• Demonstrates progress. Incremental progress is readily measurable and visible to stakeholders through product demos and information radiators like burn-down charts.
	• Encourages the people doing the work to set the pace so they're not overworked and enjoy an increased role in decision making.
	• Enables an adjustable workload based on team-set capacity and stakeholders-set priorities.
	• Encourages transparency of technical and intrapersonal issues so that they are uncovered before becoming endemic.
	• Gives team members authority to make decisions.
	• Encourages team members to consult and collaborate with stakeholders.
	• Subdivides large tasks into granular tasks that are readily worked and quality-testable.
	• Gives team members a *get-it-done attitude* by cutting bureaucratic excess and having management clear progress impediments.
	• Encourages team members to behave like owners in a start-up company.
	• Challenges organizational standards and process.
Weaknesses	• Overemphasizes velocity and product delivery often at the expense of building the right product with the best product features and the highest consumer value.
	• Often relies on a single Product Owner (Scrum) who must give product direction and set priorities.
	• Misinterpretation of the essence of Agile allows business domain experts and stakeholders to be disengaged, lax about ferreting out essential product needs, or scatter-brained about setting direction for the team.
	• Misinterpretation of the essence of Agile tends to down-play technical debt that can threaten product quality and slow progress.
	• Overreliance on geographically distributed teams, business experts, and stakeholders can diminish productivity and quality.
	• Vertical silo-ing of technical and business domain knowledge can become debilitating if left unattended particularly if there is turnover.
	• Tendency for inexperienced or poorly coached Agile teams to emphasize gratuitous ceremony. For example, retrospectives are wasteful if team members are not forthright and constructively self-critical.
	• Challenges organizational standards and process.
Opportunities	• For product-driven organizations, Agile is a way to revolutionize how your organization does business. Agile is a means to increase productivity and to inspire commitment.
	• Agile features demonstrable progress realized through frequent, incremental production releases. As such, it is ideal for start-up companies trying to attract and maintain investors.
	• An adoption of Agile represents an opportunity to challenge organizational standards and process by delivering tangible results.

(Continued)

Threats

- Threats are most likely to emerge from outside the team.

- Compliance and legal issues in large organizations are always looming (e.g., legal team needs to review content).

- Security issues in large organizations pose a threat because work product requires a security review.

- Jealously from non-Agile teams can be a threat.

- If an organization is not fully Agile, a perception of preferential treatment might emerge.

- Compensation issues can occur because internal team members, or contracted team members, typically do not work for the same person giving their salary review or impacting their hourly rate.

- Revolutionary change does not suit all people in the organization. Many people resist change.

- Some organizations are not patient or disciplined enough to realize the advantages of Agile.

 GROUP REFLECTION Each project methodology has its strengths, weaknesses, opportunities, and threats. Compare Agile methods to other project methods using a SWOT analysis.

Agile Design

Before the Agile movement gained popularity in the early 2000s, most software teams followed some form of the *Waterfall Model*. The Waterfall Model assumes a *Big Design Up Front* (BDUF) approach whereas the Agile approach to design is more fluid and dependent on the real-time discovery of requirements. Most Agile teams use some form of *Emergent Design*. Many find the move from the rigidity of Waterfall to fluidity of Agile to be liberating.

Waterfall Model

The waterfall model is a software development method that borrows from the process commonly used in the manufacturing and construction industries. Waterfall is characterized by the sequential phases of Conception, Initiation, Analysis, Design, Construction, Testing, Production/Implementation and Maintenance. Progress is seen as flowing downward, like a waterfall, through each of the phases.

Big Design Up Front assumes that all phases of application design (e.g., Conception, Initiation, Analysis, and Design) have been completed and perfected before implementation (e.g., Construction) is started.

Emergent Design

Agile coach David Hussman pointed out to me during an informal conversation that ancient Egyptians practiced evolutionary design while building pyramids. Here is my paraphrase of his comment:

The first pyramids were merely burial mounds. The next version was the step pyramid (e.g., Djoser's tomb) and the next version the "bent" pyramid (a design in rock that they had to refactor during construction). These were all the forerunners to the Giza structures. It was a progression of small, simple structures which evolved based on the learning (and failures) from the last iteration.

On Agile teams, much of the design is adaptive and occurs in real-time. Rather than imagining and designing for every contingency beforehand, Agile teams allow for design discovery.

Knowing that design occurs on the fly doesn't mean professionals don't prepare beforehand by learning as much as possible about the product, business rules, and problem domain. However, sound preparation is not the same as BDUF. Most Agile teams prepare to build a product with the tacit understanding they will adapt the design as the unforeseen emerges. Sound preparation allows for informed improvisation.

Like performers, well-prepared Agile teams are freer to improvise because preparation considers the eventualities—not all eventualities, but some. Preparation frees the team to be creative without mucking things up, even if all we start with are a few baseline considerations like

- Why are we building this product?
- Who's going to use it?
- What do they need most?
- What do they like or dislike most?

As a successful emergent designer, I want to:

- Be receptive to discovery;
- Have ample time for up-front research;
- Be given clear and verifiable benchmarks for customer and business value;
- Have enough information, and ongoing feedback, to allow for informed improvisation once the project commences.

The Lean Startup

Minimum Viable Product

Minimum Viable Product is a strategy used for rapid quantitative market testing of a product or product feature, popularized by Eric Ries. A similar term is Minimum Desirable Product. Minimum Desirable Product is the simplest "experience" necessary to prove a high-value, satisfying product experience. Yet another term is Minimum Feasible Product which hints at the technical or engineering limits.

All the Minimum Product terms, whether Viability, Desirability, or Feasibility focused, are hypothesis-driven approaches to product development.

- *Viability* focuses on the business proposition (e.g., convergence on a viable profit-making outcome).
- *Desirability* focuses on the experience (e.g., convergence on the simplest experience to prove a high value, satisfying product experience).
- *Feasibility* focuses on engineering (e.g., convergence on the smallest engineering effort to prove a high value suite of product features).

That is, with a product hypothesis, or hypotheses, one builds as much as needed to test the product hypotheses.

Hypothesis Testing

Hypothesis testing is the primary iterative construct espoused by the Lean Startup community. Hypothesis testing encompasses:

1. **Make a Proposition or Hypothesis**—Our customers will prefer A over B.
2. **Devise and Perform a Suitable Test**—Make a prototype featuring A and a prototype featuring B. Interview potential customers about their preferences with directed questions about the positives and negatives about both prototypes.
3. **Evaluate Test Results**—Weigh the negatives and positives of both prototypes.
4. **Take Action**
   a. Refine the test to learn more, or
   b. Change your business model
5. **Repeat**—Propose and test another hypothesis.

 GROUP REFLECTION One principle of the Agile Manifesto follows a less-is-better motto of simplicity:

> *"Simplicity—the art of maximizing the amount of work not done—is essential."*

How does Minimum Viable Product *maximize the amount of work not done?*

One weakness in many Agile projects has been the challenge of assigning meaningful priorities to backlog stories. In the Scrum method, the Product Owner, as a proxy to the Business Stakeholders and product users, must prioritize tasks. Often the Product Owner must set priorities based on seat-of-the-pants guesses of what's valuable, rather than on something measurable or verifiable. Hypothesis testing is one approach to helping set priorities where features become a business proposition, much like a startup company. Part of the Lean Startup philosophy is continuous testing and refinement as you converge to a better business model.

Appendix A: Agile Manifesto

The Principles of the Agile Manifesto are:

- Our highest priority is to satisfy the customer through early and continuous delivery of valuable software.
- Welcome changing requirements, even late in development. Agile processes harness change for the customer's competitive advantage.
- Deliver working software frequently, from a couple of weeks to a couple of months, with a preference to the shorter timescale.

- Business people and developers must work together daily throughout the project.
- Build projects around motivated individuals.
- Give them the environment and support they need, and trust them to get the job done.
- The most efficient and effective method of conveying information to and within a development team is face-to-face conversation.
- Working software is the primary measure of progress.
- Agile processes promote sustainable development.
- The sponsors, developers, and users should be able to maintain a constant pace indefinitely.
- Continuous attention to technical excellence and good design enhances agility.
- Simplicity—the art of maximizing the amount of work not done—is essential.
- The best architectures, requirements, and designs emerge from self-organizing teams.
- At regular intervals, the team reflects on how to become more effective, then tunes and adjusts its behavior accordingly.

References

Cockburn, Alistair. 2004. *Crystal clear: A human-powered methodology for small teams*. Addison-Wesley Professional.

Derby, Esther, Diana Larsen, and Ken Schwaber. 2006. *Agile retrospectives: Making good teams great*. The Pragmatic Bookshelf.

Gladwell, Malcolm. 2000. *The tipping point*. New York: Little, Brown and Company.

Highsmith, Jim. 2004. *Agile project management: Creating innovative products*. Addison-Wesley Professional.

Hussman, David. 2011. *Cutting an agile groove: The live sessions*. The Pragmatic Bookshelf. (A video series recorded in front of a live audience, divided into three sections: *Planning to Coach; Developing Customers and Products;* and *Discovery and Delivery*, each of which contains multiple episodes.)

Principles behind the Agile Manifesto. 2001. *Manifesto for agile software development*. http://agilemanifesto.org/principles.html

Sliger, Michele, and Stacia Broderick. 2008. *The software project manager's bridge to agility*. Addison-Wesley Professional.

Tabaka, Jean. 2006. *Collaboration explained: Facilitation skills for software project leaders*. Addison-Wesley.

Wysocki, Robert K. 2009. *Effective project management: Traditional, agile, extreme*, 5th ed. New York: Wiley.

Project Management Principles and Practices

This chapter discusses what a project is, introduces project-scoping strategies, and explains why projects and project management are receiving a lot of attention right now. The emphasis is primarily traditional project management.

The number of books and articles on project management is growing almost exponentially. An example of this growth is membership in the Project Management Institute (PMI). In 2007 PMI had over 150,000 members in 150 countries. According to the 2011 annual report PMI has more than 600,000 members and credential holders in more than 184 countries. Yet, many of the basic challenges of project management have not changed. An article in *The Economist* (July 9, 2005), titled "Overdue and Over Budget, Over and Over Again," opened with the following statement: "When George Stephenson built a railway from Liverpool to Manchester in the 1820s, it cost 45% more than budget and was subject to several delays."

Today only a fraction of technology projects in the United States finish on time. In the United States, we spend more than $250 billion each year on IT application development of approximately 175,000 projects. A great many of these projects will fail (by fail I mean fail to meet estimate expectations). The Standish Group research shows a staggering 31.1 percent of projects will be canceled before they ever get completed (which may represent a good decision rather than failure). Further results indicate 52.7 percent of projects will cost 189 percent of their original estimates (Standish Group, 1995). The situation in 2004 is not much better with the Standish Group reporting 29 percent of IT projects "succeeding," cost overruns averaging 56 percent of original budgets, and projects on average taking 84 percent more time than initially scheduled. Ouch!

Good project management can make a difference, according to the *Economist* report. They cite the BP experience of converting its exploration division, BPX, into a portfolio of projects, each with more or less free reign from central control. The "asset federation" approach, as they call it, means that project managers must build their own teams.

The situation has changed a lot since the development of scheduling tools and strategies such as CPM (critical path method) and PERT (program evaluation and review technique) in the 1950s. Laufer, Denker, and Shenhar (1996) have outlined the evolution in the nature of project management.

Table 9.1 Evolution of Models of Project Management

Central Concept	Era of Model	Dominant Project Characteristics	Main Thrust	Metaphor	Means
Scheduling (control)	1960s	Simple, certain	Coordinating activities	Scheduling regional flights in an airline	Information technology, planning specialists
Teamwork (integration)	1970s	Complex, certain	Cooperation between participants	Conducting a symphony orchestra	Process facilitation, definition of roles
Reducing uncertainty (flexibility)	1980s	Complex, uncertain	Making stable decisions	Exploring an unknown country	Search for information, selective redundancy
Simultaneity (dynamism)	1990s	Complex, uncertain, quick	Orchestrating contending demands	Directing a three-ring circus with continuous program modification based on live audience feedback	Experience, responsiveness, and adaptability

A summary of the changes is shown in Table 9.1. Laufer et al. emphasize that projects have become more complex and the time to accomplish them has become shorter; thus, many projects require simultaneous management.

 REFLECTION Take a moment to reflect on the current nature of project management from your experience. Think about the project and project management environment you will enter when you graduate (especially if you're close to graduation). Try to describe your project in terms of the categories in Table 9.1—central concept, dominant project characteristics, main thrust, metaphor, and means.

I ask students in many of my project management classes to complete this reflection exercise. I know it is difficult to predict the future (to paraphrase Yogi Berra and Niels Bohr), but thinking about the kind of project management future we want is important, too. As Alan Kay (1971) said, "The best way to predict the future is to invent it." Alan Kay worked at Xerox Palo Alto Research Lab from 1972 to 1983 where he coined the term "Object Oriented Programming," invented the Smalltalk programming language, conceived the laptop computer, and was the architect of the modern windowing GUI (graphical user interface). Here's what a couple recent groups came up with:

Central concept—Virtual, nonlinear

Dominant project characteristics—Leveraged chaos

Main thrust—Melding innovation

Metaphor—Adhocracy

Means—Open-ended management

Central concept—Global projects

Dominant project characteristics—Cross-time, cross-geography

Main thrust—Parallelism

Metaphor—Concurrent engineering on steroids

Means—Electronic sharing

Ed Yourdon claims in his book *Death March Projects* (1997) that many projects must be completed in half the time, with half the budget, or with half the resources initially planned, hence the phrase "death march projects." Yourdon also claims that it is almost exciting at times to be a part of this type of project.

REFLECTION Think about your involvement with projects both in school and in other aspects of your life. Have you been involved in more and more projects in school? Think about some of these projects. What are the distinguishing features of the projects you've been involved with? For example, did you have to make a presentation or write a report? Did you have to give a performance, as in the production of a dramatic event such as a play? Have you participated in a science fair project or a design project? Please take a few minutes to reflect on changes in your involvement in projects and make a list of the distinguishing features of these projects.

What's on your list? Does it include items such as "common, overriding purpose and established goals," "temporary" (i.e., clear beginning and end), "one-time activity," "requires coordinating many interrelated activities," and "involves several people"?

What Is a Project?

A dictionary of project management terms (Cleland and Kerzner, 1985) defines a project as follows:

> [A project is] a combination of human and nonhuman resources pulled together in a temporary organization to achieve a specified purpose.

Project is defined by Snead and Wycoff (1997) as "a nonroutine series of tasks directed toward a goal" (p. 10). In their helpful guide, the authors claim that "success depends on the ability to effectively complete projects" (p. 11).

A textbook (Nicholas, 1990) that I have used in my project management classes lists the following features of projects:

- Definable purpose with established goals
- Cost, time, and performance requirements
- Multiple resources across organizational lines
- One-time activity
- Element of risk
- Temporary activity
- Process of phases/project life cycle

My current favorite definition is "A project is a sequence of unique, complex and connected activities that have one goal or purpose and that must be completed by a specific time, within budget, and according to specifications" (Wysocki, 2012).

Based on Wysocki's definition and Nicholas's list of features, you can see that projects are quite different from the ongoing, day-to-day work that most of us do. Each project is unique, is temporary, has an element of risk, and has a definable purpose with established goals. Three features of projects that I'd like to explore further are (1) exploration versus exploitation projects, (2) cost, time, and performance requirements, and (3) project phases or life cycle.

Exploration versus Exploitation Projects

As described in Chapter 2, Framing and Aligning the Project and Team, a common tension I've encountered working with students on project management topics is between (1) doing old things better and (2) doing new things. Civil engineering construction projects often involve improving the effectiveness and efficiency of current practices, whereas mechanical engineering product design projects emphasize developing new ideas. James March's (1991) distinction between exploration and exploitation activities, summarized in Table 9.2, provides some guidance on the differences.

Table 9.2 Exploiting Old Ways versus Exploring New Ways

Exploiting Old Ways: Organizing for Routine Work	Exploring New Ways: Organizing for Innovative Work
Drive our variance	Enhance variance
See old things in old ways	See old things in new ways
Replicate the past	Break from the past
Goal: Make money now	Goal: Make money later

Source: March, 1991.

Keys to Project Success

Traditionally, project success has been measured according to three criteria: cost, time, and performance. Although students in classes often negotiate time (especially due dates) and performance requirements, there is often less flexibility in professional life. For example, the due dates for submitting research proposals to funding agencies are rigid. One must get the proposal in before the deadline or wait until next year (and hope the agency still is making grants in that particular area). In many large construction projects there are significant incentives for finishing on time, and there are major penalties for finishing late. Some projects have been terminated when there were cost overruns—note the tragic demise of the Superconducting Supercollider (the multibillion-dollar particle accelerator in Texas that was terminated by the U.S. Congress).

Subsequent chapters of this book will explore how cost, time, and performance are operationalized—that is, how they are put into practice. Briefly, cost is operationalized by budgets, time by schedules, and performance by specifications and requirements.

Cost, time, and performance. Is this it? Is this all that we need to attend to for successful projects? Many project management experts are discussing a fourth aspect of project success—client acceptance. Pinto and Kharbanda (1995), for example, argue that there is this quadruple constraint on project

Figure 9.1 Project Success: Quadruple Constraint

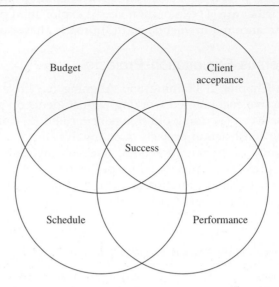

success, which of course increases the challenge of completing projects successfully (see Figure 9.1).

The most common way of operationalizing client acceptance is by involving the client throughout the project. One of the most famous examples of this is Boeing's 777 project, in which customers were involved early on and throughout the project. These customer airlines had a significant influence on how the 777 was designed and built. Boeing's vision was to build a high-quality aircraft in an environment of no secrecy and no rivalry. These new values were clarified in the following three statements (cited in Snead and Wycoff, 1997, p. 59):

1. Use a style of management unheard of in the industry: working together while building trust, honesty, and integrity.
2. In the past, people were afraid to state a problem because of the practice of killing the messenger. We will instead celebrate our problems and get them out into the open so we can work on them.
3. We must come with no limitations in our mind. We must have a shared thought, vision, appreciation, and understanding of what we are going to accomplish together.

The creation of the environment described above was enabled by Boeing's long-range goals for the 777 (Snead and Wycoff, 1997, pp. 59–60):

- Design, develop, and produce a plane safer and more reliable than any other plane in aviation history that is state-of-the-art and service-ready on delivery, to be called the 777.
- Design, develop, and produce a program to empower a massive team of people to implement the "working together" philosophy while creating the 777.

Phil Condit, Boeing's CEO during the 777 project, said, "The task for us at Boeing is to provide a massive change in thinking throughout the company—this is a cultural shift, and it isn't easy!" Boeing experienced many positive changes (and outcomes) during this process. The 777 was delivered on time and under budget. Most significantly, however, the process positively changed the "management-teamwork" paradigm from a hierarchical relationship to a "lateral relationship" (cited in Snead and Wycoff, 1997, p. 59).

Other significant changes that Boeing incorporated in the development of the 777 were: (1) using a virtual design environment (CATIA, a sophisticaed CAD program) and not building a physical prototype, (2) switching to fly-by-wire (a computer control system) from the traditional hydraulic control system, (3) including representatives of customers' companies on the design team, and (4) investing more time and resources in the design phase to save from fixing things on the factory floor. One story that was particularly compelling in this "fixing it on the factory floor" problem was that of the aircraft doors. In justifying more resources for design, the door team investigated the number of change orders during manufacturing for the previous aircraft, the Boeing 767. They found over 13,000 change orders during manufacturing and argued that if they could cut that number in half they could save millions of dollars. They made their case (Sabbagh, 1995, 1996).

If you'd like to explore Boeing's 777 project in more detail, the book *21st Century Jet* by Karl Sabbagh (1996) and the six-part PBS (1995) video series *21st Century Jet: The Building of the 777* provide rich insight into the process. Also, Jim Lewis's 2002 book *Working Together* is based on the 12 guiding principles of project management that Alan Mulally, current CEO at Ford Motor Company and former President of Commercial Airlines Division of Boeing, used in the Boeing 777 project.

Project Life Cycle

 REFLECTION Please reconsider the projects that came to mind during the Reflection on page 156. Did each project seem to go through a series of stages? If so, how would you characterize them? Think about how the activities and work on the project changed from beginning to end. Jot down your reflections.

The prevailing view of the project life cycle is that projects go through distinct phases, such as these:

1. Conceiving and defining the project
2. Planning the project
3. Implementing the plan
4. Completing and evaluating the project
5. Operating and maintaining project

A typical construction project has the following seven phases (Kerzner, 1998):

1. Planning, data gathering, and procedures
2. Studies and basic engineering
3. Major review

4. Detail engineering
5. Detail engineering/construction overlap
6. Construction
7. Testing and commissioning

Some people, however, perhaps in moments of frustration, have described the phases of a project in more cynical terms:

1. Wild enthusiasm
2. Disillusionment
3. Total confusion
4. Search for the guilty
5. Punishment of the innocent
6. Praise and honors for the nonparticipants

These faults could often be avoided if project managers would think about resource distribution over the project life cycle.

I usually use a hands-on building exercise to help students experience project management throughout the life cycle. For example, a project devised by Billy Koen involves building a simply supported newsprint beam that will support a concentrated load of 250 grams in the center of a span that is at least 65 centimeters long. The students find it very challenging, but most succeed—as shown in Figure 9.2. As you examine the three paper beam design images in Figure 9.2, think about important heuristics for managing a successful paper beam design project.

Another project that I now routinely use is building an index card tower. The framing for this design-build project is

- Teams of 3–4 members randomly assigned.
- Experience entire project life cycle in about 30 minutes.
- Goal is for all teams to meet the specification (design requirement).
- Attend to both the task and the team work.

The following team member roles are randomly assigned: task recorder, process recorder, time monitor, and materials manager.

The design objective and rules are specified as are the materials (one 100-card pack of 3 × 5 inch index cards and one roll of 1/2 inch × 300 inches clear tape):

Design objective

Design and build a tower at least 25 cm high that can support a stack of textbooks. The tower is built from index cards and office tape.

Design rules

Materials are 100 index cards and one roll of office tape
Cards can be folded but not torn
No piece of tape can be longer than 2 inches
Tower cannot be taped to the floor
Tower must be in one piece, and easily transported in one hand
Time to design and build: 15 minutes
Height is measured from the ground to the lowest corner of the book
placed on top

Tower must support book for at least 10 seconds before the measurement is made

Room must be cleaned up before measurements are made.

As you can see from the designs shown in Figures 9.2 and 9.3 most teams meet the design objective and there is great variety in the designs.

Figure 9.2 Simply Supported Beam Building Exercise

Figure 9.3 Index Card Tower Building Exercise

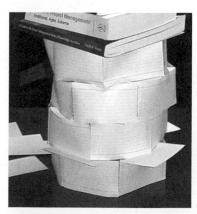

REFLECTION Consider the paper beam or index card tower project and the first four phases of the project life cycle described above (conceiving, planning, implementing, and completing) and sketch a graph of how you think resources (people, money, etc.) are distributed throughout the life of a project.

What did you come up with? Continually increasing resources? Increasing, then decreasing? Why did you draw the shape of graph you did? A typical distribution of resources is shown in Figure 9.4.

Project managers must also consider how their ability to make changes and the cost of those changes vary over the project life cycle. Figure 9.5 shows the relationship between these two factors. Consider the essential message in Figure 9.5: You have considerably more flexibility early in a

Figure 9.4 Resource Distribution over the Project Life Cycle

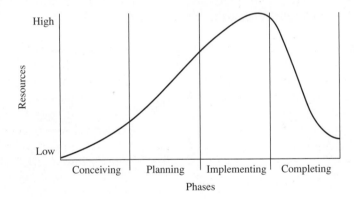

Figure 9.5 Ability to Change, and Cost to Make Changes, over the Project Life Cycle

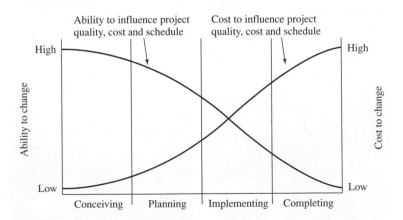

project and it's cheaper to make changes then, so don't skimp on planning during the early stages. This essential message probably makes a lot of sense, but it's hard to implement. Many project managers and project team members have such extraordinary eagerness to "get going," they often neglect to plan carefully and thoroughly. This essential message could also be described as a project management heuristic. (See Chapter 1 for elaboration on the meaning of *heuristics* and the importance of heuristics in engineering.) Following are examples of project management heuristics that students typically synthesize from the simply supported beam-building exercise:

1. *Allocate resources to the weak link.* Students are more likely to succeed if they recognize that the beam usually fails at the point where the load is applied and at the ends, and apply reinforcement (their one file folder label) to these areas.
2. *Freeze the design.* At some stage in the project (when about 75 percent of the time or resources are used up) the design must be frozen. Students who individually strive to create successful prototypes without comparing designs with one another or discussing strategy often fail to create a working design as a group—they are still working individually when time is called.
3. *Periodically discuss the process and ask meta-level questions, such as, What are we doing? Why are we doing it? How does it help?* Students who reflect out loud with one another during the design process produce better designs more quickly than those who don't.

Heuristics are essential for successful project management, because every project is unique and requires its own approach. Ravindran, Phillips, and Solberg (1987) present a superb collection of modeling heuristics (that are highly relevant for project management):

1. Do not build a complicated model when a simple one will suffice.
2. Beware of molding the problem to fit the technique.
3. The deduction phase of modeling must be conducted rigorously.
4. Models should be validated prior to implementation.
5. A model should never be taken too literally.
6. A model should neither be pressed to do, nor criticized for failing to do, that for which it was never intended.
7. Beware of overselling a model.
8. Some of the primary benefits of modeling are associated with the process of developing the model.
9. A model cannot be any better than the information that goes into it.
10. Models cannot replace decision makers.

The heuristics given in both of the above lists are important when thinking about the project life cycle, and they will become crucially important when we look at the use of project scheduling models in Chapter 11.

Project Scoping and Planning

Projects typically start with a Statement of Work (SOW) provided by the client. The statement of work is a narrative description of the work required for the project. A Project Charter is often developed. Planning starts with the development of a Work Breakdown Structure (WBS). A WBS is "a deliverable-oriented grouping of project elements which organizes and defines the total scope of a project" (Project Management Institute, 2004, 2008). There are typically three to six levels in WBSs—program, project, task, subtask, etc. Developing a work breakdown structure is important for scoping a project, i.e., determining the specific tasks that have to be completed, choosing appropriate groupings for these activities, and setting precedence and interdependence (what has to follow what and what can be going on at the same time). In engineering classes, the statement of work is provided by the faculty member.

Project planning starts in response to the statement of work. This process can be very detailed, as in Mantel, Meredith, Shafer, and Sutton's (2001) project master plan, which has the following elements:

Overview
  Brief description of project
  Deliverables
  Milestones
  Expected profitability and competitive impact
  Intended for senior management

Objectives
  Detailed description of project's deliverables
  Project mission statement

General Approach
  Technical and managerial approaches
  Relationship to other projects
  Deviations from standard practices

Contractual Aspects
  Agreements with clients and third parties
  Reporting requirements
  Technical specifications
  Project review dates

Schedules
  Outline of all schedules and milestones

Resource Requirements
  Estimated project expenses
  Overhead and fixed charges

Personnel
  Special skill requirements
  Necessary training
  Legal requirements

Evaluation Methods

165

Chapter 9:
Project Management
Principles and
Practices

Evaluation procedures and standards
Procedures for monitoring, collecting, and storing data on project
  performance

Potential Problems

List of likely potential problems

Another common format for project planning is the project charter, and in this area there has been a radical change recently. I've asked participants in executive project management workshops over the years how they go about planning a project. Ten years ago no one mentioned project charters, but in the past few years almost every participant has had experience with sophisticated project-planning systems. Some treat their systems as intellectual property and are reluctant to share them.

Martin and Tate (1997) describe the following elements in a typical project charter:

1. Write an overview of the project scope.
2. Determine the team's boundaries for creating the deliverables.
3. Define the customer's criteria for acceptance.
4. Determine the required reviews and approvals.
5. Establish risk limits.
6. Select the project leader and team members.
7. Set deadlines for delivery of the final deliverables.
8. Set limits on staffing and spending.
9. Create a list of required reports.
10. Identify organizational constraints and project priorities.

Examples of project charters are available on Jim Lewis's project management website (http://www.lewisinstitute.com/) and there is a thorough project charter template on Microsoft Office templates (http://office.microsoft.com/en-us/templates/TC011414181033.aspx?pid=CT101445011033).

The next level of detail in the planning process is the development of a work breakdown structure (WBS). A WBS is "a deliverable-oriented grouping of project elements which organizes and defines the total scope of a project" (Duncan, 1996). Typically a WBS has three to six levels, such as program, project, task, and subtask. Developing a work breakdown structure is important for scoping a project—that is, determining the specific tasks that have to be completed, choosing appropriate groupings for these activities, and setting precedence and interdependence (what has to follow what, and what can be going on at the same time).

A simple approach for creating a WBS is to (1) gather the project team, (2) provide team members with a pad of sticky notes, (3) ask team members to write down all the tasks they can think of, (4) have team members place their sticky notes on chart paper, and (5) have members work together to rearrange them. I've used the following Post-It Note Project Planning exercise in my classes and workshops:

Figure 9.6 Post-It Note Project Planning

 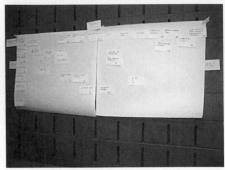

Statement of Work (SOW)—Activities Needed to Complete Office Remodeling

1. One activity per Post-It note. Include name, description, and estimated duration (initial each Post-It).
2. Arrange Post-Its on chart paper.
3. Work together to rearrange Post-Its.
4. Draw arrows to indicate precedence.

Figure 9.6 shows typical results of this activity.

These two parts of project planning in response to the statement of work—the Project Charter and work breakdown structure—are often neglected in older project management textbooks and classes, perhaps due to an eagerness to get to the nitty-gritty of doing project scheduling using critical path analysis. However, carefully considering these two initial aspects of project scoping is an important part of thorough planning.

Reflection on Project Management

Project management is a relatively new profession and is growing at a remarkable rate. *Fortune* magazine called project management "Career Number 1" for the 1990s, and in the twenty-first century there is even more emphasis on project management. When I was in engineering school in the 1960s, project management courses weren't offered. Because I now teach several project management courses, I've had to learn it by experience and research. Several of the books I've found useful and have used as texts in my courses are listed in the references (see Culp and Smith, 1992; Eisner, 1997; Frame, 1994, 1995; Grady, 1992; Graham and Englund, 1997; Kerzner, 1998; Lewis, 1993, 1998, 2001; Lientz and Rea, 1995; Meredith and Mantel, 1994; Nicholas, 1990; Pinto and Kharbanda, 1995; Snead and Wycoff, 1997).

Recently I've looked closely at Gray and Larson (2008), the provocative books of Berkun (2005, 2008) and many others, including revisiting Peters (2010); however, the books I've found to be most helpful and relevant are those of Wysocki (2011, 2012). Wysocki's (2012) *Effective Project Management: Traditional,*

Agile, Extreme, sixth edition, is the book I use in courses for professional master's students and I've been using earlier editions for about the past five years. My view is that Wysocki's work represents the current state of the art (SOTA) of best practice in project management; however, because project management is an emerging field and is changing quite rapidly, I encourage you to continue honing your skills and competencies. The SOTA will change!

Questions

1. What is a project? What are the key characteristics of projects? How does project management differ from management in general?
2. What are the three cardinal conditions of project success?
3. What has been your experience in completing projects "on time, under budget, within specifications, and acceptable to the client"? What is your "batting average"? Is it better than the 10 percent figure cited by the Project Management Institute survey?
4. How has your distribution of effort varied over the life of projects that you've worked on? Do you start strong and taper off? Do you start slowly and build? Sketch out a graph that has effort on the ordinate (y) and time on the abscissa (x) for a typical project. Is your effort curve consistent with the "bell-shaped" curve described earlier in the chapter? Is it different? Does most of your effort happen during the last few hours before the project is due? If much of your effort is applied in the closing hours of the project, perhaps you are freezing the design too late. How does your enthusiasm vary over the project life cycle?
5. Start developing a list of your own "project management heuristics." There are several books of rules of thumb, which are one type of heuristic. One of my favorites is Grady (1992).

Exercises

1. Project Planning

Now that you've had an opportunity to think about projects, project management, project life cycles, and project scoping, I'd like you to try applying what you've learned.

Suppose you have two tickets to a fabulous concert and are planning a special dinner for two prior to the concert. Your menu consists of a very special soup and a baked chicken entrée. The soup must be boiled for 35 minutes and you should allow 15 minutes to serve and consume it. The chicken dish requires a fair amount of preparation: you have to boil the rice for 30 minutes, brown the chicken in the frying pan for 15 minutes, and bake the rice and chicken in a baking dish in the oven for 15 minutes. It takes 5 minutes to prepare a sauce in the frying pan and 15 minutes to boil the peas. (You have only two pots and one frying pan.) For the good red wine you've bought, you must allow 5 minutes to uncork it (very carefully) and let it stand for 30 minutes before serving it. You plan to allow 25 minutes to serve and eat the entrée and drink the wine.

How much time do you need to prepare and consume the meal? What representation (model) did your group use to determine the time? How did you keep track of which activities had to follow others and which could be going on at the same time?

2. Playground Project Planning

Student professional organizations (American Society of Civil Engineering, ASCE) are often involved in community service projects, such as the following school playground construction project. Assume that you are a project team member and that the following activities must be accomplished to build a playground.

Activity	Estimated Duration (Quarter Days)
Construct playground pads and slides	1
Construct playground walls	2
Design playground	3
Drill foundation holes	1
Excavate site	1
Place sand	1
Place support frame	2
Procure cement	5
Procure playground materials	7
Procure tools	1
Wash playground	1

You have been assigned by the project manager to complete the following tasks:

Deliverables:
1. Develop a brief statement of work or project mission statement.
2. Complete a work breakdown structure.

3. **General Project Scoping**

Select a project (or subproject) from your workplace or experience, and assume the following roles and prepare the appropriate documents.

Project Deliverables
1. Assume the role of client: Develop a statement of work (SOW) or project mission statement. Write the SOW as the client directing the engineer-consultant-contractor to perform prescribed project details and requirements.
2. Assume the role of engineer/consultant/contractor. Create a project charter using the Martin and Tate (1997) format (see page 165), the Lewis Institute charterform (www.lewisinstitute.com/pdf/charterform.pdf), or a form from your experience or workplace.
3. Complete a work breakdown structure (WBS) for the project.
4. Write a one-page executive summary of the project.

References

Berkun, S. 2005. *The art of project management.* Sebastopol, CA: O'Reilly.

———. 2008. *Making things happen: Mastering project management.* Sebastopol, CA: O'Reilly.

Cleland, D. I., and H. Kerzner. 1985. *A project management dictionary of terms.* New York: Van Nostrand Reinhold.

Culp, G., and A. Smith. 1992. *Managing people (including yourself) for project success.* New York: Van Nostrand Reinhold.

Duncan, William R. 1996. *A guide to the project management body of knowledge.* Newton Square, PA: Project Management Institute.

Economist Magazine. 2005. Overdue and over budget, over and over again. July 9.

Eisner, H. 1997. *Essentials of project management and systems engineering management.* New York: Wiley.

Frame, J. D. 1994. *The new project management.* San Francisco: Jossey-Bass.

———. 1995. *Managing projects in organizations.* San Francisco: Jossey-Bass.

Grady, Robert B. 1992. *Practical software metrics for project management and process improvement.* Englewood Cliffs, NJ: Prentice Hall.

Graham, Robert J., and Randall L. Englund. 1997. *Creating an environment for successful projects.* San Francisco: Jossey-Bass.

Gray, C. F., and E. W. Larson. 2008. *Project management: The managerial process*, 4th ed. Boston: McGraw-Hill.

Kay, Alan. 1971. The origin of the quote came from an early meeting in 1971 of PARC, Palo Alto Research Center, folks and the Xerox planners. "In a fit of passion I uttered the quote!"—Alan Kay, in an e-mail on September 17, 1998, to Peter W. Lount (http://www.smalltalk.org/alankay.html, accessed 3/9/03).

Kerzner, H. 1998. *Project management: A systems approach to planning, scheduling, and controlling*, 6th ed. New York: Van Nostrand Reinhold.

Laufer, A., G. R. Denker, and A. J. Shenhar. 1996. Simultaneous management: The key to excellence in capital projects. *International Journal of Project Management* 14 (4), 189–199.

Lewis, James P. 1993. *The project manager's desk reference: A comprehensive guide to project planning, scheduling, evaluation, control and systems.* New York: Probus.

———. 1995. *Fundamentals of project management.* New York: AMACOM.

———. 1998. *Mastering project management: Applying advanced concepts of systems thinking, control and evaluation, resource allocation.* New York: McGraw-Hill.

———. 2000. *Working together: 12 principles for achieving excellence in managing projects, teams, and organizations.* New York: McGraw-Hill.

———. 2001. *Project planning, scheduling, and control: A hands-on guide to bringing projects in on time and on budget*, 3rd ed. New York: Probus.

Lientz, Bennet, and Kathryn Rea. 1995. *Project management for the 21st century.* San Diego: Academic Press.

March, James G. 1991. Exploration and exploitation in organizational learning. *Organizational Science* 2, 71–87.

Martin, P., and K. Tate. 1997. *Project management memory jogger.* Lawrence, MA: GOAL/QPC.

Mantel, S. J., J. R. Meredith, S. M. Shafer, and M. M. Sutton. 2001. *Project management in practice.* New York: Wiley.

Meredith, J. R., and S. J. Mantel. 1994. *Project management: A managerial approach.* New York: Wiley.

Nicholas, J. M. 1990. *Managing business and engineering projects: Concepts and implementation.* Englewood Cliffs, NJ: Prentice Hall.

Peters, T. J. 2010. *The little big things.* New York: Harper-Collins.

Pinto, J. K., and O. P. Kharbanda. 1995. *Successful project managers: Leading your team to success.* New York: Van Nostrand Reinhold.

Project Management Institute. 2004. *A guide to the project management body of knowledge (PMBOK guide)*, 3rd ed. Newton Square: PA: Project Management Institute.

———. 2008. *A guide to the project management body of knowledge (PMBOK guide)*, 4th ed. Newton Square: PA: Project Management Institute.

Ravindran, A., D. T. Phillips, and J. J. Solberg. 1987. *Operations research: Principles and practice.* New York: Wiley.

Sabbagh, Karl. 1995. *21st century jet: The building of the 777.* PBSHome Video.

———. 1996. *21st century jet: The making and marketing of the Boeing 777.* New York: Scribner's.

Snead, G. L., and J. Wycoff. 1997. *To do, doing, done! A creative approach to managing projects and effectively finishing what matters most.* New York: Fireside.

Standish Group. 1995. The Standish Group Report. http://www.scs.carleton.ca/~beau/PM/Standish-Report.html (accessed 3/11/03).

Wysocki, Robert K. 2011. *Executive's guide to project management: Organizational processes and practices for supporting complex projects.* New York: Wiley.

———. 2012. *Effective project management: Traditional, agile, extreme*, 6th ed. New York: Wiley.

Yourdon, E. 1997. *Death march projects.* Reading, MA: Addison-Wesley.

The Project Manager's Role

Project management is undergoing enormous changes, as Table 9.1 indicated, and thus the role of the project manager is changing. Before we explore the changes that are occurring in project management, let's explore broader changes that are occurring in business, industry, government, and education.

 INDIVIDUAL AND GROUP REFLECTION Think about changes that have occurred in the workplace (or school, if that is your principal area of experience) in the past five years. Make a list of some of the most notable changes and compare it with other team members' lists.

Students in my project management classes who do the above Reflection come up with lots of changes they're noticing—communications technology, computers, the global marketplace, emphasis on quality, shortened time frames, and the changing role and importance of knowledge workers.

Changes in the Workplace

Changes in the workplace have been studied and summarized by numerous authors, including Byrne (1992, 2000). Changes occurring in how engineers work in business and industry, summarized in Table 10.1, have serious implications for how we prepare engineering graduates for working in the twenty-first century.

The changes that are occurring in business and industry suggest that we should consider changes in engineering education to prepare our graduates to function effectively in the "new paradigm" companies. The "Made in America" study (Dertouzos, Lester, and Solow, 1989) recommended that MIT should do the following:

1. Broaden its educational approach in the sciences, in technology, and in the humanities, and educate students to be more sensitive to productivity, to practical problems, to teamwork, and to the cultures, institutions, and business practices of other countries.
2. Create a new cadre of students and faculty characterized by (1) interest in, and knowledge of, real problems and their societal, economic, and political context; (2) an ability to function effectively as members of a team creating new products, processes, and systems; (3) an ability to operate

Table 10.1 What a Difference a Century Can Make: Contrasting Views of the Corporation

Characteristic	20th Century	21st Century
Organization	The pyramid	The web or network
Focus	Internal	External
Style	Structured	Flexible
Source of strength	Stability	Change
Structure	Self-sufficiency	Interdependencies
Resources	Atoms—physical assets	Bits—information
Operations	Vertical integration	Virtual integration
Products	Mass production	Mass customization
Reach	Domestic	Global
Financials	Quarterly	Real-time
Inventories	Months	Hours
Strategy	Top-down	Bottom-up
Leadership	Dogmatic	Inspirational
Workers	Employees	Employees and free agents
Job expectations	Security	Personal growth
Motivation	To compete	To build
Improvements	Incremental	Revolutionary
Quality	Affordable best	No compromise

Source: Byrne, 2000.

effectively beyond the confines of a single discipline; and (4) an integration of a deep understanding of science and technology with practical knowledge, a hands-on orientation, and experimental skills and insight.

3. Revise subjects to include team projects, practical problems, and exposure to international cultures. Encourage student teaching to instill a stronger appreciation of lifelong learning and the teaching of others. Reinstitute a foreign-language requirement in the undergraduate admissions process.

Although progress has been made in the past 12 years, largely due to the emphasis by the Accreditation Board for Engineering and Technology (ABET) on graduates' skills and abilities, the changes Dertouzos et al. called for in 1989 are extremely important.

The changes outlined above characterizing the 21st century organization are mirrored by the "Desired Attributes of a Global Engineer" that are listed in Table 10.2. Some of these attributes were mentioned in Chapter 1, but this time the perspective is different, that is, your role is as a project manager and project team member. More and more you will be expected to demonstrate competence in attributes such as these and will need to be looking for them in team members as you assemble project teams.

Changes like those outlined by Dertouzos and his colleagues and those boldly described by Gaynor (1998) are enormously difficult to implement in a direct, linear manner. The nature of change is described in Katzenbach and Smith (1993) using the metaphor of a whitewater raft ride. The authors also list behavioral changes that are demanded by change.

Major change, by its nature, is intentionally disruptive and largely unprogrammable. In comparing the management of major versus normal change,

Table 10.2 Desired Attributes of a Global Engineer[1]

- A good grasp of these engineering science fundamentals, including:
  - Mechanics and dynamics
  - Mathematics (including statistics)
  - Physical and life sciences
  - Information science/technology
- A good understanding of the design and manufacturing process (i.e., understands engineering and industrial perspective)
- A multidisciplinary, systems perspective, along with a product focus
- A basic understanding of the context in which engineering is practiced, including:
  - Customer and societal needs and concerns
  - Economics and finance
  - The environment and its protection
  - The history of technology and society
- An awareness of the boundaries of one's knowledge, along with an appreciation for other areas of knowledge and their interrelatedness with one's own expertise
- An awareness of and strong appreciation for other cultures and their diversity, their distinctiveness, and their inherent value
- A strong commitment to team work, including extensive experience with and understanding of team dynamics
- Good communication skills, including written, verbal, graphic, and listening
- High ethical standards (honesty, sense of personal and social responsibility, fairness, etc.)
- An ability to think both critically and creatively, in both independent and cooperative modes
- Flexibility: the ability and willingness to adapt to rapid and/or major change
- Curiosity and the accompanying drive to learn continuously throughout one's career
- An ability to impart knowledge to others

[1]*A Manifesto for Global Engineering Education*, Summary Report of the Engineering Futures Conference, January 22–23, 1997. The Boeing Company & Rensselaer Polytechnic Institute.

one top executive said, "It used to be like I-75. You'd lay it out from Toledo to Tampa. Now it's more like a whitewater raft ride. You try to get the right people in the raft and do the best you can to steer it. But you never know what's just around the bend." (p. 208)

Katzenbach and Smith suggest several behavioral changes that will help us make the necessary changes; these are listed in Table 10.3.

Several recent studies of essential stills for the twenty-first century workplace have been conducted. The National Research Council report "Exploring the Intersection of Science Education and 21st Century Skills" identified 5 twenty-first century skills that have emerged as important (National Research Council, 2010):

1. Adaptability
2. Complex communication/social skills
3. Nonroutine problem-solving skills
4. Self-management/self-development
5. Systems thinking

Table 10.3 Behavioral Changes Demanded by Performance in the 1990s and Beyond

From	To
Individual accountability	Mutual support, joint accountability, and trust-based relationships *in addition to* individual accountability
Dividing those who think and decide from those who work and do	Expecting everyone to think, work, and do
Building functional excellence through each person executing a narrow set of tasks ever more efficiently	Encouraging people to play multiple roles and work together interchangeably on continuous improvement
Relying on managerial control	Getting people to buy into meaningful purpose, to help shape direction, and to learn
A fair day's pay for a fair day's work	Aspiring to personal growth that expands as well as exploits each person's capabilities

Refer to the online document for an elaboration of each of these skills from the report (see: http://www.nap.edu/catalog.php?record_id=12771).

The most recent National Research Council report on this topic (2012), *Education for Life and Work: Developing Transferable Knowledge and Skills in the 21st Century,* advocated for more emphasis on deep learning and argued that the essential skills fall into three categories:

1. The Cognitive Domain includes three clusters of competencies: cognitive processes and strategies; knowledge; and creativity. These clusters include competencies such as critical thinking, information literacy, reasoning and argumentation, and innovation.
2. The Intrapersonal Domain includes three clusters of competencies: intellectual openness; work ethic and conscientiousness; and positive core self-evaluation. These clusters include competencies such as flexibility, initiative, appreciation for diversity, and metacognition (the ability to reflect on one's own learning and make adjustments accordingly).
3. The Interpersonal Domain includes two clusters of competencies: teamwork and collaboration; and leadership. These clusters include competencies such as communication, collaboration, responsibility, and conflict resolution.

Although this book has cognitive domain aspects, the principal emphasis is on the intrapersonal and the interpersonal domains.

Peter Drucker (1993), who has written more articles for the *Harvard Business Review* than anyone else, has described the changing views of the "manager" concept. Drucker stresses the idea of the "knowledge worker" and, consistent with this concept, focuses on skills and strategies for "managing the knowledge worker." In the 1920s, a manager was seen as a person who was responsible for the work of subordinates; in the 1950s, a manager was responsible for the performance of people; and in the 1990s and beyond, a manager is responsible for the application and performance of knowledge.

INDIVIDUAL REFLECTION How are you reacting to these impending changes? Take a minute to reflect. What is your level of mastery of each of the "Attributes of a Global Engineer" (Table 10.2)? What is your level of development and expertise in the intrapersonal and interpersonal domains? How well is your engineering education preparing you along these dimensions? Is your college education on the cutting edge of modern practice? Are you gaining mastery from other activities, for example, internships and co-ops? Discuss with others in your group.

Lots of people have noted, often with a sense of frustration, that today's classroom is one of the few settings that would be recognizable to someone working in the "same" setting 100 years ago. Few, if any, other settings—transportation, hospitals, factories—would be recognizable to someone who worked in them 100 years ago. Perhaps the classroom is a "place that time forgot and that the decades can't improve" (to paraphrase Garrison Keillor from Prairie Home Companion), but I think there is room for improvement. And your education and preparation for success in the global workplace is at stake.

Changes in Project Management

With all the changes that are occurring in the workplace—including downsizing, rightsizing, and attending to the customer—is there any question that change is also occurring in project management? Management guru Tom Peters (1991) makes bold claims about the importance of project management: "Those organizations that take project management seriously as a discipline, as a way of life, are likely to make it into the 21st century. Those that do not are likely to find themselves in good company with dinosaurs" (p. 128). As an engineering graduate student, Peters wrote a masters thesis on PERT charts. He has also made the following statements (Peters, 1991):

- "Tomorrow's corporation is a 'collection of projects.'"
- "Everyone needs to learn to work in teams with multiple independent experts—each will be dependent upon all the others voluntarily giving their best."
- "The new lead actor/boss—the Project Manager—must learn to command and coach; that is, to deal with paradox." (p. 64)

Tom Peters's recent work is on the WOW project (Peters, 1999a). He writes in *Fast Company* (Peters, 1999b): "In the new economy, all work is project work. And you are your projects! Here's how to make them go WOW!" (p. 116).

In the area of project management, several authors have summarized the most notable changes. Pinto and Kharbanda (1995) refer to our age as "The Age of Project Management." The following are key features of this age:

1. Shortened market windows and product life cycles
2. Rapid development of third world and closed economies
3. Increasingly complex and technical products
4. Heightened international competition
5. The environment of organizational resource scarcity

Lientz and Rea (1995) list several trends that affect projects:

Global competition	Empowerment
Rapid technological change	Focus on quality and continuous improvement
Product obsolescence	
Organizational downsizing	Measurement
Business reengineering	Interorganizational systems

Furthermore, Lientz and Rea remind us that projects are set in time. They are also set in the contexts of organization, a legal system, a political system, a technology structure, an economic system, and a social system. How do these environmental factors affect projects? How should a project manager and project respond? Outside factors impact the project, and the project must respond to the resulting challenges.

If I haven't convinced you that there are many changes occurring in the business world and that the emergence of project management is one of them, try the following reflection.

 INDIVIDUAL REFLECTION What does it take to be a good project manager? Take a few minutes to think about the skills and competencies (and perhaps the attitudes) needed for effective project management. Make a list. Compare your list with the lists of other students.

Do you know any project managers? Do you have relatives or friends who do project work? Try to find someone you can interview to help you get your bearings on project management. (See the exercise at the end of this chapter.) Then revise your list.

Skills Necessary for Effective Project Managers

Barry Posner (1987) conducted a survey of project managers, asking them what it takes to be a good project manager. He got the following results:

1. Communications (84 percent of respondents listed it)
   a. Listening
   b. Persuading
2. Organizational skills (75 percent)
   a. Planning
   b. Goal setting
   c. Analyzing
3. Team-building skills (72 percent)
   a. Empathy
   b. Motivation
   c. Esprit de corps
4. Leadership skills (68 percent)
   a. Setting example
   b. Energy
   c. Vision (big picture)
   d. Delegating
   e. Positive outlook
5. Coping Skills (59 percent)
   a. Flexibility
   b. Creativity
   c. Patience
   d. Persistence
6. Technological Skills (46 percent)
   a. Experience
   b. Project knowledge

Several authors have surveyed project managers and conducted extensive literature searches to learn about essential project management skills. Pinto and Kharbanda (1995) list the following skills necessary for effective project managers:

Planning: work breakdown; project scheduling; knowledge of project management software; budgeting and costing.

Organizing: team building; establishing team structure and reporting assignments; defining team policies, rules, and protocols.

Leading: motivation; conflict management; interpersonal skills; appreciation of team members' strengths and weaknesses; reward systems.

Controlling: project review techniques; meeting skills; project close-out techniques.

Lientz and Rea (1995) provide the following list of keys to success as a project manager:

Communicate regularly *in person* with key team members.
Keep management informed.
Keep informed on all aspects of the project.
Delegate tasks to team members.
Listen to input from team members.
Be able to take criticism.
Respond to and/or act on suggestions for improvement.
Develop contingency plans.
Address problems.
Make decisions.
Learn from past experience.
Run an effective meeting.
Set up and manage the project file.
Use project management tools to generate reports.
Understand trade-offs involving schedule and budget.
Have a sense of humor.

 INDIVIDUAL REFLECTION How do these lists compare with yours? Was there a lot of overlap? Were there categories of items that were on your list but not on these, and vice versa?

Research by Jeffrey Pinto (1986) sought to quantify some of these factors by correlating them with their importance for system implementation (see the box "Critical Success Factors and Their Importance for System Implementation"). "System implementation" may be interpreted as a successful project outcome.

How does one implement all of the characteristics of effective project managers? There are so many. One way is to employ a common modeling strategy, called *salami tactics*, in which a complex problem is broken into smaller, more manageable parts (Starfield, Smith, and Bleloch, 1994). The "slices" that I'll use are the phases in a typical project life cycle—planning, organizing, staffing, directing, and controlling.

Participating in and Managing Multidisciplinary Teams

Due to the complexity of problems and projects, the urgency to understand multiple perspectives and to represent them accurately and fairly, and the need to manage trade-offs and make decisions, more and more project teams will be multidisciplinary. Multidisciplinary teams are not yet a common feature of undergraduate engineering experiences, unless you happen to participate in a large-scale project team, such as the Solar Vehicle Project.

I encourage you to gain multidisciplinary team experience as an undergraduate student. As I've repeated several times, I encourage you to develop a set of heuristics for participating in and managing multidisciplinary teams. To help you get started with your list of heuristics, I once again turn to my colleague and co-author, Tony Starfield, who co-authored a paper, "Ten Heuristics for Interdisciplinary Modeling" (Nicolson, Starfield, Kofinas, and Kruse, 2002). Here is a version of their list of heuristics that Tony Starfield sent me:

1. Carefully choose the interdisciplinary team. Make sure participants are committed to the project (i.e., the study of the system) rather than to their own disciplines. Also make sure they understand some of the problems inherent in interdisciplinary projects (such as what to publish and where to publish it—in fact, have publications in mind from the start of the project).
2. Make sure the problem is well-defined. So as to focus on the system from the start, begin with a set of hypotheses about the system and define a suite of system experiments. Make sure that the linkages are

177

strong (i.e., system behavior is not dominated by only one component). Think outside the box—look for good questions to ask about the system. Develop the habit of looking from the system to the components rather than from the components to the system.

3. Do not allocate all the funding at the start of the project. It is likely that the relative importance of the components will emerge only during the study. In fact it would be ideal if funding agencies first awarded preliminary planning funds (for one year, say) and then funded the project only when it was demonstrated that an effective team was attacking a well-defined problem.

4. Use rapid prototyping for all modeling efforts. The emphasis should be on getting a system model up and running within the first year. Then throw it away and begin again, or refine it.

5. Ban all models or model components that are inscrutable. Invest in model presentations (such as spreadsheets) that are accessible and understandable to all. Do not accept component sub-models that are "black boxes."

6. Invest in a suite of models (each with a well-defined objective) rather than concentrating on one all-purpose synthesis model.

7. Work hard at communication within the project and building a team. Do not assume that people from different disciplines are able to communicate. Even when they appear to reach an understanding, confirm that all have the same understanding.

8. A system model is a balancing act between what one knows and understands and what one does not know. People like to concentrate on what they know. It is essential to ensure that participants are simplifying what they know (where it is appropriate to do so) and are making educated guesses (where necessary) at what they do not know. This implies strong control and leadership. There might in fact be an advantage to having an outside modeling consultant who facilitates key workshops—partly to have a refreshing outside viewpoint, partly to avoid ego conflicts within the project.

9. Sensitivity analysis is a vital component (at all stages) of the modeling effort. This involves an analysis of not only parameter values, but also assumptions and the effect of alternative educated guesses on the outcome of the model. Sensitivity analysis is the only tool one has for determining what goes into the model and what level of detail is necessary. It is also the only tool for dealing with the likely effects of alternative educated guesses.

10. Finally, be humble. Remember that while the participants may all be experts in their component fields, they are all likely to be amateurs as far as the system as a whole is concerned. A distinguished group of component experts does not guarantee a distinguished system team. Members of the team must be willing to probe each other's approaches and assumptions; more importantly they must be willing to have their assumptions and ex-cathedra statements probed. The purpose (and excitement) of the project lies in uncovering the unknown, namely, the behavior of the system.

**Project Manager's Role over
the Project Life Cycle**

179

*Chapter 10:
The Project
Manager's Role*

Planning

During the planning stage, you as the project manager must establish project objectives and performance requirements. Remember to involve key participants in the process (because, according to an old rule of thumb, involvement builds commitment). Establish well-defined milestones with deadlines. Try to anticipate problems and build in contingencies to allow for them. Carefully outline responsibilities, schedules, and budgets.

Organizing

The first step in organizing is to develop a work breakdown structure that divides the project into units of work. If the project is large and complex, then the next step is to create a project organization chart that shows the structure and relationships of key project members. Finally, schedules, budgets, and responsibilities must be clearly and thoroughly defined.

Staffing

Most project successes depend on the people involved with the project. You must define work requirements and, to the extent possible, seek appropriate input when selecting team members. Be sure to orient team members to the big picture of the project. Seek each team member's input to define and agree upon scope, budget, and schedule. (Remember, involvement builds commitment and usually yields a better product.) Set specific performance expectations with each team member.

Directing

The day-to-day directing of projects involves coordinating project components, investigating potential problems as soon as they arise, and researching and allocating necessary resources. Be sure to remember to display a positive can-do attitude, and to be available to team members. Recognize team members' good work and guide necessary improvement.

Controlling

Keeping the project on course with respect to schedule, budget, and performance specifications requires paying attention to detail. The following factors usually help:

1. Communicate regularly with team members.
2. Measure project performance by maintaining a record of planned and completed work.
3. Chart planned and completed milestones.

4. Chart monthly project costs.
5. Document agreements, meetings, telephone conversations.

This summary of the project manager's role over the project life cycle is intended to provide guidance and is not intended to be followed linearly or exhaustively. Each project is unique and requires its own approach. However, the suggestions above are likely to improve project success.

Reflection on Change

Enormous changes are occurring in the way work and learning are done. You are probably experiencing some of these changes in your classes as you are asked to work on projects in groups and formulate and solve open-ended problems. If you're working at an engineering job, you are surely experiencing some of these changes.

I've tried to provide a perspective on changes that are occurring both in the classroom and in the workplace. One of the most popular references on change is Stephen Covey's *Seven Habits of Highly Effective People* (Covey, 1989), which has sold millions of copies. Covey lists these habits as follows:

1. *Be pro-active.* Take the initiative and the responsibility to make things happen.
2. *Begin with an end in mind.* Start with a clear destination to understand where you are now, where you're going, and what you value most.
3. *Put first things first.* Manage yourself. Organize and execute around priorities.
4. *Think win/win.* See life as a cooperative arena, not a competitive one, where success is not achieved at the expense or exclusion of the success of others.
5. *Seek first to understand.* Understand then be understood to build the skills of empathic listening that inspire openness and trust.
6. *Synergize.* Apply the principles of cooperative creativity and value differences.
7. *Renewal.* Preserve and enhance your greatest asset, yourself, by renewing the physical, spiritual, mental, and social/emotional dimensions of your nature.

Some students in my classes have said "Covey's book changed my life!" Stephen Covey had an early influence on my professional work. I attended a management development program he conducted in Moab, Utah, in 1969–1970 as a part of my first full-time engineering job. The roles of project managers in engineering school and in the workplace are complex and varied. Covey's list provides a good set of heuristics to guide project managers. Another classic that you may want to read is Frederick P. Brooks's *The Mythical Man-Month*. If Brooks's book about software project management intrigues you, then you may want to check out Steve McConnell's *Software Project Survival Guide*. More and more engineers are involved in software development, and these two books will help you in that area.

I tend to think of each course I teach as a project. And in terms of beginnings and endings, and resource loading during the semester, each course clearly has project characteristics. I think about the goals and outcomes, that is, what I want students to know and be able to do at the end of the course, and what evidence I'll gather through monitoring and assessment to document that students have learned; and finally I design the instructional aspects of the course. Mainly I try to orchestrate variety during the class sessions to keep things interesting and to provide help for students who learn in a myriad of ways. In the fall 2002 semester, two students wrote a paper on the project management aspects of the course. I was hesitant to read it, but as I delved in, I found from their perspective that I had succeeded in treating the course as a project. This paper by Luke Heaton and Greg Williams, *An Analysis of Project Management CE 4101W as a Project,* is available from me at ksmith@umn.edu. Undergraduate students have joined me on several projects to design and teach new courses (Smith, Mahler, Szafranski, and Warner, 1997), reflect on and devise strategies for learning difficult concepts (Starfield, Butala, England, and Smith, 1983), construct knowledge bases for learning to synthesize (Smith, Starfield, and MacNeal, 1985) and integrate writing into the required civil engineering project management course (Smith and Kampf, 2004). Please note that the writing collaboration with chapter authors Bob MacNeal and Connie Kampf began many years ago.

Questions

1. What changes have you noticed in the workplace or at school? Has your school undergone a schedule change recently (e.g., from quarters to semesters)? How do the changes you've noted compare with those listed in this chapter?
2. This chapter emphasized the changing nature of the workplace and of engineering work, and the needed project management skills, based on past (and sometimes current) practice. What do you anticipate project management skills will be in the future? What do the futurists (John Naisbitt, Watts Walker, Esther Dyson, etc.) have to say about this?
3. What skills are essential for effective project managers? How can they be enhanced and developed?
4. What does the literature identify as keys to project success? How does this list compare with your experience?
5. This chapter organized the project manager's role around the life cycle. Are there other ways that come to mind for organizing the project manager's role? What are they? What are their advantages and disadvantages?

Exercise

Interview a project manager, or someone who is involved with project work. Potential interview questions developed by students in my project management classes are listed below. This exercise not only will give you a chance to find out more about project management in practice (and refine your list of essential skills, competencies, and attitudes), but also may help you decide whether it is a career path you'd like to pursue.

1. What is the main thrill or interesting reason for being a project manager?
2. Describe a typical work schedule during the week, including number of hours.
3. What directed you to become a project manager? Why not stay in engineering or some other form of business management?
4. Discuss examples of the project manager's role as a team leader and a team member.
5. Discuss the realm and responsibilities of the project manager.
6. What personal characteristics are the project manager's best allies during the job's activities?
7. What skills have you had to develop or refine since becoming a project manager?
8. What goals are you striving for personally and professionally?
9. What are the things that slow you down?
10. What are a few of the frustrations of the job?
11. Describe the project manager's professional credibility and its value.
12. How does the company you work for conceive the project manager and her or his responsibilities/opportunities?
13. Describe any battles you've experienced to complete tasks in the most economical manner and still maintain quality or integrity.
14. How important is the project schedule and what purposes does it serve?
15. Discuss the extent of your interaction with project owners or clients.
16. What is your level of involvement with contract negotiations?
17. Discuss your interaction with other professionals (e.g., engineer or architect).
18. Describe methods you use to monitor adequate communication between project owner, architect, client, etc., and the jobsite crew.
19. Describe the accounting practices you use for project budget and regular reviews.
20. Is your financial compensation commensurate with the work you do? What other benefits are there?

References

Brooks, Frederick P., Jr. 1995. *The mythical man-month: Essays on software engineering—Anniversary edition.* Reading, MA: Addison-Wesley.

Byrne, J. A. 1992. Paradigms for postmodern managers. *BusinessWeek* (Special Issue on Reinventing America), pp. 62–63.

———. 2000. Management by web: The 21st century corporation. *BusinessWeek,* August 28, p. 87.

Covey, Stephen R. 1989. *The seven habits of highly effective people.* New York: Simon & Schuster.

Dertouzos, M. L., R. K. Lester, and R. M. Solow. 1989. *Made in America: Regaining the productive edge.* New York: Harper.

Drucker, Peter F. 1993. *Post-capitalist society.* New York: Harper Business.

Gaynor, G. H. 1998. The dawning of a new age: Crossroads of the engineering profession. *Today's Engineer* 1 (1), 19–22.

Katzenbach, Jon R., and Douglas K. Smith. 1993. *The wisdom of teams: Creating the high-performance organization.* Cambridge, MA: Harvard Business School Press.

Lientz, Bennet, and Kathryn Rea. 1995. *Project management for the 21st century.* San Diego: Academic Press.

McConnell, Steve. 1998. *Software project survival guide: How to ensure your first important project isn't your last.* Redmond, WA: Microsoft Press.

National Research Council. 2010. *Exploring the intersection of science education and 21st century skills: A workshop summary.* Margaret Hilton, Rapporteur. Board on Science Education, Center for Education, Division of Behavioral and Social Sciences and Education. Washington, DC: The National Academies Press.

————. 2012. *Education for life and work: Developing transferable knowledge and skills in the 21st century.* Committee on Defining Deeper Learning and 21st Century Skills, James W. Pellegrino and Margaret L. Hilton, Editors. Board on Testing and Assessment and Board on Science Education, Division of Behavioral and Social Sciences and Education. Washington, DC: The National Academies Press.

Nicolson, Craig R., Anthony M. Starfield, Gary P. Kofinas, and John A. Kruse. 2002. Ten heuristics for interdisciplinary modeling. *Ecosystems* 5, 376–384.

Oberlender, G. D. 1993. *Project management for engineering and construction.* New York: McGraw-Hill.

Peters, Thomas J. 1987. *Thriving on chaos: Handbook for a management revolution.* New York: Knopf.

————. 1991. Managing projects takes a special kind of leadership. *Seattle Post-Intelligence,* April 29, 1991, p. 64.

————. 1999a. *The Project 50.* New York: Knopf.

————. 1999b. The WOW project: In the new economy, all work is project work. *Fast Company* 24, 116–128.

Pinto, J. K. 1986. *Project implementation: A determination of its critical success factors, moderators, and their relative importance across stages in the project life cycle.* Unpublished Ph.D. dissertation, University of Pittsburgh.

Pinto, J. K., and O. P. Kharbanda. 1995. *Successful project managers: Leading your team to success.* New York: Van Nostrand Reinhold.

Posner, Barry. 1987. Characteristics of effective project managers. *Project Management Journal* 18 (1), 51–54.

Smith, K. A., M. Mahler, J. Szafranski, and D. Warner. 1997. *Problem-based freshman engineering course.* American Society for Engineering Education Annual Conference Proceedings, Paper 2530.

Smith, Karl A., and Alisha A. Waller. 1997. *New paradigms for engineering education.* Pittsburgh: ASEE/IEEE Frontiers in Education Conference Proceedings. Adapted from K. A. Smith and A. A. Waller, Afterword: New paradigms for college teaching, in *New paradigms for college teaching,* edited by W. E. Campbell and K. A. Smith (Edina, MN: Interaction, 1995).

Smith, Karl A., and Constance Kampf. 2004. Developing writing assignments and feedback strategies for maximum effectiveness in large classroom environments. In *International Professional Communication Conference,* Minneapolis, Minnesota, USA, September 29–October 1, 2004.

Smith, K. A., A. M. Starfield, and R. Macneal. 1985. Constructing knowledge bases: A methodology for learning how to synthesize. In L. P. Grayson and J. M. Biedenbach (eds.), *Proceedings Fifteenth Annual Frontiers in Education Conference,* Golden, CO, Washington: IEEE/ASEE, 374–382.

Starfield, A. M., K. L. Butala, M. M. England, and K. A. Smith. 1983. Mastering engineering concepts by building an expert system. *Engineering Education,* 104–107.

Starfield, A. M., K. A. Smith, and A. L. Bleloch. 1994. *How to model it: Problem solving for the computer age.* Edina, MN: Interaction Book Company.

CHAPTER **11**

Project Scheduling

Project scheduling is a central yet often overrated aspect of project management. For some the feeling is "We've got a schedule; we're done." Getting a schedule is just one important step in the process of project management. The real work begins when circumstances cause delays and pressures mount to revise the schedule.

INDIVIDUAL REFLECTION Think about how you typically schedule complex projects, such as completing a major report for a class. Do you make a list of things to do? An outline? Do you draw a concept map? Or do you just start writing? Do you develop a timeline?

In this chapter, we'll work our way through the details of the scheduling process. We'll learn the basics of the critical path algorithm and experience firsthand the ideas of forward pass, backward pass, critical path, and float. As you develop an understanding of these concepts and procedures, you will gain insight into managing projects with complex schedules. I first encountered these concepts as an undergraduate engineering student in about 1964. The critical path method was presented in an engineering systems class as a network algorithm. The approach was purely mechanical; no reference was made to its potential usefulness in scheduling projects.

Let's revisit the meal-planning exercise from Chapter 9 (Exercise 1 at the end of Chapter 9). If you haven't done that exercise yet, go back and think about how you would tackle this task. We'll use this exercise as the project example throughout this chapter.

REFLECTION What representation (model) did your group use to determine the time needed to cook and eat the meal? How did you keep track of which activities had to follow others and which could be going on at the same time? How did you go about determining the total time the meal preparation and eating would take? Did you make a list? a timeline? Or did you approach the problem in some other way?

A common approach for scoping a project is to prepare a work breakdown structure (WBS) (see Chapter 9). The WBS can be presented as a list or an organization chart. A one-level WBS would be "Prepare the meal," but this wouldn't be too helpful in figuring out what had to be done. A two-level WBS would include:

Preparation
    Boil soup
    Boil rice
    Boil peas
    Brown chicken
    Prepare sauce
    Bake chicken, rice, and sauce
    Open wine and let it breathe

Eating
    Eat soup
    Eat entrée

This two-level WBS provides more specific guidance but still leaves a lot up to the chef (which is OK in many cases).

A more elaborate approach to preparing a WBS is to use Post-It notes to sort out the sequences. There are several possible sequences for the activities for this WBS, depending on your interpretation of the proper order in which to prepare this meal. One possible WBS showing precedence relationships (technically this is now a *precedence network*) is shown in Figure 11.1.

Figure 11.1 A Post-It Note Precedence Network

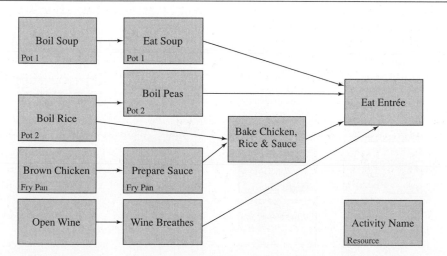

In this WBS only the activity names and the resources (Pot 1, etc.) needed for the activities are listed. Notice that I've made decisions about placing the sauce on the entrée before putting it in the oven, and having the wine with the entrée rather than with the soup. You may have chosen a different sequence, perhaps to have the wine with the soup or to place the sauce on entrée after it is served. Later we'll explore how these choices affect the schedule.

REFLECTION Have you used the WBS idea for scoping projects? If not, are there places in your personal and professional life where you can immediately apply the WBS idea? How about an engineering course or design project you're working on? If you want more practice, try the office-remodeling project example at the end of the chapter.

Critical Path Method

Now that we have a precedence network for the meal-planning project, we can determine the minimum time it will take to complete it. To do this, we go through Figure 11.1, number each node, and list the time it takes (see Figure 11.2). Examine the precedence network in Figure 11.2 to determine the minimum time to complete the project. Sum the individual activity durations along each path; for example, path 1 + 5 + 10 is 35 + 15 + 25 = 75 minutes. Which path is longest?

Provided that the number of activities is not too large, problems of this type can often be solved by hand. By sketching the relationships between the individual tasks, and taking into account the amount of time each requires for completion, we can determine the total amount of time needed to get the whole process completed.

When the number of tasks gets large—say, over 20—then it's quite challenging to keep track of everything by hand. A simple and systematic way of

Figure 11.2 A Precedence Network

Boil Soup 1 35 P1	**Eat Soup** 5 15 P1	
	Boil Peas 6 15 P2	**Eat Entrée** 10 25
Boil Rice 2 30 P2		**Bake Chicken Rice & Sauce** 9 15
Brown Chicken 3 15 FP	**Prepare Sauce** 7 5 FP	
Open Wine 4 5	**Wine Breathes** 8 30	**Activity Name** Act.# Duration

doing this is provided by the critical path method (CPM). This method represents the flow of tasks in the form of a network. To use it, we simply have to know the duration of each of the activities, and the predecessors of each—that is, the set of activities that must have terminated before a given activity can begin.

Forward Pass—Early Start (ES) and Early Finish (EF)

The first step in the procedure is to run through the network from beginning to end and mark the earliest time at which each activity can start—the early start (ES) time. In Figure 11.3, this time is in the upper left-hand corner of each activity. This is clearly obtained by adding the earliest start of its latest-starting predecessor to that predecessor's duration. When two or more activities must be completed before the next one can start (such as Boil Rice and Brown Chicken and Prepare Sauce before Bake Entrée), then the maximum must be used. The early finish (EF) time is determined by summing the early start (ES) and the duration (see Figure 11.3).

Backward Pass—Late Start (LS) and Late Finish (LF)

Similarly, a backward pass is made, establishing the latest possible starting time (late start, LS) that an activity can have, which is the latest start of the earliest starting successor, less the duration of the activity under consideration (see Figure 11.4). The result is the late finish (LF) time.

Critical Path

Activities for which the earliest and latest times turn out to be equal are called *critical*. That is, these activities cannot be delayed without increasing the duration of the entire project. The path that these activities lie on in the network is known as the *critical path*. The remaining *noncritical* activities have some "float" (sometimes referred to as slack) and can have their durations increased by some amount before they would become critical and delay the completion of the entire project.

Figure 11.3 CPM: Forward Pass—Early Times

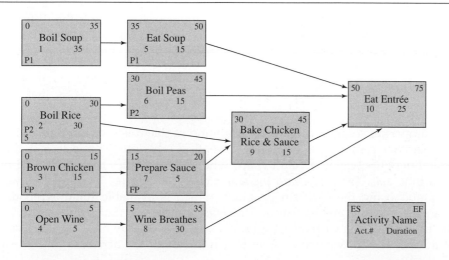

Figure 11.4 CPM: Backward Pass—Late Times

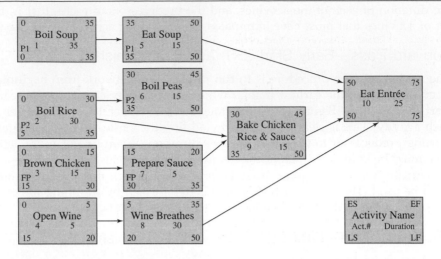

Floats

The amount by which termination of a noncritical activity can be delayed before it causes one of its successors to be delayed is called the *free float* of that activity. Technically, the free float (FF) is based on early start (ES) times, and for any activity *i*, the free float is equal to the minimum early start for activities following activity *i* minus the early start for *i* minus the duration (D) for *i*. Algebraically, the free float (FF) is determined as follows:

$$FF_i = (ES_{i+1})_{min} - ES_i - D_i$$

The amount of slack an activity has before it would cause the path on which it lies to become critical is called the *total float*. The total float of an activity is the minimum (out of all of the paths on which it lies) of the sum of its free float and those of all activities ahead of it on the path. Thus an activity is critical if its total float is zero. Technically, the total float (TF) is the difference between the late times and the early times—late start minus early start or late finish minus early finish. Algebraically, the total float (TF) for an activity *i* is determined as follows:

$$TF_i = LS_i - ES_i = LF_i - EF_i$$

The numerical solution to the meal planning problem is given in Table 11.1.

Another common model for representing scheduling projects is a time-scaled network, called a Gantt chart, where the activities have been laid out on a time axis. Table 11.1 and the Gantt charts in Figures 11.5 and 11.6 were prepared using the CritPath program, which is available for downloading from my website and is featured in *How to Model It* (Starfield, Smith, and Bleloch, 1994). The CritPath program is set up to display only eight activities at a time. If you want to be able to scroll though the activities and change

Table 11.1 Meal Planning Exercise—Critical Path Method Results

Activity	Name	Duration	Resources	Early Start	Early Finish	Late Start	Late Finish	Float Total	Float Free	Current Start	Critical Path
1	Boil soup	35	1	0	35	0	35	0	0	0	Yes
2	Boil rice	30	1	0	30	5	35	5	0	0	No
3	Brown chicken	15	1	0	15	15	30	15	0	0	No
4	Open wine	5	1	0	5	15	20	15	0	0	No
5	Eat soup	15	1	35	50	35	50	0	0	35	Yes
6	Boil peas	15	1	30	45	35	50	5	5	30	No
7	Prepare sauce	5	1	15	20	30	35	35	15	10	No
8	Wine breathes	30	1	5	35	20	50	15	15	5	No
9	Bake entrée	15	1	30	45	35	50	5	5	30	No
10	Eat entrée	25	1	50	75	50	75	0	0	50	Yes

them, download the CritPath program from my website (www.ce.umn. edu/~smith) and play with it.

If you are still having difficulty understanding the differences between free float and total float or are struggling with the critical path calculations,

Figure 11.5 Gantt Chart, Activities 1–8

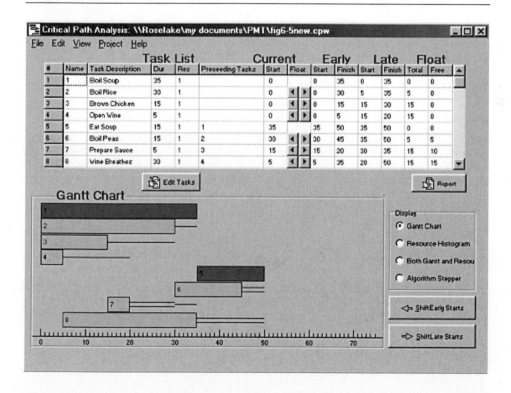

Figure 11.6 Gantt Chart, Activities 3–10

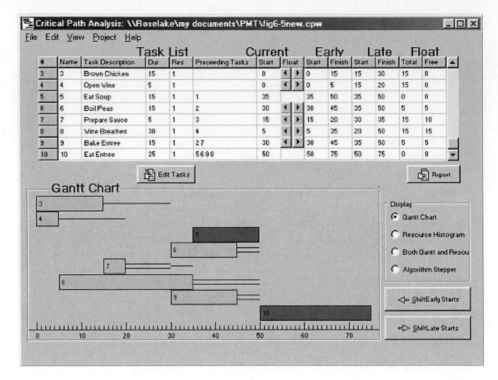

use the algorithm stepper in the CritPath program. It will walk you through the process using a graphical representation (see Figure 11.7).

Notice that there is no gap in the path that includes activities Open Wine (1), Eat Soup (5), and Eat Entrée (10). That means, of course, that they are on the critical path. Also notice how there is a gap after activities Wine Breathes (8), Prepare Sauce (7), Bake Entrée (9) and Boil Peas (6), which means they have free float in addition to having total float. The activities Brown Chicken (3) and Open Wine (4) are followed by a gap farther down the path, but not by an immediate gap; this means that they have total float but not free float.

 INDIVIDUAL REFLECTION Take a few minutes to think about the advantages and disadvantages of the two representations of the meal-planning project—the precedence network (Figure 11.4) and the Gantt chart (Figures 11.5 and 11.6). What are the unique features of each? What specific features does each represent? Where is each appropriate?

In the above Reflection, you may have concluded that both the precedence network and the Gantt chart are essential for understanding complex

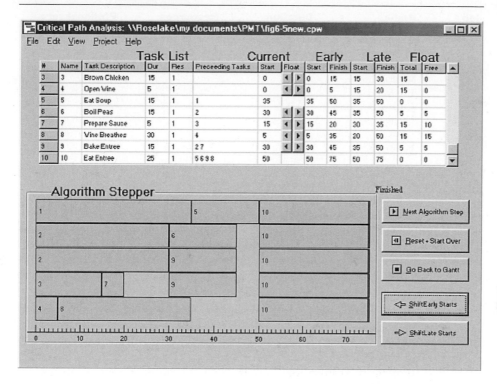

projects and communicating project information. The Gantt chart is a time-scaled network, because it represents time directly. It gives a clear picture of the duration of events, but it doesn't directly show the nature of the interdependence—that is, what has to follow what. The precedence network, on the other hand, clearly shows the interdependence—precedence and simultaneity—that is, what has to follow what and what can be going on at the same time, but it doesn't directly show the time required for each activity.

The CritPath program and most project-scheduling software use the precedence network representation to do the critical path calculations. Many people find the Gantt chart most useful for tracking project progress.

Critical Path Method Summary

In summary, the sequence of steps to apply the critical path method to project scheduling is as follows:

1. Develop a work breakdown structure (WBS).
2. Connect the activities in the WBS by arrows that indicate the precedence.
3. Perform the critical path analysis calculations either by hand for a simple problem or using computer software.
4. Create graphical representations—precedence network and Gantt chart—that suit your purposes.

Table 11.2 Bus Shelter Construction Example

Job	Name	Duration	Resources	Predecessors
1	Shelter Slab	2	2	5
2	Shelter Walls	1	1	1
3	Shelter Roof	2	2	2,4
4	Roof Beam	3	2	2
5	Excavation	2	3	
6	Curb and Gutter	2	3	5
7	Shelter Seat	1	2	4,6
8	Paint	1	1	7
9	Signwork	1	2	2,6

Bus Shelter Construction Example

Now that we've worked through the meal-planning exercise in some detail, let's try another example. Consider the construction project outlined in Table 11.2. Note that the precedence relationships are specified, so you don't have to create a work breakdown structure; however, developing a precedence network is an important step. The Resources column specifies the number of people required for each task.

Determine the minimum time required to complete the bus shelter. Develop a precedence network. Identify the critical path. Draw a Gantt chart for the project. Give it a try before reading further. (A precedence network is sketched out in Figure 11.8.)

Next, perform the critical path analysis calculations. You may do this by hand if you want more practice, or you can use CritPath or another commercial project-scheduling program. The table and Gantt chart for the first eight activities are shown in Figure 11.9.

Look carefully at the critical path method results and the Gantt chart. Notice that there is more than one critical path. The presence of multiple critical paths can be seen on the Algorithm Stepper, because it displays all the paths through the network. Get the CritPath software and try it. Table 11.3 shows the entire set of results for the bus shelter construction project.

Figure 11.8 Precedence Network for Bus Shelter Construction

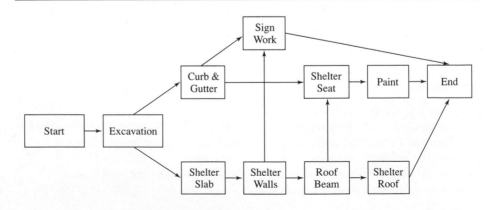

Figure 11.9 Gantt Chart for Bus Shelter Construction

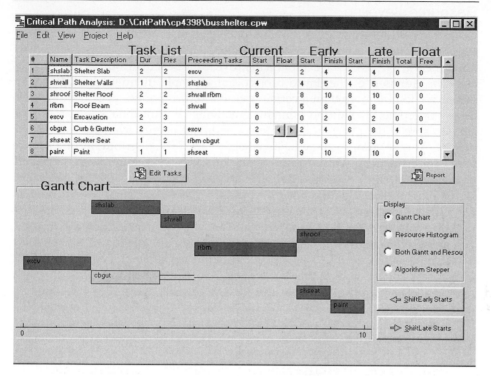

Try developing and setting up your next project using the critical path method. Do the calculations by hand a couple of times to familiarize yourself with the forward pass and backward pass of the algorithm. Then use CritPath or another commercial project-scheduling program.

Table 11.3 Bus Shelter Construction—Critical Path Method Results

Activity	Name	Duration	Resources	Early Start	Early Finish	Late Start	Late Finish	Float Total	Float Free	Current Start	Critical Path
1	Shelter Slab	2	2	2	4	2	4	0	0	2	Yes
2	Shelter Walls	1	1	4	5	4	5	0	0	4	Yes
3	Shelter Roof	2	2	8	10	8	10	0	0	8	Yes
4	Roof Beam	3	2	5	8	5	8	0	0	5	Yes
5	Excavation	2	3	0	2	0	2	0	0	0	Yes
6	Curb and Gutter	2	3	2	4	6	8	4	1	2	No
7	Shelter Seat	1	2	8	9	8	9	0	0	8	Yes
8	Paint	1	1	9	10	9	10	0	0	9	Yes
9	Signwork	1	2	5	6	9	10	4	4	5	No

Project Resource and Cost Considerations

Resource Leveling

Critical activities, having no slack, cannot be extended or shifted without upsetting the scheduled completion of the project. However, the slack afforded by noncritical activities can be exploited to provide the best distribution of resources over the duration of the entire project. For example, it might be difficult or expensive to hire more than a certain number of programmers or tradespeople at any one time. By shifting noncritical activities within their floats, it is possible to spread the distribution of personnel more evenly over the span of the project. At other times it may be beneficial to load the distribution in a certain way—for example, if work over a holiday period is to be minimized. Decisions of these kinds can be made only when the constraints (i.e., earliest and latest start times) of the schedule have been determined. Look at what happens to the resource histogram for the bus shelter project when you shift all activities to their early start times (Figure 11.10). What do you expect would happen if you shifted all activities to their late start times? See Figure 11.11.

Compare Figures 11.10 and 11.11 to help decide what you think would be the best allocation of resources. Notice that there is not too much that you can do to level the resources in this case, which is sometimes the situation with real projects.

Figure 11.10 Resource Histogram for Bus Shelter Construction

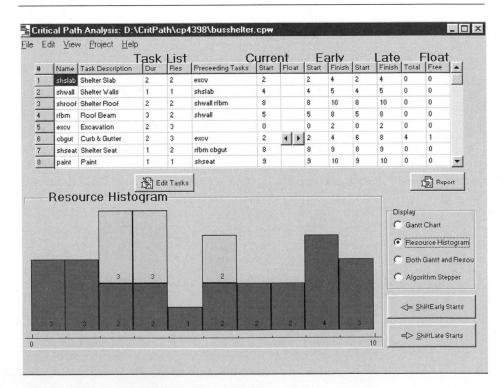

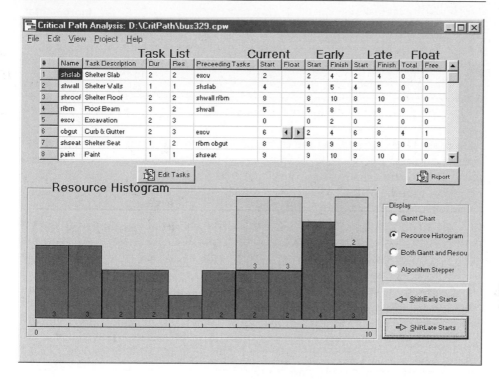

Cost Considerations

On some projects you might work through the critical path calculations and find that the required project duration is greater than the time you have available. Or, more commonly, you might get behind during the project due to weather, late deliveries, work delays, and so on. In such cases, you could, of course, go to your supervisor or professor and ask for an extension.

Alternatively, you could add resources (e.g., people, overtime) to activities on the critical path to decrease their duration, thus decreasing the time for the entire project. Technically, this is known as "crashing" a project. Why wouldn't we add resources to noncritical activities? Let's work through the example shown in Table 11.4 to get a better sense of how this works.

Figure 11.12 shows the "normal" schedule duration. The normal schedule cost is just the sum of the normal costs for the four activities—$2700.

As the project manager, you would have to choose which activities along the critical path to add resources to, in order to decrease their duration. What criteria would you use to choose the activities? Would you crash activities early in the schedule first? The cost-conscious project manager would crash the activities that had the minimum cost per unit of time saved. Often convenience, availability, and other factors must be considered.

Let's look at what happens as we decrease the duration of activities on the critical path for the example above (see Figure 11.12). The lowest-cost choice

Table 11.4 CPM/Cost Example

Task	Precedence	Normal Time	Crash Time	Normal Cost	Incremental Cost/Day
A	–	8	4	800	300
B	–	4	3	600	100
C	B	2	1	1000	400
D	A, C	3	2	300	200

is Activity D. By decreasing the duration of Activity D from 3 to 2, the overall project duration decreases to 10 and the cost increases to $2700 + $200 = $2900. Next we can add resources to Activity A to decrease it to 7. The overall project duration becomes 9 and the cost increases to $3000. Adding more resources to A to decrease it to 6 decreases the overall project duration to 8 and increases the cost to $3300. The updated Gantt Chart is shown in Figure 11.13. We can continue to decrease the duration of the overall project, but now we must add resources to more than one activity and hence the cost increases at a higher rate.

As you add resources to critical activities and decrease the duration along the critical path, eventually more and more activities become critical.

Figure 11.12 Gantt Chart for Cost Example

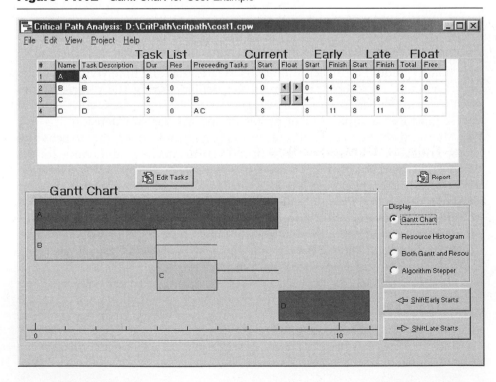

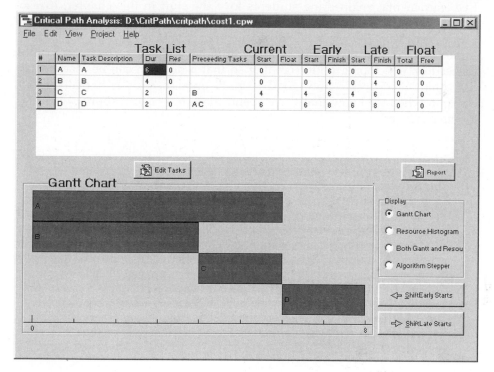

 INDIVIDUAL AND GROUP REFLECTION What are some good strategies for using the float over the life of a project? Do you let things slide early on, thus using the float up early? Do you wait until later in the project to use the float? As a project manager, how do you recommend that the float be utilized?

The Role of Computer-Based Project Management Software

It is not hard to see that if we were to add a few more activities, the problem would soon become unmanageable by hand. Further, if changes have to be made to either the order in which activities must occur or the time in which they can be completed, the entire process would have to be repeated. The advantage of the critical path method is that it is indeed systematic. It can be described as a formal set of instructions that can be followed by a computer. Alterations in the data can be made repeatedly and the problem quickly solved, again by the machine. This would enable us to obtain the benefit of what-if analysis, the process of making changes and seeing effects of those changes immediately. Such analysis gives the user an intuitive feel for the problem. The role of the computer will be addressed in more detail in Chapter 14.

Reflection: Avoiding Analysis Paralysis

I've learned that engineering students love the stuff in this chapter; it resonates with them. I've also seen students get so involved in the analysis that they forget what they're analyzing, and why they're doing it. Analysis is important, but in engineering, analysis must be purposeful—it must be focused on developing understanding so that a decision can be made. Also, it's essential to decide how good is good enough. This is a really tough decision when we know that if we spend more time and resources we'll get a better answer.

Questions

1. What is a work breakdown structure (WBS)? Why is it important? What are some of the types of WBS?
2. What is the critical path method (CPM)? What are free float and total float?
3. Explain the differences between resource leveling and crashing a project.
4. How have you typically managed complex projects in the past? How well did the approach work? Not all projects merit taking the time to develop a schedule, because they can be managed by a list or by using your day planner. Where could you apply the critical path method and how do you expect it might help?
5. How does the CritPath program compare with other software packages you've used (spreadsheet, for example)?
6. What are some of the advantages and disadvantages of relying on project-scheduling algorithms?

Exercises

1. Work Breakdown Structure Example—Office Remodeling Project

The following activities must be accomplished to complete an office remodeling project:

Activity	Estimated Duration (Days)
Procure paint	2
Procure new carpet	5
Procure new furniture	7
Remove old furniture	1
Remove old carpet	1
Scrub walls	1
Paint walls	2
Install new carpet	1
Move in new furniture	1

Part 1: Work Breakdown Structure (WBS)
1. Create a possible work breakdown structure (WBS) for the remodeling project.

Part 2: Scheduling
1. When can the new furniture be moved in?
2. What is the minimum project duration?
3. Which activities do you have to pay close attention to if you want to finish at the earliest possible time?

2. Resource Leveling

Given the following set of project data, determine the smoothest distribution of resources. Assume that resources are transferrable.

Task	Duration	Resources	Predecessor
1	7	8	
2	5	6	
3	4	4	2
4	2	4	1,3
5	3	6	2
6	1	6	5

3. Crashing

Given the following project data, determine the normal schedule cost.
Crash the project as far as possible. List the project duration and cost for each step along the way.

Task	Precedence	Normal Time	Crash Time	Normal Cost	Incremental Cost Per Day
A	–	5	3	500	300
B	A	4	2	600	100
C	A	6	4	1000	400
D	B, C	3	2	300	200

4. Scheduling Case Study

Develop a work breakdown structure, precedence network, and Gantt chart for a project you're involved with. Complete the critical path analysis calculations. Use these representations to guide the project and to review progress.

5. A Minnesota Dream Project—Lakeside Cabin Cost Estimate

Imagine you've just inherited a lakeside lot in northern Minnesota (beautiful in the summer) that has an access road, electricity, water, and sewage disposal. You've also inherited a modest sum with which to buy building materials. If you're having trouble imagining yourself being so lucky, suppose that a friend or neighbor has asked you for an estimate on how much it would cost to build a cabin and for help in designing and building. Engineers are often expected to know such things. How much would it cost for a modest, say, 24-foot-square, cabin? How long would it take you to build it?

The cabin cost estimate project is a favorite of students in my project management classes. We haven't done much here with cost estimating (this is usually done in engineering economics courses), so I'll provide a little guidance. I suggest you take the following steps:

1. Guess. Take a wild guess at what it would cost for materials for a modest cabin.
2. Look up the square-foot costs for typical residential construction ($50–70 per square foot) and adjust it down for a modest cabin. Many students use $30 per square foot for a modest cabin.
3. Use a unit cost approach:
   1. Develop a floor plan.
   2. Create a detailed list of materials with associated quantities.

3. Find the cost of the materials in a local building center brochure (or cost manual).
4. Use a spreadsheet to list and calculate the total cost of the materials.
4. Compare the three cost estimates—guess, cost per square foot, and unit cost.

Use the procedures outlined in this chapter to determine how long it would take you to build it; that is, develop a WBS and a schedule using the critical path method.

Reference

Starfield, A. M., K. A. Smith, and A. L. Bleloch. 1994. *How to model it: Problem solving for the computer age.* Edina, MN: Interaction Book Company.

CHAPTER 12

Project (and Team) Monitoring and Evaluation

Two important parts of project management are keeping on top of projects through monitoring and conducting end-of-the-project review through evaluation. There are many ways to keep informed, keep others informed, and coordinate projects. Informal one-on-one meetings, e-mail, and phone and video conversations are the most common. Other simple forms include voice messages and handwritten notes. Emerging forms of communication include web-based video conference meetings, instant messaging (Internet and smartphone), and web-based project discussion systems. More involved forms of information exchange are groupware, enterprise systems, informal reports, formal memos and meetings, and formal presentations. Each has advantages and disadvantages.

 REFLECTION What is your experience with face-to-face, phone, chat, video conference, e-mail, and handwritten communications? Under what conditions do you prefer each? What is your experience with web-based information exchange? How well do all of these work for you?

Tom Peters (1989) popularized the idea of "management by wandering around" (MBWA), which has become an important aspect of most project managers' daily lives. Effective project managers stay in touch. More recently, Peters (1999) has said that "all work is project work" and that individuals are identified and recognized by their project work.

This chapter begins by discussing meetings, progresses through successively more complex ways to monitor the work of projects and teams, and ends with strategies for evaluating projects.

Meetings

Although meetings are a principal way of keeping up-to-date, they are also one of the banes of project managers and many others. Dressler (cited in Lewis, 1998) lists some of the major complaints people have about meetings:

- Their purpose is unclear.
- Participants are unprepared.

- Key people are absent or missing.
- The conversation veers off track.
- Participants don't discuss issues but instead dominate, argue, or take no part at all.
- Decisions made during the meeting are not followed up on.

 INDIVIDUAL REFLECTION Think about some of your best (and worst) experiences in meetings. How do the complaints listed above compare with your experiences in meetings? What additional challenges have you encountered? What conditions contribute to best and worst experiences? What are some of the strategies you use or have seen used to counter the worst experiences?

Five guidelines from the book *Meetings: Do's, Don'ts, and Donuts* (Lippincott, 1994) can help alleviate some of the most common problems:

1. State in a couple of sentences exactly what you want your meeting to accomplish.
2. If you think a meeting is the best way to accomplish this, then distribute an agenda to participants at least two days in advance.
3. Set ground rules to maintain focus, respect, and order during the meeting.
4. Take responsibility for the meeting's outcome.
5. If your meeting isn't working, try other tools, such as brainstorming.

Using a meeting process, such as the one outlined in *The Team Handbook* (Scholtes, Joiner, and Streibel, 1996), also can help. The authors describe the three-part process as follows:

Before
Plan.
Clarify meeting purpose and outcome.
Identify meeting participants.
Select methods to meet purpose.
Develop and distribute agenda.
Set up room.

During
Start: check-in, review agenda, set or review ground rules, clarify roles.
Conduct: cover one item at a time, manage discussions, maintain focus and pace.
Close: summarize decisions, review action items, solicit agenda items for next meeting, review time and place for next meeting, evaluate the meeting, thank participants.

After
Follow-up: distribute or post meeting notes promptly; file agendas, notes, and other documents; do assignments.

The nearby box "How to Run a Meeting" also provides good advice for running effective meetings.

How to Run a Meeting

PLAN THE MEETING
- Be clear on objectives of the meeting.
- Be clear WHY you need the meeting.
- List the topics to be addressed.

INFORM
- Make sure everyone knows exactly what is being discussed, why, and what you want from the discussion.
- Anticipate what people and information may be needed and make sure they are there.

PREPARE
- Prepare the logical sequence of items.

- Allocate time on the basis of importance, not its urgency.

STRUCTURE AND CONTROL
- Put all evidence before interpretation and action.
- Stop people from jumping back and going over old ground.

SUMMARIZE AND RECALL
- Summarize all decisions and record them with the name of the person responsible for any action.

Source: Adapted from "Meetings, Bloody Meetings," starring John Cleese, 1993.

Shannon Ciston provides insight into her experience in documenting meetings in the nearby box "Meeting Minutes (and Agendas)."

Meeting Minutes (and Agendas)

My first year on the job as an assistant professor, I had a crash course in writing meeting minutes. As a junior member of several committees, I wanted to make a contribution while learning the ropes. I thought that recording meeting minutes was the perfect way to do this. Applying my note-taking style from my days as a student, I recorded every detail by hand in a notebook. Who was there, who said what, what decisions were made and points of view were discussed. I thought of these like a legal court transcript. I'd then spend at least one hour per hour of meeting time organizing and transcribing these minutes before sending them to the members of the committee and archiving them. I was proud of my minutes, which were thorough and well formatted. I developed a reputation for taking good minutes, and asked to take minutes at yet more meetings.

It wasn't until I had observed a few senior colleagues taking a much more efficient approach that I began to re-examine my style. Beginning with a clear agenda, they edited the file electronically in real time to include attendance, final decisions, action items, and any other important main ideas that arose. In some cases, these minutes were sent out instantly at the end of the meeting to all attendees, so that it was in our e-mail inbox by the time we got back to our respective desks. What an efficient and effective way to communicate the important points of a meeting!

Shannon Ciston

One emerging idea in this area is that of virtual meetings. John Leeper, information services director at Ryan Construction, reported recently that Ryan Construction is making extensive use of Webex for meetings (Leeper, 2002).

I currently spend several hours each week engaged in video conversations with colleagues around the world. What started a few years ago with one-on-one Skype conversations has morphed into multi-person conversations on a variety of platforms. Recently we have been using Google+ Hangouts for project meetings. Although video conferences are not the same as being present in person, they do seem to support more and better interaction than phone conferences or e-mail exchanges; also they reduce the amount of travel.

Team Charters

Just as project charters are important for getting projects off to a good start, team charters are excellent tools for getting a team off to a good start. The idea and examples of team charters were introduced in Chapter 4, and in this chapter the emphasis is on the use of charters for developing a framework for monitoring and evaluation. A key element of team charters is the development of team norms, which set up the criteria upon which the team can be monitored and assessed.

 INDIVIDUAL REFLECTION Review the team charter description from Mathieu and Rapp (2009) in the nearby box "The Team Charter" and note connections with your experiences. Have you developed and used team charters? If so, what were their strengths and weaknesses? What features of the Mathieu and Rapp team charter resonate with you?

The Team Charter

The Team Charter was a lengthy, structured exercise that was introduced and explained during class time. It was framed in terms of how the team would function to compete in the business simulation. It contained three major parts, as detailed below.

Teams could complete it in any way they chose (methods ranged from completing it together in person to exclusive use of virtual communications). Teams had a week to complete the assignment outside of class time.

Part 1: Individual Preparation
(Each member completed separately.)

Members were asked to detail, in writing, their personal characteristics in terms of their personal background (whatever they chose to share; usually, it was where they grew up, major, hobbies, personality features); contact information and preferred medium or mediums (e.g., text, e-mail, voice, face-to-face); availability in terms of hours and days, as well as preferred work times; individual business-related strengths and weaknesses, including factors such as content knowledge and work experiences; preferred work styles, particularly as related to teamwork; and anything else they believed the team should know.

Part 2: Team Roles, Expectations, and Processes
(One version for the entire team.)

Members were to meet and share their individual information from Part 1 and then to determine, as a team, how they would operate and what types of norms they wished to establish. They were provided with a series of questions to prompt such a discussion:

- What are your goals for the simulation, performance and otherwise?
- Who will be responsible for what activities (including, perhaps, backup roles)? and
- What is your timetable for activities?

As for norms, they were prompted to address specific expectations regarding

- Meeting attendance; task performance and quality;
- Idea contributions;
- Cooperation and attitudes; and
- Anything else they wanted.

Part 3: Rewards and Sanctions
(One version for the entire team.)

Members also determined, as a group, how they would

- Ensure expected contributions and performance levels;

- Reward members and the team for successes; and
- Manage or sanction poor performance (often tied to peer evaluations, which contributed to students' course participation grades).

Teams were required to circulate a single copy to all members and to incorporate any edits or changes that were warranted. The final integrated document was passed in for the team grade and was posted in their team web space.

Mathieu, John E., and Tammy L. Rapp. 2009. Laying the foundation for successful team performance trajectories: The role of team charters and performance strategies. *Journal of Applied Psychology* 94 (1), 90–103.

Monitoring Team Effectiveness

An important part of any team meeting is taking time to reflect on how well the team worked together. One common method for monitoring the effectiveness of teamwork is the plus/delta team processing approach typically attributed to Boeing. Near the end of the meeting the team stops working on the task and spends a few minutes discussing how well they worked. The team makes a list that records what went well on one side (+) and what they could do even better on the other (Δ). Other methods include individual reflection using instruments such as the one in Figure 12.1. Team members each fill in the chart and then discuss each other's scores and comments. Another approach is a narrative background assessment using questions such as those developed by Zou and Ko (2012):

1. What is your conception of teamwork? What are its major components?
2. What do a group of people have to do in order to become a performing team?
3. What personal strengths can you bring to your team in order to improve the team performance?
4. How can you deal with problems arising from your interactions with your teammates?
5. What is your plan/strategy to be an effective team member?

The next simplest monitoring approach is the use of checklists, which serve as a reminder, a way to document, and to assess. An example of a

Figure 12.1 A Sample Individual Reflection Instrument

For each trait, rate the team on a scale of 1 to 5:
1 = Not present (opposite trait present)
2 = Very poor (not much evidence of positive trait)
3 = Poor (some positive trait seen)
4 = Good (positive trait evident more than opposite trait)
5 = Very good (lots of evidence of positive trait)

Positive Trait	Score	Comments
Safety		
Inclusion		
Free interaction		
Appropriate level of interdependence		
Cohesiveness		
Trust		
Conflict resolution		
Influence		
Accomplishment		
Growth		

Source: Uhlfedler, 1997.

thorough checklist is shown in Figure 12.2. It was contributed by Ko and Leung (2012) and is used extensively at the Hong Kong University of Science and Technology.

More complex monitoring involves collecting data on individual participation in the team. Several observation forms are available. The one I start students with in my project management classes is shown in Figure 12.3. Any of the task and maintenance behaviors (see Chapter 4) may be listed in the rows. Team members take turns observing the team and recording each member's participation. They then provide feedback about the team's functioning during the processing phase. A rule of thumb that I commonly use is "Keep the feedback specific, descriptive, immediate, and positive." I give negative feedback only if the person requests it. If negative feedback is requested, the person is usually ready to hear it. Only then will it be helpful. More rules of thumb for feedback include the following, from Scholtes (1988):

Guidelines for Constructive Feedback
- Acknowledge the need for feedback.
- Give positive feedback (give negative feedback only if the recipient asks for it).
- Understand the context.
- Know when to give feedback.
- Know how to give feedback.
- Be descriptive.
- Don't use labels.
- Don't exaggerate.
- Don't be judgmental.

- Speak for yourself.
- Talk first about yourself, not about the other person.
- Phrase the issue as a statement, not a question.
- Restrict your feedback to things you observed.
- Help people hear and accept your compliments when giving positive feedback.

Figure 12.2 Checklist for Facilitating Discussions (Ko and Leung, 2012)

Checklist for facilitating discussions
(Please check if the facilitator does the following items appropriately)

Preparing yourself

- ☐ Familiarize with the content and background
- ☐ Identify key learning points and objectives
- ☐ Anticipate questions from participants
- ☐ Identify the relationship with key issues/other learning points, if any
- ☐ Check the time allotted
- ☐ Check participants' background and experience with the topic
- ☐ Learn the procedures/instructions/rules of the discussion/activity
- ☐ Prepare the necessary materials

Starting the discussion

- ☐ Introduce yourself and participants
- ☐ State the purpose and instructions clearly
- ☐ Set the time allotted and ground rules
- ☐ Identify roles of participants (e.g. note taker, presenter, characters in a role-play, etc)

Engaging participants

- ☐ Make eye contact with every participant
- ☐ Solicit ideas and suggestions from all participants of the group
- ☐ Identify less vocal participants and invite them to contribute
- ☐ Ask participants to respond to each others' ideas
- ☐ Provide feedback to group on how well they are communicating and interacting
- ☐ Encourage and recognize participants' involvement

Listening actively

- ☐ Identify common or different points of view regularly
- ☐ Check for understanding frequently
- ☐ Recognize divergent, unpopular ideas or minority views
- ☐ Ask participants to clarify when necessary
- ☐ Address non-verbal communication patterns
- ☐ Ask "why" and check assumptions, if necessary

Handling challenges

- ☐ Acknowledge distractions and move the focus back to the objective
- ☐ Identify dominators and make sure others have opportunities to contribute
- ☐ Steer intellectual rather than personal conflicts
- ☐ Check progress frequently and make cuts if you are behind schedule
- ☐ Invite participants directly to respond when there's lengthy idle time (dead air)
- ☐ Motivate participants to respect others' opinions (as ground rules), even when they disagree with them
- ☐ Focus on moving the discussion forward, when unresolved arguments arise

Consolidating the discussion

- ☐ Ensure the completion of tasks/goals
- ☐ Acknowledge participants' effort
- ☐ Summarize what has been done
- ☐ Take note on points that have not been fully discussed or areas that are confused
- ☐ Give participants opportunity to ask questions, if time allows

Things that were done well:	Things that could have been done better:	Other comments/ questions:

Figure 12.3 Observation Sheet

Observation Category	Names	Total
Task Contributes ideas		
Maintenance Encourages		
Total		

Notes:

Observation Directions

- Move your chair so you can see each member of the team clearly without interacting with them.
- Write the name of each person in the team at the top of one of the columns on the Observation Sheet.
- Watch each person systematically. As you see each person display one of the two behaviors specified (contributes ideas or describes feelings) place a hatch mark below his/her name, in the box to the right of the appropriate behavior.
- *Task* means anything that helps the team accomplish its task. For example, *Contributes ideas* means giving an idea related to one of the questions on the worksheet and/or to something said by another team member related to the task.
- *Maintenance* means anything that helps improve working relationships in the team. *Encourages* means praising others' ideas or inviting others to contribute.
- You may make some notations below the grid that may help you explain some scoring.
- When time is called, total the hatch marks in each column and across each row.
- When you give feedback to the team you will only give them the column totals and the row totals. Let them see the sheet. DO NOT INTERPRET WHAT YOU SAW, OR WHAT THE TOTALS MIGHT SUGGEST. You may be tempted to soften what you say. Don't allow this to happen. You are not criticizing, you are only reporting what you saw, related to very specific behaviors.
- It is the job of the team to discuss what the totals might suggest about how they functioned as a team, and to develop one or two sentences that capture this thought.

The idea of observing teams in action and trying to document their interactions and effectiveness is a common research approach (Bucciarelli, 1996; Cuff, 1991; Donnellon, 1996; Minneman, 1991; Brown and Duguid, 1991; Wenger and Snyder, 2000). It is also common in business and industry. A form that I've found very useful is shown in Figure 12.4. This was developed by Xerox and is included in their interactive skills workbook (Xerox Corporation, 1986). The second part of the figure provides definitions and examples of behavior categories in the worksheet.

The purpose of collecting data on team functioning by observing and other means is not only to provide data for monitoring but also to help each member learn how to attend to how the team is performing. Even if you don't have an opportunity to systematically observe a team, read the definitions and examples in Figure 12.4 and think about how you can expand your repertoire of behaviors.

Figure 12.4 Xerox's Interactive Skills Coding Worksheet

Behavior								Totals	%
Initiating									
Proposing									
Building									
Reacting									
Supporting									
Disagreeing									
Defending/attacking									
Clarifying									
Testing understanding									
Summarizing									
Seeking information									
Giving information									
Totals									
Process									
Shutting out									
Bringing in									

Definitions and Examples

Behavior Category	Definition	Examples
Proposing	A behavior that puts forward a new suggestion, proposal, or course of action.	"Let's deal with that one tomorrow." "I suggest we add more resources to . . ."
Building	A behavior that usually takes the form of a proposal, but that actually extends or develops a proposal made by another person.	". . . and your plan would be even better if we added a second reporting stage." "If I can take that further, we could also use the system to give us better cost control."

Figure 12.4 Xerox's Interactive Skills Coding Worksheet (Continued)

Behavior Category	Definition	Examples
Supporting	A behavior that makes a conscious and direct declaration of agreement with or support for another person, or for their concepts and opinions.	"Yes, I go along with that." "Sounds OK to me." "Fine. I accept that."
Disagreeing	A behavior that states a direct disagreement or that raises obstacles and objections to another person's concepts or opinions. Disagreeing is about issues.	"No, I don't agree with that." "Your third point just isn't true." "What you're suggesting won't work."
Defending/ attacking	A behavior that attacks another person, either directly or by defensiveness. Defending/ attacking usually involves value judgments and often contains emotional overtones. It is usually about *people*, not issues.	"That's stupid." ". . . and your third point is either stupid or an out-and-out lie." "Don't blame me, it's not my fault; it's *John's* responsibility."
Testing understanding	A behavior that seeks to establish whether or not an earlier contribution has been understood. It differs from seeking information in that it is an attempt to ensure agreement or consensus of some kind, and refers to a prior question or issue.	"Can I just check to be sure we're talking about the same thing here?" "Can I take it that we all now agree on this?"
Summarizing	A behavior that summarizes or restates, in a compact form, the content of previous discussions or events.	"So far, we have agreed (a) To divide responsibilities, (b) To meet weekly, (c) To finish the draft proposal by . . ."
Seeking information	A behavior that seeks facts, opinions, or clarification from another person.	"What timeline did we agree to?" "Can anyone tell me what page that table is on?" "Have you checked that thoroughly?"
Giving information	A behavior that offers facts, opinions, or clarification to other people.	"I remember a case like that last year." "There are at least three alternatives."
Bringing in*	A behavior that invites views or opinions from a member of the team who is not actively participating in the discussion.	"Dick, have you anything to say on this one?" "Cheryl has been very quiet. I wonder whether she has anything she would like to say here."
Shutting out*	A behavior that excludes another person or persons, or reduces their opportunity to contribute. Interrupting is the most common form of shutting out.	Jose: "What do you think, Bob?" Karl: "What I think is. . ." (Karl is shutting out Bob)

*Characteristic of a process behavior.

The Team Diagnostic Survey (TDS) (Wageman, Hackman, and Lehman, 2005) is a validated and reliable instrument to assess teams. The developers describe the instrument as follows: "The TDS is based explicitly on existing research and theory about the conditions that foster team effectiveness. It provides an assessment of how well a team is structured, supported, and led as well as several indicators of members' work processes and their affective reactions to the team and its work." Although it is one of only a few reliable and valid instruments for team diagnosis, it appears to be infrequently used in engineering.

Team Talk Analysis

An even more sophisticated approach to processing the work of teams was developed by Donnellon (1996), who claims, "Not all groups are teams." Although, as I mentioned in Chapter 3, the words *group* and *team* are often used interchangeably, it is important to distinguish between the gathering of people into groups and the purposeful formation of a team. A *team*, according to Donnellon, is "a group of people who are necessary to accomplish a task that requires the continuous integration of the expertise distributed among them" (p. 10).

Donnellon studied team talk and devised six dimensions along which to assess teams: identification (with what group team members identify); interdependence (whether team members feel independent from or interdependent with one another); power differentiation (how much team members use the differences in their organizational power); social distance (whether team members feel close to or distant from one another socially); conflict management tactics (whether members use the tactics of force or collaboration to manage their conflicts); and negotiation process (whether the team uses a win–lose or a win–win process). Donnellon then used these dimensions to differentiate between nominal teams and real teams, as shown in Table 12.1.

The dimensions shown in the table are consistent with the underlying conceptual framework in this book—the importance of interdependence, low power differentiation, close social distance (trusting relationships), constructive conflict management strategies, and win–win dynamics. I encourage you

Table 12.1 Nominal versus Real Teams

	Nominal Team	**Real Team**
Identification	Functional group	Team
Interdependence	Independence	Interdependence
Power differentiation	High	Low
Social distance	Distant	Close
Conflict management tactics	Forcing, accommodating, avoiding	Confronting, collaborating
Negotiation process	Win–lose	Win–win

Source: Donnellon, 1996.

Table 12.2 Team Talk Dimensions

Identification	Inter-dependence	Power Differentiation	Social Distance	Conflict Negotiation	Management	Profile
Team	High	Low	Close	Win–Win	Collaborative	Collaborative
Team	Moderate	Low	Close	Win–Win	Force–Avoid	Mostly Collaborative
Team	Moderate	High	Close			Emergent
Both	High	High	Distant	Win–Lose	Force–Avoid	Adversarial
Both	Low	High	Distant	Win–Lose	Force–Avoid	Adversarial
Function	Low	Low	Distant			Nominal
Function	Low	High	Distant	Win–Lose	Force–Avoid	Doomed

to examine the groups and teams you are a member of along these dimensions. Donnellon's team talk audit for assessing team dynamics is included in her book. Use this instrument to attend to the team talk, reflect on what it tells you about the team, and then plan how you will discuss the assessment with the team.

Donnellon also described five types of teams, based on the categorization in her six dimensions. In Table 12.2, I've summarized some of the more direct paths. Think about where your team fits.

Donnellon's work indicates that there are very few paths to collaborative team profiles, a conclusion borne out in the work of Katzenbach and Smith (1993) and Bennis and Beiderman (1997), whose case studies note that very few teams perform at the highest levels. With these dimensions in mind, carefully examine your group and team experiences and then explicitly discuss the performance (functioning) of your team to help you decide (1) to leave if your team is doomed, (2) refine the team if you're in the middle, or (3) celebrate and continue performing if you're a collaborative team.

Using the monitoring and processing formats described above to systematically reflect on the team's performance on both the task and their work with one another will help the team achieve its goals and help the members get better at working with one another. Group (or team) processing takes time and commitment and is typically difficult for highly motivated, task-oriented individuals. Spending a little carefully structured time on how the team is functioning can make an enormous difference in the team's effectiveness and the quality of the work environment.

Peer Assessment

Peer assessment, a process of rating other team members, often anonymously, is becoming more common in engineering teams. There are several resources for peer assessment, such as *The Team Developer* (McGourty and De Meuse, 2001), and the Comprehensive Assessment of Team-Member Effectiveness (CATME) (www.catme.org). Many engineering faculty members use an anonymous computer-based peer assessment system in which each individual rates each of the other team members in four team effectiveness dimensions—communication, decision making, collaboration, and self-management—using a 5-point scale. Each member then has access to her or his own rating as well as the overall average for the team. Matthew Ohland, as well as McGourty and De Meuse (2001), stress the importance of using the information for development. They recommend that the individual and the team focus on using the information to help them improve and solve problems. Matthew Ohland's extensive experience with the development and use of the CATME peer assessment system is summarized in the nearby box.

Focus on What Your Teammates Do Rather than on What You Think of Them

It is challenging to give a team member a single rating on their effectiveness as a teammate because some team members will be helpful to the team in some ways, but engage in some behaviors that hinder the team. Another difficulty is that each team member is likely to consider some ways of contributing more valuable than others, so the evaluation of a particular teammate will be overly influenced by that teammate's performance in certain areas. The only way to be fair is to focus on behaviors—what your teammates do—rather than on opinions such as how you feel about them. One way to focus on behaviors would be to ask you to take an inventory of what behaviors your teammates demonstrate and how often. The result would be that you might need to answer 50 or more questions about each member of the team. It is difficult to stay focused on answering accurately when completing such a long survey. A better way to focus on behaviors is by using sample behaviors to anchor each point of a rating scale. A peer evaluation instrument that is widely used in engineering education is the Comprehensive Assessment of Team-Member Effectiveness (CATME, see www.catme.org). CATME measures five different types of contributions to a team using such a behaviorally anchored rating scale. Each scale includes representative behaviors describing exceptional, acceptable, and deficient performance in each area. Recognizing that an individual team member may exhibit a combination of behaviors, the CATME instrument also includes "in between" ratings. The five types of contributions and are described below, along with associated behaviors.

Contributing to the Team's Work describes a team member's commitment to the effort, quality, and timeliness of completing the team's assigned tasks.

- A student who is exceptional at contributing to the team's work
  - does more or higher-quality work than expected.
  - makes important contributions that improve the team's work.
  - helps to complete the work of teammates who are having difficulty.
- A student who does an acceptable job at contributing to the team's work
  - completes a fair share of the team's work with acceptable quality.
  - keeps commitments and completes assignments on time.
  - fills in for teammates when it is easy or important.
- A student who is deficient at contributing to the team's work
  - does not do a fair share of the team's work, delivers sloppy or incomplete work.
  - misses deadlines, is late, unprepared, or absent for team meetings.
  - does not assist teammates, quits if the work becomes difficult.

Interacting with Teammates measures how a team member values and seeks contributions from other team members.

- A student who is exceptional at interacting with teammates
  - asks for and shows an interest in teammates' ideas and contributions.

- improves communication among teammates, provides encouragement or enthusiasm to the team.
- asks teammates for feedback and uses their suggestions to improve.
- A student who does an acceptable job at interacting with teammates
  - listens to teammates and respects their contributions.
  - communicates clearly, shares information with teammates, participates fully in team activities.
  - respects and responds to feedback from teammates.
- A student who is deficient at interacting with teammates
  - interrupts, ignores, bosses, or makes fun of teammates.
  - takes actions that affect teammates without their input, does not share information.
  - complains, makes excuses, or does not interact with teammates, accepts no help or advice.

Keeping the Team on Track describes how a team member monitors conditions that affect the team's progress and acts on that information as needed.

- A student who is exceptional at keeping the team on track
  - watches conditions affecting the team and monitors the team's progress.
  - makes sure that teammates are making appropriate progress.
  - gives teammates specific, timely, and constructive feedback.
- A student who does an acceptable job at keeping the team on track
  - notices changes that influence the team's success.
  - knows what everyone on the team should be doing and notices problems.
  - alerts teammates or suggests solutions when the team's success is threatened.
- A student who is deficient at keeping the team on track
  - is unaware of whether the team is meeting its goals.
  - does not pay attention to teammates' progress.

- avoids discussing team problems, even when they are obvious.

Expecting Quality is about voicing expectations that the team can and should do high-quality work.

- A student who is exceptional at expecting quality
  - motivates the team to do excellent work.
  - cares that the team does outstanding work, even if there is no additional reward.
  - believes that the team can do excellent work.
- A student who does an acceptable job at expecting quality
  - encourages the team to do good work that meets all requirements.
  - wants the team to perform well enough to earn all available rewards.
  - believes that the team can fully meet its responsibilities.
- A student who is deficient at expecting quality
  - is satisfied even if the team does not meet assigned standards.
  - wants the team to avoid work, even if it hurts the team.
  - doubts that the team can meet its requirements.

Having Relevant Knowledge, Skills, and Abilities accounts for both the talents a member brings to the team and those talents a member develops for the team's benefit.

- A student who has exceptional knowledge, skills, and abilities
  - demonstrates the knowledge, skills, and abilities to do excellent work.
  - acquires new knowledge or skills to improve the team's performance.
  - is able to perform the role of any team member if necessary.
- A student who has an acceptable level of knowledge, skills, and abilities
  - has sufficient knowledge, skills, and abilities to contribute to the team's work.
  - acquires knowledge or skills needed to meet requirements.
  - is able to perform some of the tasks normally done by other team members.

- A student who has deficient knowledge, skills, and abilities is
  - missing basic qualifications needed to be a member of the team.
  - unable or unwilling to develop knowledge or skills to contribute to the team.
  - unable to perform any of the duties of other team members.

Sample Team Member Descriptions for Practice Evaluation

Research shows that team performance can be enhanced if team members reflect on their own and their teammates' performance and give each other high-quality feedback. "High-quality" ratings are consistent with observed behavior, which may or may not be "high" ratings. We also know that rating quality (again, consistency with observed behavior) improves with practice. Guided practice in giving and receiving feedback and in practicing self- and peer-evaluations using behavioral criteria will help you improve. Please take your time in evaluating the members of the fictitious team below. Then, you will have the chance to compare your performance as a rater to ratings provided by experts (and get feedback on why the experts rated each team member that way).

The section below describes each member of a four-person team. Other descriptions are found at https://www.catme.org/.

- *Pat:* Friendly and very well-liked, makes working fun, and keeps everyone excited about working together. Relies on teammates to make sure everything is going okay. Pays attention to keeping the team upbeat but doesn't seem to notice if the team's work is getting done. Struggles to keep up with the rest of the team and often asks teammates for explanations. The team has to assign Pat the least difficult jobs because Pat doesn't have the skills to do more complex work. Offers ideas when able, but does not make suggestions that add anything unique or important to the final product. Always shows up for meetings, prepares beforehand, and does everything promised. Is confident that the team can do everything that is essential. Agrees that the team should meet all explicit task requirements.

- *Chris:* Okay as a person and doesn't interfere with the contributions of others but rubs teammates the wrong way by frequently griping about the work and making excuses for not following through on promises to the team. Chris has the brains and experience to make a unique and valuable contribution, but doesn't try. The fact that Chris is so smart frustrates some teammates who have to try hard to accomplish tasks that would be easy for Chris. Ignores assigned tasks or does a sloppy job because "Robin will redo the work anyway." Misses meetings or shows up without assigned work. Contributes very little during meetings. Was late to one meeting because "no one told me the meeting time." Missed another meeting because "the alarm clock didn't go off." After missing meetings asks lots of questions to make sure that everyone is making progress and the team's work is being accomplished. Spends more time checking that everyone else is doing their work than getting the job done. Chris always seems sure that the team will do fine and says that the team should do good work that fully meets the standards for acceptable performance. In response to a teammate's question about Chris's failure to deliver a promised piece of work, Chris said, "Why should I bother? Robin won't let the team fail."

- *Robin:* Very bright. Has far greater knowledge of the subject than any of the other team members. Extremely skilled in problem solving. Robin has very high standards and wants the team's work to be impressive, but Robin worries whether the team's work will be good enough to stand out. Robin completes a big chunk of the team's work and takes on a lot of the really difficult work. Does the work that Chris leaves unfinished. The quality of Robin's work is consistently outstanding. Tends to just work out the solutions and discourages teammates' attempts to contribute. Reluctant to spend time explaining things to others. Doesn't like to explain "obvious" things. Is particularly impatient with Pat's questions and once told Pat, "You are not smart enough to be on this team." Complains that Chris is a "lazy freeloader." Sometimes gets obsessed with

215

grand plans and ignores new information that would call for changes. Does not pay attention to warning signs that the current plan might not be effective until the problems are obvious. Then handles the situation as a crisis and takes over without getting team input. Robin is reluctant to acknowledge or discuss problems in the team until they affect Robin's work.

- *Terry:* Not nearly as bright as Robin, but works to develop enough knowledge and skills to do the assigned tasks. Terry can usually fill in for other team members if given specific directions, but does not understand most of the tasks that other team members normally perform. Does more grunt work than any of the other team members, but doesn't do as good a job as Robin and doesn't take on difficult tasks. Sometimes makes mistakes on the more complex work. Super responsible, spends a lot of time giving one-on-one help to Pat. Always on time to meetings. Often calls to remind everyone (especially Chris) about meetings and usually makes some nice comment about one of the teammate's strengths or a valuable contribution that the teammate has recently made. Terry is outgoing and highly supportive of teammates when well-rested, but is sometimes too tired to get excited about teammates' ideas. Is not defensive when teammates offer feedback, but doesn't ask for teammates' suggestions, even when teammates' input could help Terry to do

better work. Terry thinks that the team can do great work and encourages teammates to do their best. When Robin expresses doubts if the team can do superior work, Terry reassures everyone that the team is capable of outstanding work. When the team is headed in the wrong direction, Terry is quick to notice and say something, but usually doesn't suggest a way to fix it. Terry reviews the team's objectives and alerts the team to anything that comes up that would affect the team. Terry was reluctant to press the issue when Robin's plan ignored one of the guidelines specified for the project.

Practice

To test your ability to focus on individual behaviors, go to https://www.catme.org/login/survey_instructions and rate each team member on each type of contribution to the team.

On the Scenario Results page, a green arrow indicates that your rating matches the expected rating. Good work! If your rating doesn't match the expert rating, the blue arrow shows your rating and the red arrow indicates the rating experts would have assigned. If you count one point for every level separating your rating from the expert rating on the five different types of contribution, a low score is best, indicating the greatest agreement with the expert ratings. You can "Mouse over" the red arrows to read the rationales underlying the expert ratings.

Matthew Ohland

Peer assessment has also been used in merit review (as in merit reviews for raises and promotions). The most common system is the 360-degree evaluations that were used extensively at GE. GE abandoned the 360s because "Like anything driven by peer input, the system is capable of being 'gamed' over the long haul. People began saying nice things about one another so they would all come out with good ratings" (Welch and Byrne, 2001, p. 183). GE currently uses 360s only in special situations. Peer assessment of team members is subject to the same concern—everyone might be too nice and give others a high rating, which makes the assessment of limited value for improvement. Effective development results from a climate that promotes improvement. Peer assessment might help create such a climate, but it needs to be used with real care.

One way to ensure that it is used with real care is to use peer assessment for constructive criticism focused on improvement and not as a part of a final evaluation, that is, a grade.

There are many examples for constructive and creative collaborations throughout history. One of the best known is that between the artists Pablo Picasso and Georges Braque (Johnson and Johnson, 2004). Picasso and Braque met almost every day and talked constantly about their new style. They would have intense discussions about what they planned to paint, and then they would spend all day painting separately. Each evening, they would eagerly review each other's work and criticize each other's work intensely. Here are descriptions of their interactions:

> *Almost every evening, either I went to Braque's studio or Braque came to mine. Each of us had to see what the other had done during the day. We criticized each other's work. A canvas wasn't finished unless both of us felt it was.*

> PABLO PICASSO (in a letter to Françoise Gilot)

> *The things Picasso and I said to one another during those years will never be said again, and even if they were, no one would understand them anymore. It was liked being roped together on a mountain.*

> GEORGES BRAQUE

As Picasso and Braque did, you need to assess your teammates and be assessed by them, but it needs to be in a climate of creative interdependence as that of "two mountaineers roped together."

Self-Assessment

Know thyself, the motto inscribed on the sixth-century B.C.E. temple of Apollo at Delphi (*The Oxford Dictionary of Proverbs*, 2003), is as important today as it was when it was written over 2500 years ago.

Although peer assessment and professor assessment are important and hopefully helpful, it is self-assessment that has lasting value and will endure. The better you become at realistic self-assessment, the better you will be able to match your skills and knowledge to the tasks at hand and the more satisfying your accomplishments will become.

Apparently realistic self-assessment about generosity and cooperation are hard to come by in the West. Epley and Dunning (2000) found that undergraduate students typically overrated themselves. Dunning's (2005) book *Self-insight* further elaborates on how difficult it is to gain a realistic understanding of ourselves.

Here's a self-assessment form that may help you improve the accuracy of your perceptions (Johnson and Johnson, 2004). Complete this form comparing your self-assessment with the assessment of your teammates. Discuss the results with your team. Ask for clarification when your rating differs from the ratings given by your teammates.

Rate yourself on the following scale:

(5 = Excellent, 4 = Proficient, 3 = Adequate, 2 = Limited, 1 = Inadequate)

	Self	Peer
1. Take a position, contribute ideas, opinions		
2. Ask for others' positions, ideas, opinions		
3. Use evidence to support a position		
4. Differentiate the positions proposed		
5. Integrate the different positions		
6. Encourage others to participate		
7. Check for others' understanding		
8. Listen attentively		
9. Contribute energy and enthusiasm		
10. Show consideration for others		
11. Respect work and ideas of others		
12. Keep work neat and easy for others to follow		
13. Overall contribution to team effort		
What specific action will you take next time?		

Practice with self-assessment will almost surely result in improvement. Self-assessment involves a comparison and mostly I've referred to peers. However, the comparison can be one's own past performance, a preset criterion, or the performance of others. All three are important and can be helpful.

Project Evaluation

At the end of a project it is important, and often a requirement, to conduct an evaluation. Typically a set of project evaluation questions guides this process. The following, generated by Haynes (1989), is a typical set of questions:

1. How close to scheduled completion was the project actually completed?
2. What did we learn about scheduling that will help us on our next project?
3. How close to budget was the final project cost?
4. What did we learn about budgeting that will help us on our next project?
5. Upon completion, did the project output meet client specifications without additional work?
6. If additional work was required, please describe.
7. What did we learn about writing specifications that will help us on our next project?
8. What did we learn about staffing that will help us on our next project?
9. What did we learn about monitoring performance that will help us on our next project?
10. What did we learn about taking corrective action that will help us on our next project?

11. What technological advances were made?

12. What tools and techniques were developed that will be useful on our next project?

13. What recommendations do we have for future research and development?

14. What lessons did we learn from our dealings with service organizations and outside vendors?

15. If we had the opportunity to do the project over, what would we do differently?

Continual Evaluation

Evaluation doesn't have to occur only at the end of the project; it is often initiated when a project falls behind schedule or goes over budget. My recommendation is that evaluation be an integral part of the project. You have probably been involved in team projects that got behind schedule or used more resources than were initially allocated.

 INDIVIDUAL REFLECTION How have you dealt with projects that got behind schedule or required more resources than were initially allocated? What are some of the strategies you've used? Take a few minutes and reflect on dealing with delays and cost overruns.

When progress is monitored, three questions should always be asked (Lewis, 2000):

1. What is the actual status of the project?
2. If a deviation exists, what caused it?
3. What should be done about it?

In answering the third question, there are three responses that can be made:

1. Ignore the deviation.
2. Take corrective action to get back on target.
3. Revise the plan.

A key question concerning project deviations involves understanding the source of the deviation (or what Deming, the quality guru, referred to as *variation*). Deming (1993) identified two sources of variation:

Common causes produce points on a control chart that over a long period all fall inside the control limits.

Special causes are something special, not part of the system of common causes, but detected by a point outside the control limits.

Furthermore, Deming identified mistakes that result from misidentified sources of variation.

Mistake 1. To react to an outcome as if it came from a special cause, when actually it came from common causes of variation.

Mistake 2. To treat an outcome as if it came from common causes of variation, when actually it came from a special cause.

The following table summarizes the consequences of making the wrong attributions:

Efforts Directed	Type of Variation	
	Common Cause	**Special Cause**
Common cause	Good	Disappointment (Mistake 2)
Special cause	Disappointment (Mistake 1)	Good

Making changes during the project is a necessary and costly part of most complex projects. Several project "change systems" are available. Change protocols from Lewis (2000), Wysocki and McGary (2004), and the Project Management Institute (2004) involve a description of the requested change as well as a budget justification. The Change Approval Form from the Lewis Project Management Institute is shown below (http://www.lewisinstitute.com/_store/download.asp):

Project Change Approval		
Project Name:	Project Number:	Date: May 19, 1999
Project Manager: Requested by:	Department:	Change in: I Scope II Schedule I Budget Performance
Deviation Information		
Description of change being requested: Reason for change: Effect on schedule: Effect on cost (budget): Effect on performance (quality): Effect on scope: Justification:		
Class	Distribution of Estimated Cost Deviation	The Requested Change Is:
Capital		I Absolutely necessary to achieve desired results | I Scope reduction that will not impact original targets
Non-capital		I Discretionary - provides benefits beyond the original target | I Scope reduction that will impact original targets
Required Approvals		
I Project Leader/Manager (type name)	Sign:	Date:
I General Manager (type name)	Sign:	Date:
I Concerned Dept. Manager (type name)	Sign:	Date:
I Controller (type name)	Sign:	Date:
I Concerned Vice President (type name)	Sign:	Date:
I President (type name)	Sign:	Date:
I Other (type name)	Sign:	Date:

There are lots of internal things you can do with your project team to address delays and resource excesses. Sometimes it's necessary to try to change external conditions to address delays and overruns. Here's a list of some things you can do:

1. *Recover later in the project.* If there are early delays or overruns, review the schedule and budget for recovery later. This is a common strategy in many projects. How often have you done extraordinary work at the last minute, especially the night before the project is due?
2. *Reduce project scope.* Consider eliminating nonessential elements or containing scope creep. Engineers often find better ways of doing things during projects and are sometimes perfectionists, so there is a tendency for the scope to creep.
3. *Renegotiate.* Discuss with the client the possibility of extending the deadline or increasing the budget. How often have you asked a professor for an extension? This is a common strategy, but sometimes there is no flexibility.
4. *Add additional resources.* Adding more resources—people, computers, and so on—to a project (activities along the critical path, as you learned in Chapter 11) can reduce the duration. The increased costs must be traded off with the benefits of the reduced schedule.
5. *Offer incentives or demand compliance.* Sometimes by offering incentives (provided you don't endanger people's lives or sacrifice performance specifications) you can get a project back on track. Other times you may have to demand that people do what they said they would do.
6. *Be creative.* If the delay is caused by resources that have not arrived, you may have to accept substitutions, accept partial delivery, or seek alternative sources.

Building Quality into Projects

Evaluation and continual improvement often become an ongoing part of projects and company culture. This aspect of company or organizational culture is commonly described as a quality initiative. Table 12.3 provides a set of insightful contrasts about old and new thinking about quality.

Engineers are often required to help develop a quality initiative in their organization. You may have been involved in a quality initiative in your work or school. Although there has been some attention paid to quality in schools (see Langford and Cleary, 1995, for example), much of the emphasis on quality has been in the workplace. Business and industry have taken the lead, as indicated by Ford Motor Company's motto "Quality Is Job One."

Some quality basics include a systems perspective, emphasis on the customer, and understanding variation. It is essential to have knowledge of sources of variation, especially ways of measuring and documenting them, and strategies for reducing variability and maintaining consistent quality.

The current quality movement started with work by W. Edwards Deming in the 1940s and progressed through a series of initiatives—continuous quality improvement (CQI), total quality management (TQM), and presently,

Table 12.3 Thinking About Quality

Old	New
Competition motivates people to do better work	Cooperation helps people do more effective work
For every winner there's a loser	Everyone can win
Please your boss	Please your customer
Scapegoating pinpoints problems	Improve the system
Focus improvements on individual processes	Focus on the purpose of the overall system, and how the processes can be improved to serve it better
Find the cause and fix the problem	First, acknowledge there is variation in all things and people. See if the problem falls in or outside the system.
The job is complete if specifications have been met	Continual improvement is an unending journey
Inspection and measurement ensure quality	A capable process, shared vision and aim, good leadership, and training are major factors in creating quality
Risks and mistakes are bad	Risks are necessary and some mistakes inevitable when you practice continual improvement
You can complete your education	Everyone is a lifelong learner
Bosses command and control	Bosses help workers learn and make improvements
Bosses have to know everything	The team with a good leader knows more and can do more
Short-term profits are best	Significant achievement in a complex world takes time
You don't have to be aware of your basic beliefs	You must be conscious of your beliefs and constantly examine and test them to see if they continue to be true
Do it now	Think first, then act

Source: Dobyns and Crawford-Mason, 1994.

Six Sigma. Each successive phase seems to provide enhanced features for focusing on quality. These are the essential themes of Six Sigma (Pande, Neuman, and Cavanagh, 2000):

- A genuine focus on the customer
- Data- and fact-driven management
- Process focus, management, and improvement, as an engine for growth and success
- Proactive management
- Boundaryless collaboration
- A drive for perfection, and yet a tolerance for failure

Another central feature of Six Sigma is the Six Sigma improvement model DMAIC—Define, Measure, Analyze, Improve, Control. Many students (especially those who work for 3M, Honeywell, Seagate, Medtronic, and so forth) in the Management of Technology master's program course I teach have in their bag a copy of Rath and Strong's *Six Sigma Pocket Guide* (2000), which is based on the DMAIC model.

Further readings on quality can be found in the references in Deming (1993, 1986), Bowles and Hammond (1991), Dobyns and Crawford-Mason (1994), Brassand (1989), Sashkin and Kiser (1993), and Walton (1986). You may also want to consult a basic textbook on quality, such as Summers (1997).

Reflection on Paying Attention

I am often reminded of the advice of the talking mynah birds in Aldous Huxley's *Island* (1962). These birds periodically called out "Attention, attention; Here and now." Huxley is emphasizing awareness, as indicated in the following dialogue:

> "Listen to him closely, listen discriminatingly. . . ." Will Farnaby listened. The mynah had gone back to its first theme. "Attention," the articulate oboe was calling. "Attention." "Attention to what?" he asked, in the hope of eliciting a more enlightening answer than the one he had received from Mary Sarojini. "To attention," said Dr. MacPhail. "Attention to attention?" "Of course." (p. 16)

We often get so wrapped up in achieving our goals and completing our tasks that we forget to pay attention to what's going on around us. My sense is that successful project managers have refined their skills for paying attention.

Questions

1. Where did you develop skills for monitoring the work on project teams? Have you had an opportunity to observe a project team? If so, where? What did you learn from the experience? Do you try to attend to what's happening within the team while it is working?
2. What can you do to improve the functioning of teams during "boring and useless" meetings? List things you can do and strategies for doing them. Try them out.
3. Check out some of the ethnographic research on work in organizations, such as Brown and Duguid (1991). This paper is also available on the Xerox Palo Alto Research Center website. How does research affect your view of work in organizations?
4. What are some strategies for building quality into projects?
5. How can project evaluation, which is often seen as a punitive process, become a more positive and constructive process? What things can project team members and managers do to make evaluation an ongoing part of project work?

References

Bennis, W., and P. W. Biederman. 1997. *Organizing genius: The secrets of creative collaboration.* Reading: Addison-Wesley.

Bowles, J., and J. Hammond. 1991. *Beyond quality: How 50 winning companies use continuous improvement.* New York: Putnam.

Brassand, Michael. 1989. *The memory jogger plus+: Featuring the seven management and planning tools.* Methuen, MA: GOAL/QPC.

Brown, John Seely, and Paul Duguid. 1991. Organizational learning and communities-of-practice: Toward a unified view of working, learning, and innovation. *Organizational Science* 2 (1), 40–56.

Bucciarelli, Louis L. 1996. *Designing engineers.* Cambridge, MA: MIT Press.

Cuff, Dana. 1991. *Architecture: The story of practice.* Cambridge, MA: MIT Press.

Deming, W. E. 1986. *Out of crisis.* Cambridge, MA: MIT Center for Advanced Engineering Study.

———. 1993. *The new economics for industry, government, education.* Cambridge, MA: MIT Center for Advanced Engineering Study.

Dobyns, Lloyd, and Clare Crawford-Mason. 1994. *Thinking about quality: Progress, wisdom, and the Deming philosophy.* New York: Times Books.

Donnellon, Anne. 1996. *Team talk: The power of language in team dynamics.* Cambridge, MA: Harvard Business School Press.

Dunning, D. 2005. *Self-insight: Roadblocks and detours on the path to knowing thyself.* New York: Psychology Press.

Epley, N., and D. Dunning. 2000. Feeling "holier than thou": Are self-serving assessments produced by errors in self or social prediction? *Journal of Personality and Social Psychology* 79, 861–875.

Haynes, M. E. 1989. *Project management: From idea to implementation.* Los Altos, CA: Crisp.

Huxley, Aldous. 1962. *Island.* New York: Harper & Row.

Johnson, David W., and Roger T. Johnson. 2004. *Assessing students in groups: Promoting group responsibility and individual accountability.* Thousand Oaks, CA: Corwin Press.

Katzenbach, Jon R., and Douglas K. Smith. 1993. *The wisdom of teams: Creating the high-performance organization.* Cambridge, MA: Harvard Business School Press.

Langford, David P., and Barbara A. Cleary. 1995. *Orchestrating learning with quality.* Milwaukee: ASQC Quality Press.

Leeper, John. 2002. Personal communication. November 7.

Leung, W. K., and E. I. Ko. 2011. *Checklist for facilitating discussions.* Presented in a workshop for students in Vocational Training Council in Hong Kong on October 29.

Lewis, James P. 1998. *Team-based project management.* New York: AMACOM.

———. 2000. *Working together: 12 principles for achieving excellence in managing projects, teams, and organizations.* New York: McGraw-Hill.

Lippincott, S. 1994. *Meetings: Do's, don'ts, and donuts: The complete handbook to successful meetings.* Pittsburgh: Lighthouse Point Press.

Mathieu, John E., and Tammy L. Rapp. 2009. Laying the foundation for successful team performance trajectories: The role of team charters and performance strategies. *Journal of Applied Psychology* 94 (1), 90–103.

McGourty, Jack, and Kenneth P. De Meuse. 2001. *The team developer: An assessment and skill building program.* New York: Wiley.

Minneman, Scott. 1991. *The social construction of a technical reality: Empirical studies of group engineering design practice.* Xerox Corporation Palo Alto Research Center Report SSL-91-22. Palo Alto, CA: Xerox Corporation.

The Oxford Dictionary of Proverbs. 2003. Ed. Jennifer Speake. Oxford: Oxford University Press.

Pande, Peter S., Robert P. Neuman, and Roland D. Cavanagh. 2000. *The six sigma way: How GE, Motorola and other top companies are honing their performance.* New York: McGraw-Hill.

Peters, Thomas J. 1989. *A passion for excellence* (with Nancy Austin). New York: Knopf.

———. 1999. The WOW project: In the new economy, all work is project work. *Fast Company,* May, 116–128.

Project Management Institute. 2004. *A guide to the project management body of knowledge (PMBOK guide),* 3rd ed. Newton Square, PA: Project Management Institute.

Rath, and Strong. 2000. *Six sigma pocket guide.* Lexington, MA: Rath and Strong Management Consultants.

Sashkin, Marshall, and Kenneth J. Kiser. 1993. *Putting total quality management to work.* San Francisco: Berrett-Koehler.

Scholtes, Peter. 1988. *The team handbook: How to use teams to improve quality.* Madison, WI: Joiner Associates.

Scholtes, P. R., B. L. Joiner, and B. J. Streibel. 1996. *The team handbook.* Madison: Joiner Associates.

Summers, Donna C. S. 1997. *Quality.* Upper Saddle River, NJ: Prentice Hall.

Uhlfedler, H. 1997. Ten critical traits of group dynamics. *Quality Progress* 30 (4), 69–72.

Wageman, Ruth, J. Richard Hackman, and Erin Lehman. 2005. Team diagnostic survey development of an instrument. *The Journal of Applied Behavioral Science* 41 (4), 373–398.

Walton, M. 1986. *The Deming management method.* New York: Putnam.

Welch, John F., Jr., and John A. Byrne. 2001. *Jack: Straight from the gut.* New York: Warner.

Wenger, E., and W. Snyder. 2000. Communities of practice: The next organizational frontier. *Harvard Business Review.*

Wysocki, Robert K., and Rudd McGary. 2004. *Effective project management: Traditional, adaptive, extreme.* New York: Wiley.

Xerox Corporation. 1986. *Leadership through quality: Interactive skills workbook.* Stamford, CT.

Zou, T. X. P., and E. I. Ko. 2012. Teamwork development across the curriculum for chemical engineering students in Hong Kong: Processes, outcomes and lessons learned. *Education for Chemical Engineers* 7 (3), e105–e117.

CHAPTER 13

Skills and Strategies for Effective Project Documentation*

When the explorer Roald Amundsen began his race to the South Pole, he documented his course carefully by placing 20 black flags on either side of his supply depot for several miles, so that he would be able to find his way back even if he miscalculated. In contrast, his competitor, Robert Falcon Scott, used a single red flag as a marker. At the end of the race, Scott and his team froze to death 10 kilometers from their supply depot. In contrast, Amundsen won, and survived, the race, aided by his careful preparation and documentation practices (Collins and Hansen, 2011).

So what does exploration have to do with engineering? Engineering design can be thought of as a form of exploration. Like explorers, designers need to both arrive at good design and make their way back to where they started. Making your way back requires careful preparation and documentation. Creating a good design is only half the work. Engineers also need to be able to reproduce and protect their designs with document production techniques and patents. In engineering environments, effective documentation practices are like Amundsen's black flags—they help you "find your way back" to key concepts needed to (re)create and (re)contextualize your design.

One of the theses of this book is that most engineering is (re)engineering, and most design is (re)design. Regardless of whether you are working on an airplane, building, bridge, software, hardware, or consumer product design, it is rare to begin from a blank slate. Most designers begin with the current state of the art, and then improve it. So how do you know what the current state of the art is? The best place to start is by looking at documentation.

This chapter is organized into three sections—Skills and Strategies for Project Documentation, Project Communication Practices, and Communication Patterns of Engineers.

Skills and Strategies for Project Documentation

Why are project documentation and record keeping important? Have you ever had to try to pick up the pieces from a group project that went wrong? Did you wish that others had documented their work so you could have done

---

*By Constance Kampf.

your job more easily? How about your own note-taking and learning habits? Have you ever studied for an exam and wished you had taken better notes during class?

Like your experiences in school projects and exams, project documentation involves both writing for yourself and writing for others. Because engineering involves complex ideas and designs, writing for yourself is an essential first step in the process. Writing for yourself is often done in the form of journaling and laboratory notes. Writing for others is often done with the help of shared documents such as laboratory reports, project schedules, progress reports, meeting minutes, patents, reports, and websites. These documents provide touchstones for and crystallizations of project-related communication during a project. They are also useful after a project has finished because they contain information about the state of the art at the time they were written, and document key issues.

Latour (2008) emphasizes that "to design is always to redesign." He goes on to say that "There is always something that exists first as a given, as an issue, as a problem. Design is a task that follows to make something more lively, more commercial, more usable, more user friendly, more acceptable, and so on, depending on the various constraints to which the project has to answer. In other words, there is always something remedial in design." So, for the people that follow you in a workplace, how can you make available as much information and insight as possible so that the redesign in later projects can begin from the "state of the art" and use the best of your work as a starting point? In the same way, how can you look to previous work so that your work begins from the "state of the art" as well?

 REFLECTION What are some skills and strategies you use to communicate with yourself? What are some skills and strategies you use to communicate with others?

Writing for Yourself

Writing for yourself is often easier than writing for others because you can easily see when it doesn't work and change your strategies until you find ones that do work. One written form of self-communication that you can start with as an engineering student is journaling. *Journaling* is a useful skill for developing your critical thinking habits. It differs from note taking in that it focuses on your ideas and understanding instead of what other people say. Writing in your private journal offers you a space for transforming the information in readings, lectures, lab exercises, as well as classroom debates and discussions into knowledge.

If you prefer a public audience for your reflections and insights, you can also consider blogging. Interesting blogs for engineers include How to Geek (http://www.howtogeek.com/) which offers technology related information as well as technology fun; Hello Engineers Blogspot (http://hello-engineers.blogspot.dk/), which contains descriptions of engineering student project ideas, presentations, and seminars from Europe; and the Zen College Life Blog, which offers a list of the top 50 engineering blogs (http://www.zencollege life.com/50-top-engineering-blogs/), which include blogs from top engineering schools such as MIT, as well as Princeton and many others. These blogs offer resources and connect information from many sources together for you. In a personal blog, you can both connect to resources and reflect on your learning, sharing insights with others. You might consider beginning with a small audience of your peers to see what they think of your insights. If your ideas prove popular enough, you may be able to use a personal blog both for your own learning and to interact with a broad group of other people around your insights and knowledge from your engineering classes and experiences.

The importance of journaling is not new. Famous inventors such as Thomas Edison and Leonardo da Vinci kept journals. As part of the Rutgers Thomas Edison Papers Project (http://edison.rutgers.edu/index.htm), you can access scans of Thomas Edison's papers and journals. Leonardo da Vinci's papers are available electronically through the Biblioteca Leonardiana in Italy at http://www.leonardodigitale.com/index.php?lang=ENG. To see the journals, choose the "search in the text" option from the menu across the top of the page. Notice that da Vinci, even back in the 1500s, was aware of journaling for private and public audiences, given that he wrote "in mirror" for private journals. "Writing in mirror" meant that the text was readable only with a mirror, thus making the content much harder for others to take even if they had the journal in their own hands. Take a look at both Edison and da Vinci's journals online. Why is so much time and energy being spent to make them available today? Why do you think that Leonardo da Vinci was so aware of the distinction between writing for himself and for others? What can you learn from this distinction to support your engineering career? (See the Activity box "Establishing a Blog and/or Journal" nearby.)

Activity: Establishing a Blog and/or Journal

Work with a partner to answer the following questions and set up your personal plan for self-communication.

Part 1: Consider whether blogging or journaling is best for you. Blogging is public, and journaling is private. What are the advantages to each? What are the disadvantages? Discuss what kinds of information and insights you would want to be public. What should be private? Why?

Part 2: Consider how to write. Writing reflects your voice. I remember co-writing a book with two other authors, and when I was proofreading, I could tell who wrote what, because it reflected the way they talked. As I read, I could actually hear each voice in my head. You have a voice too. So don't worry about mechanics or even

being grammatical when you write for yourself privately, just focus on the ideas. The act of writing is both about quantity and quality. As Professor Victoria Mikelonis used to say, "How do I know what I think, until I see what I write?" It takes a combination of the quality of your ideas and the patience to simply write what comes to mind so you can pick out "the diamonds" from the rest.

Part 3: Based on your answers, make a plan for how you will communicate with yourself. Answer the following questions to help you build your plan:

1. Will you do it privately or publicly? Or both?
2. How will you organize your journal or blog?

3. Will you use technology or write in a book by hand?
4. How will you organize it so you can access it when you study for exams?
5. Who else will read or view it? (Is it something that you might share with your professors, study buddies or friends? Or even future employers?)
6. How will you schedule your writing? Usually, journals work best with short, systematic writing. For example, you might spend 15–20 minutes after a class, reflecting on insights and key ideas before you forget them. Or you might spend time at the beginning or end of the work day, or work week—depending on how often you choose to write.
7. How will you back up the contents so you don't lose them right before you begin studying for your exams or working on a key assignment?

Part 4: Interaction with your professors, fellow students, and summarizing significant findings.

In this part, you can set up a formal agreement with your professor, fellow students or other audiences to react to your writing and help you see the significance of some of your insights.

Interaction–Professor: Examine the journal twice during the term—reading entries you select, and responding or arguing with them to give you an outside perspective on your ideas.

Interaction–Correspondent: Choose a fellow student from your friends to read and respond to your journal entries.

Interaction–Conclusions: Make a table of contents with links to or page numbers for the significant entries. At the end of the term, write a two-page summary of the significant ideas from your journal. Finally, submit an evaluation of whether the journal enhanced or distracted from your learning experience. Was it worth the effort?

Source: Adapted from T. Fulwiler, *Teaching with Writing* (Portsmouth, NH: Boynton/Cook Publishers, 1987). Revised by B. S. Thompson in consultation with K. A. Smith and R. C. Rosenberg in 1998. Revised by C. Kampf in 2012.

The blog/journal activity indicated in the Activity box is an effective way to lay the groundwork for your engineering career. Getting used to writing and also interacting with others about what you write is a key skill for engineers. This is because at least half of good engineering work is writing—laboratory notes, patents, proposals for funding bridges or roads, proposals to management or clients for developing a product, etc. Notice that writing is typically linked to money-generating activity such as proposals and patents. The organizations that engineers work for depend on good writing to get patents approved, win proposals, etc. So your ability to write is a core part of your ability to do good engineering design.

Writing for Others

In contrast to writing for yourself, writing for others involves more preparation and analysis. Like blogging, you need to be aware of your audience and polish your writing so people believe you are credible. Polishing includes editing and checking your grammar and spelling, as well as organizing your ideas so they are easy for others to read.

It is not that easy to predict who will be looking at your blog. However, in project management, you can predict who will be looking at your documents. Although you cannot control other people's reactions to your writing, you can use analysis to predict them. Key concepts to consider in writing for others include "pre-writing" and problem-solving perspectives. "Pre-writing" offers you a way of thinking your ideas through before and during writing.

Problem-solving perspectives offer you a way of demonstrating to your audience why they should be interested in your idea—helping the audience make sense of the idea with your insights in addition to the facts.

An example of a "pre-writing" tool is the "Audience, Purpose and Action Worksheet" (Kampf and Eiler, 2004). This worksheet was developed for a writing-intensive project management course in the Civil Engineering department at the University of Minnesota. It consisted of five key questions to consider when you are writing for others:

1. Who are you audiences?
2. What is your purpose for writing?
3. What are their purposes for reading?
4. What actions should they take as a result of reading your document?
5. Why will they want to take those actions?

Notice that there are two types of purpose addressed here: both your purpose for writing and other people's purpose(s) for reading. Recognizing these different types of purpose helps you to write to both inform and persuade your audience. It also helps you take the information in your work and turn it into insights for your audience—insights about the importance of your work. These insights need to fulfill some of your audiences' expectations in order to be heard.

As you write assignments in your university courses, you may notice that your professors do not always agree with you about the quality of your work. One technique that you can develop to help your grades is to take the time to learn about their expectations for assignments and exams, and respond to those expectations. For example, if your professor expects that you show your work when you do integral and derivative problems, you will quickly find that showing your work enhances your grade. Why do professors have this expectation? Because they want to know not only what answer you arrived at, but also how you did it—even if your answer was wrong. Showing your work in calculus is an example of adapting to audience expectations because it allows your professors to assess both your answer and your understanding of the process—which is often their goal in giving exams.

This lesson in adapting to other people's expectations and purposes for reading your work is useful in your engineering career as well. One tool that organizations often use to help you both explain the state of the art during and after the project is a *template*. Templates also communicate audience expectations and guide you as you write for audiences in your workplace. Large organizations often have many templates that can help you begin your work. Examples of templates organized by the PMBOK Process Group can be found at http://www.projectmanagementdocs.com/templates.html. These templates offer organizations a place to begin using Project Management as a way of thinking about the project. They ask specific questions, such as, What is the purpose of the project? These questions encourage you to go beyond thinking about what you will do, and to reflect on why it matters for the organization. Because of the redesign interaction between past projects and new needs, project document templates are often changed as people learn from past projects. Thus, they can contain best practices and lessons learned from previous projects. This connection to past projects and lessons learned can help shape your thinking about the current project, and allows you to learn from other projects, including both successes and mistakes.

Currently, new media and software support sharing of information among project team members. One example of this is Autodesk Inventor (http://usa.autodesk.com/autodesk-inventor/) which supports sharing of notes and documents in addition to 2D and 3D renderings of product designs. In addition, products that share project information are also available, such as Microsoft Sharepoint (http://sharepoint.microsoft.com/en-us/Pages/default.aspx). The shared nature of these platforms allows engineers to write for others in a more efficient work process, encouraging engineers to be careful not only about the readability and usability of their content, but also about editing.

Many workplaces also use intranets with different tools for knowledge management. Some tools are simple, such as shared directories of files. Other tools offer a richer way of sharing, including Skype, which allows you to see another person's desktop in real time. As Smart Phones and tablets progress, the ability to use not only written documentation but also live video feeds and recorded videos will most likely change the shape of engineering documentation. But what hasn't changed since da Vinci first started journaling is that engineers must be aware of their audiences, both public and private, and adapt to the situation—whether it be communicating more clearly to share, or safeguarding engineering secrets from the wrong audience, such as your competitor.

Project Communication

Presenting your ideas in both written and oral form is an essential part of successful projects. You may, however, feel a combination of anxiety and excitement about report writing and public presentation. You are not alone. In a research project about communicating project knowledge, one focus group member from the Minnesota Department of Transportation (Mn/DOT) recalled his first visit to a city council meeting. His supervisor had asked him to come along, but had not given him any other information. So naturally the engineer figured he would observe and learn. However, when it came time to explain his project, to his surprise, his supervisor turned and introduced him as the engineer who was going to explain the project. He managed to explain the project, but never forgot what it meant to go along to a city council meeting.

Project communication is not only about the communication that goes on between project team members, but also includes communication with outside stakeholders. For civil engineers in particular, these outside stakeholders include city councils, community members, special interest groups, and anyone who is affected by or can affect project success. For mechanical and electrical engineers, the outside stakeholders can include patent lawyers, competing companies, and clients. For computer scientists, outside audiences include end users and their organizations. Understanding project communication includes being aware of all of the stakeholders, or people who hold a stake in the success or failure of the project.

An example of a project with effective communication to the community is the I-35W bridge rebuild in Minneapolis from 2007 to 2008. Here, the project responded to the disaster of the bridge's collapsing and killing people who had been on the bridge at the time (http://www.youtube.com/watch?v=osocGiofdvc). The project was quite important for the community because this bridge was the site of a tragedy, and it had been the subject of public debate on and off for decades. The bridge project set up a website to facilitate communication between the project manager, team members and the community. The archive of this site is still available at http://projects.dot.state.mn.us/35wbridge/index.html. As you look at the site, notice that the content not only includes project facts, but also insights about the project. For example, three themes that come up throughout the site are *transparency, safety, and engagement with the community*. These themes go beyond presenting facts, and help viewers make sense of the project. In addition, they portray Mn/DOT as a responsible and responsive organization with a project designed to make sure that there is no risk for the rebuilt bridge to collapse. The site uses the themes—transparency, safety and engagement with the community—to coordinate and organize information about the process of rebuilding the bridge, the project team, and features of the new bridge. How do you see these themes represented in the site? Do the representations go beyond the facts? If so how? Why do you think Mn/DOT chose to go beyond the facts and include insights about the bridge for the Twin Cities community?

In sum, writing documents and giving presentations are part of project communication, in addition to project websites. Not all projects have public audiences, but for the projects that do, project communication to the public is often done through websites—with not only facts, but also themes that help share project insights with your audience. Remember the Mn/DOT project—how did it go beyond writing and use videos and pictures? Websites offer you more opportunities and more challenges to communicate your project with outside stakeholders because you can use video, pictures, and animations.

Communication Patterns of Engineers

When I taught as part of the Project Management teaching team in the Civil Engineering Department at the University of Minnesota from 2002 to 2005, the first assignment we did each semester was to "interview an engineer in your field" about their communication practices on the job. After students had completed their interviews, they would be surprised about how much time practicing engineers worked on communication. If you have time, you might consider looking around in your network—do you know any working engineers? Take the communication survey found in Appendix A at the end of this chapter and gather your own data by asking any engineers you know about their communication and writing habits on the job.

In addition to learning from your own data, you can corroborate it with studies of engineering communication. The researchers Tenopir and King (2004) studied the communication patterns of engineers, and their insights support many of the ideas presented in this book. They discuss the role of communication in innovation, and they explain that engineering is "increasingly collaborative, multi-disciplinary, and global . . . but the goals of engineering projects are becoming progressively more refined and specialized" (p. 11). They also highlight the importance of collaboration and of communications efficiency (p. 16).

In their work, Tenopir and King (2004) also include a thorough examination of the literature on engineering communication, noting that numerous studies conclude that engineers spend the majority of their time communicating (Hailey, 2000). Estimates of how much time usually range from 40 to 60 percent of work time (Hertzum and Pejtersen, 2000) to 75 percent of the work time (Nagle, 1998). In addition to communicating, engineers were found to read an average of 280 hours per year—with 26 percent of the time spent on research journal articles, 4 percent on trade journals and bulletins, 7 percent on professional books, 21 percent on internal reports, and nearly 31 percent of their time reading other communications (including e-mail). You may wonder how to manage so much reading (or maybe you hoped you would no longer have to read much after graduating!). An often quoted piece of useful advice came from Francis Bacon: "Some books are to be tasted, others to be swallowed, and some few to be chewed and digested: that is, some books are to be read only in parts, others to be read, but not curiously, and some few to be read wholly, with diligence and attention."

Listening is one part of communication that is stressed heavily by Tenopir and King (2004). A dramatic finding they reported was that poor listening skills were the main reason that engineering applicants failed in their job interviews (Levitt and Howe, 2000). Furthermore, good communication skills and practice mean that engineers are more likely to find employment, be promoted, and advance throughout their careers (Robar, 1998).

Why are communication and listening so important to your career as an engineer? Levitt and Howe (2000) claim that communication skills are as important as technical, analytical, and problem-solving skills "because information becomes knowledge only when conclusions drawn from analysis and/ or potential solutions to problems are communicated to those who need to make decisions or implement solutions." In other words, information alone is not enough for effective communication. Engineers need to communicate knowledge as well as information. To communicate knowledge effectively, the information needs to be accompanied by insights, and adapted to audiences' needs and expectations. And as Cerri (2000) explains, "Engineers, like all technical professionals, can accomplish more if they communicate effectively."

Reflection on Documentation

In this chapter, we have looked at documentation and the role of writing in Project Management. We began with the metaphor of engineers as explorers, using documentation to help find their way back from discoveries in order to communicate them. In our brief discussion of project documentation, we touched on the challenges of both writing for ourselves and writing for others—focusing on the importance of understanding our audiences, both audiences we want to communicate with, and audiences from whom we, as Leonardo da Vinci did with his mirror writing, want to conceal information and knowledge to protect our ideas and our organization.

In looking at ways to write for ourselves and ways to write for others, we examined blogs and journals, and set up a self-communication plan for our own education. Then we examined a tool to support us in writing for others—the Audience, Purpose and Action Worksheet. We also looked at templates from the Project Management Institute as a tool to help us write project documentation for others. Then we talked about ways in which we can turn information into knowledge through project communication that includes not only the facts, but also insights about them. In addition, we discussed the importance of fitting with audience expectations. The example we examined was the Mn/DOT I-35W bridge website, which demonstrated a combination of facts and themes to help the audience understand the facts. Finally we addressed the communication patterns of engineers—highlighting the importance of both communicating and listening as part of your career.

After hearing all this emphasis on communication and its role in both project management and engineering careers, are you surprised? How can you include building your communication skills as part of your quest to become an engineer?

Appendix A: Interview Questions for Engineering Students

Instructions: Interview someone who has the job you would like to have in 5 or 10 years about communication at work. Use the following questions as a basis for your learning about the role of communication in engineering.

1. How much of your time per day is spent communicating?
2. What are the most common channels of communication that you use? (E-mail? Phone? Talking together in meetings? Casual conversation? Writing documents? Using chat or video chat? Using social media platforms? Wikis? Blogs? Twitter? Other?)
3. How much of the communication you engage in includes people from different professional or cultural backgrounds? How do you understand and adapt to their needs?
4. Whom do you communicate with most frequently? Why? How does it support you in doing your job effectively?
5. What are the most important communication skills that engineering students can learn to prepare them for their first engineering job?
6. What kinds of communication do you use when you work on projects? Is it similar to your day-to-day communication, or are there special communication tasks that you use in project contexts? If so, what are these tasks?
7. How has your understanding of the role of communication in engineering changed since you were an engineering student?

8. What are three key points about communication that you have learned on the job which you would like to share with current engineering students?
9. Do you see a connection between communication and ethics? If so, how would you describe it?
10. What is the most important aspect(s) of communication for engineers today? Why?

Questions

1. What is your experience documenting group projects? Is it a routine activity? If so, describe examples of "excellent documentation." If not, consider how you can build the development of good documentation into the ongoing processes of project work.
2. What are some types of documentation that must be maintained for projects? What are the characteristics of good documents?
3. What is your experience with electronic documentation? What are the advantages and disadvantages of electronic documents (compared with paper)?
4. Describe the characteristics of good presentations. Are good presentations the norm in your experience? Why or why not?
5. Describe your experiences keeping an academic journal or blog. What are some of the heuristics that helped make it effective for you?
6. Learning to become a better writer and presenter requires practice. How are you planning to improve your writing and presenting skills? What are some of your favorite resources?

References

Biblioteca Leonardiana. Leonardo da Vinci Papers Project, http://www.leonardodigitale.com/index.php?lang=ENG.

Cerri, Stephen. 2000. Effective communication skills for engineers. In *Proceedings of the 2000 IEEE Engineering Management Society*, 625–629.

Collins, Jim, and Morten T. Hansen. 2011. *Great by choice*. New York: Harper Collins.

The Corporation, Inc. 2012. Free project management templates (PMBOK)-PM docs, http://www.projectmanagementdocs.com/templates.html (accessed June 9, 2012).

Hailey, Jeffrey C. 2000. Effective communications for EMC engineers. In *Proceedings of the 2000 IEEE International Symposium on Electromagnetic Compatibility*, 265–268.

Hertzum, Morten, and Annelise Mark Pejtersen. 2000. Information seeking practices of engineers; Searching for documents as well as for people. *Information Processing and Management* 36, 761–778.

Kampf, C., and T. Eiler. 2004. The triple constraint of the document: Coordinating concepts in rhetoric and project management for engineering students. In *Proceedings of the Professional Communication Conference*, 83, 88. IPCC, Minneapolis, MN, September 29–October 1.

Latour, Bruno. 2008. *A cautious Prometheus? A few steps toward a philosophy of design*. Keynote, History of Design Society, Falmouth, September. Cited in *Design Dialogues Blog*, All design is redesign, September 30, 2008, http://designdialogues.com/all-design-is-redesign/ (accessed June 9, 2012).

Levitt, S. R., and R. S. Howe. 2000. Visual and statistical thinking: An essential communications curriculum for engineers. In *Proceedings of the 3rd Working Conference on Engineering Education for the 21st Century*, 155–158. Sheffield, England: Sheffield Hallam University Press.

Mathes, J. C., and Dwight W. Stevenson. 1976. *Designing technical reports: Writing for audiences in organizations.* Indianapolis: The Bobs Merrill Company.

Nagle, Joan G. 1998. Communication in the profession. *Today's Engineer* 1 (1).

Robar, Tracey Y. 1998. Communication and career advancement. *Journal of Management in Engineering* 14 (2), 26–28.

Rutgers University. Thomas Edison Papers Project, http://edison.rutgers.edu/index.htm.

Tenopir, Carol, and Donald W. King. 2004. *Communication patterns of engineers.* Piscataway, NJ: IEEE Press.

yuva.2712@gmail.com. 2012. BE projects ideas, final year engineering projects, paper presentations, engineering seminar topics, http://hello-engineers.blogspot.dk/ (accessed June 10, 2012).

Zen College Life. 2012. 50 Top engineering blogs, http://www.zencollegelife.com/50-top-engineering-blogs/ (accessed June 10, 2012).

Project Management Tools

The more time we spend on planning a project, the less total time is required for it. Don't let today's busywork schedule crowd planning time out of your schedule.

EDWARD BLISS

Getting Things Done

Allocating time up front for planning often reduces the pain later, as Bliss argues in the opening quote. Wysocki (2011) describes this phenomena as "the pain curve." Up-front planning involves significant pain early on that decreases over time. Poor or no planning involves exponentially increasing pain. Another way of illustrating this is the trade-off over time between cost to change and the flexibility to change (Chapter 9, Figure 9.5). The benefits are dramatic for traditional project management, or Big Design Up Front (as Robert MacNeal described in Chapter 8) and also, in moderation, for adaptive project management.

A wide variety of software tools is available to help the project manager and project team members accomplish their goals. These include smartphones and tablet computers, which include electronic calendars, address books, to-do lists, memo pads, and expense reports; project management programs that do scheduling, resource leveling, and tracking; and web-based project enterprise systems that manage both of the previous functions as well as drawings and specifications, budgets, contracts, and much more.

Smartphones and Tablets

Smartphones and tablet computers help project managers keep track of appointments, critical deadlines, to-do lists, notes, and expenses. Many provide for access to calendars over a network or over the Internet, a feature that makes it much easier to schedule meetings. Most provide for synchronizing of data between the phone or tablet and a computer, which makes it possible to easily take the information into the field. Paper calendars and planners are inexpensive, but they cannot be backed up easily (except by photocopying), nor can the information be shared with others very easily (which has its advantages).

INDIVIDUAL REFLECTION What type of calendar (or planner) are you currently using? Is it a small paper datebook? a leather-bound three-ring binder? Or are you using a smartphone or computer-based planner? What are the principal uses that you make of your planner?

Personal planners are mainly used to manage time, priorities, and contacts. They help project managers attend to the details that are crucial for successful teamwork and project management. As planners continue to become more powerful, and with the advent of wireless communication, they are being used for inspection and project check-off, which results in much quicker turnaround (Bryant and Pitre, 2003a; Roe, 2001; Ashby, 2009).

Project Management Software

Comprehensive project management software such as Primavera and Microsoft Project is used on complex projects to accomplish goals and complete projects on time, within budget, at a level of quality that meets the client's expectations. The basic functions of the critical path analysis aspect of these programs is summarized in Chapter 11, where the CritPath program is featured.

The two most common views used by commercial project management software are the Gantt chart and precedence network chart, sometimes referred to as a PERT chart. Figures 14.1 and 14.2 show examples of the Gantt chart and PERT chart views, respectively, from Microsoft Project.

Figure 14.1 Microsoft Project—Gantt Chart

	Task Name	Duration	Start	Finish	Pred
1	Procure Paint	2d	Wed 12/3/97	Thu 12/4/97	
2	Procure New Carpet	5d	Wed 12/3/97	Tue 12/9/97	
3	Procure New Furnature	7d	Wed 12/3/97	Thu 12/11/97	
4	Remove Old Furnature	1d	Wed 12/3/97	Wed 12/3/97	
5	Remove Old Carpet	1d	Thu 12/4/97	Thu 12/4/97	4
6	Scrub Walls	1d	Fri 12/5/97	Fri 12/5/97	5
7	Paint Walls	2d	Mon 12/8/97	Tue 12/9/97	1,6
8	Install New Carpet	1d	Wed 12/10/97	Wed 12/10/97	2,7
9	Move in New Furnature	1d	Fri 12/12/97	Fri 12/12/97	3,8

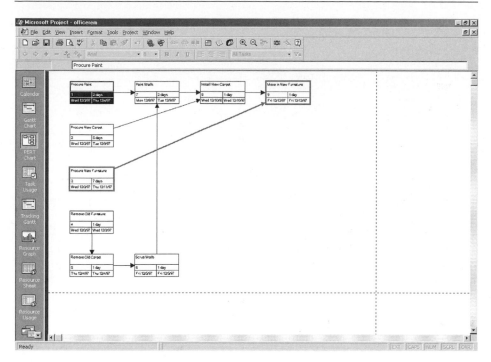

Examples of the Gantt chart and PERT chart views from Primavera are shown in Figures 14.3 and 14.4, respectively. These Primavera views show the activity detail for a highlighted activity; this allows the project manager to quickly get lots of detailed information on any activity, which makes it easy to track, manage, and update information.

Microsoft Project and Primavera are the two most widely used project management software packages. In a survey regarding project management tools by Fox and Spence (1998), 48 percent of the respondents reported using Microsoft Project and 14 percent reported using Primavera.

Pollack-Jackson and Liberatore (1998) reported similar figures—nearly 50 percent for Microsoft Project and 21 percent for Primavera—and provided extensive information on how these packages are used. The median size of projects reported by the respondents was a little over 150 activities, and the median number of resources was 16. A high percentage of respondents reported that they regularly update the information, and about 62 percent of the respondents said they use resource scheduling/leveling.

On a more personal (and perhaps mundane) level, when I taught the civil engineering project management course, I included a Gantt chart summarizing the assignments in the syllabus (see Figure 14.5). This visual approach helped many students internalize the schedule so they knew when they need to be working on the various assignments, and it especially focused them on due dates.

Figure 14.3 Primavera—Gantt Chart

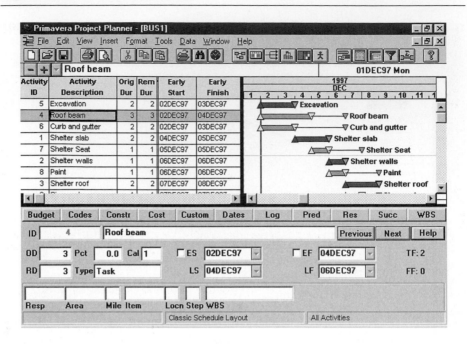

Figure 14.4 Primavera—PERT Chart

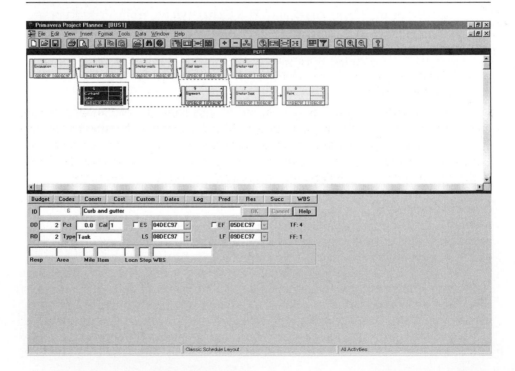

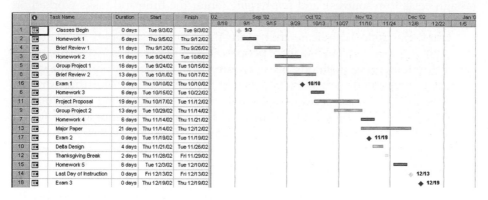

	O	Task Name	Duration	Start	Finish							
1		Classes Begin	0 days	Tue 9/3/02	Tue 9/3/02	9/3						
2		Homework 1	6 days	Thu 9/5/02	Thu 9/12/02							
4		Brief Review 1	11 days	Thu 9/12/02	Thu 9/26/02							
3		Homework 2	11 days	Tue 9/24/02	Tue 10/8/02							
5		Group Project 1	16 days	Tue 9/24/02	Tue 10/15/02							
8		Brief Review 2	13 days	Tue 10/1/02	Thu 10/17/02							
16		Exam 1	0 days	Thu 10/10/02	Thu 10/10/02			10/10				
6		Homework 3	6 days	Tue 10/15/02	Tue 10/22/02							
11		Project Proposal	19 days	Thu 10/17/02	Tue 11/12/02							
9		Group Project 2	13 days	Tue 10/29/02	Thu 11/14/02							
7		Homework 4	6 days	Thu 11/14/02	Thu 11/21/02							
13		Major Paper	21 days	Thu 11/14/02	Thu 12/12/02							
17		Exam 2	0 days	Tue 11/19/02	Tue 11/19/02				11/19			
10		Delta Design	4 days	Thu 11/21/02	Tue 11/26/02							
12		Thanksgiving Break	2 days	Thu 11/28/02	Fri 11/29/02							
15		Homework 5	6 days	Tue 12/3/02	Tue 12/10/02							
14		Last Day of Instruction	0 days	Fri 12/13/02	Fri 12/13/02					12/13		
18		Exam 3	0 days	Thu 12/19/02	Thu 12/19/02					12/19		

The Project Management Institute launched a major project management software survey, available both in print and on CD-ROM (Cabanis, 1999). The survey

- Compares and contrasts the capabilities of a wide variety of project management tools.
- Provides a forum for users and vendors to meet and match requirements and possibilities.
- Prompts vendors to become more responsive to customer needs.
- Prompts users to create a methodology for software tool selection within their own companies.
- Categorizes software tools into six areas of functionality aligned with the knowledge areas of PMI's *Guide to the Project Management Body of Knowledge (PMBOK Guide)*: scheduling, cost management, risk management, human resources management, communications management, and process management (Project Management Institute, 2000).

Like all software tools, it is important that project management software serve and not enslave the project manager. Also, if you invest the time and money in commercial project management software, you should use it to organize and manage your projects and not simply as a reporting tool. Lientz and Rea (1995) offer the following suggestions for using project management software:

1. Set up the basic schedule information: name of project file, name of project, project manager; input milestones, tasks and their estimated duration, interdependencies between tasks; input resources for each task.
2. Periodically update the schedule by indicating tasks completed, delayed, and so forth, as well as changes in resources.
3. On an as-needed basis, perform what-if analysis using the software and data.

Uses of project management software include *reporting* (use the schedule to produce graphs and tables for meetings); *tracking* (log project work and effort in terms of completed tasks); *analysis* (perform analysis by moving tasks around, changing task interdependencies, changing resources and assignments, and then seeing the impact on the schedule); *costing and accounting* (assign costs to resources); and *timekeeping* (enter the time and tasks worked on by each member of the project team).

Unofficial reports indicate that more than 1 million copies of Microsoft Project have been sold. That's a lot of people scheduling projects. Advertisements for civil engineering positions often require that applicants be familiar with project management software, especially Primavera and Meridian Project Systems. Lots of books, short courses, and multimedia training programs are available to help you learn to use these tools. Some of the books I've found useful are included in the references (see Day, 1995; Lowery, 1994; Marchman, 1998). This is a rapidly changing area, so I suggest that you stay tuned to resources such as the Project Management Institute, especially via their website (www.pmi.org), to keep current.

 REFLECTION What's your experience with project management software packages, such as Microsoft Project? Has this software been bundled with any of your textbooks? Have you used these programs to schedule project work associated with work or school? Talk about this with your friends, and work to expand your repertoire of software tools.

Project Management and the World Wide Web

Project management is continuing to develop a web presence. The documents for all collaborative projects I work on (writing projects and research projects), such as the writing of this book, are located on either Dropbox or Google Drive. The teams for my projects are geographically distributed, and resources like Basecamp (http://basecamp.com/), Dropbox or Daptiv (http://www.daptiv.com/) provide us with a place to work together. Another kind of project for which this works well is proposal or grant writing. Members of the grant-writing team can be on different continents but share documents via an electronic repository. They might meet face-to-face periodically, but most or all of the work can be conducted in an electronically mediated environment.

As mentioned above, the Project Management Institute has a very thorough website and provides access to their *Guide to the Project Management Body of Knowledge (PMBOK Guide)*. Like most other websites, project management websites update their URLs so frequently that if I had listed many here, most would already have been out of date by the time this book arrived at the bookstores. Use your favorite World Wide Web search engine (I'm partial to Google.com) and do a search on "project management."

You'll probably be amazed at the number of useful and relevant sites that come up.

Bryant and Pitre (2003b) described three broad categories of project management websites:

1. *Project collaboration networks (PCNs).* An environment for information sharing, such as eProject described above. An example in the construction industry is www.constructware.com.
2. *Project information portals (PIPs).* These contain essential project information on codes and specifications, permits, product information, cost data, and so forth. An example is www.aecdirect.com.
3. *Project procurement exchanges (PPEs).* These sites deal with the exchange of material, and are essential e-commerce. An example from the construction industry is www.buildpoint.com.

Web-enabled project management is gaining momentum and will probably change some businesses, just as it is currently changing the construction industry (Roe and Phair, 1999; Doherty, 1999). Web-enabled project management couples aspects involving communication (e-mail, fax, voice and multimedia, Intranet, Extranet, and others) and project management (scheduling, document and file management, project administration, job photos, job cost reports, and project status reports). Doherty (1999) cites several reasons for using a project Extranet:

- Fewer communication errors between project team members.
- Up-to-the-minute intelligence on all the decisions and collective information related to a project.
- Less expense for messengers, couriers, copying, and blueprints.
- Customized sites for each project and customized access for each user.
- Security.

An emerging idea in project management is the Community of Practice (COP), which is composed of three elements: a *domain* of knowledge, which is defined by a set of issues; a *community* of people who care about this domain; and the *shared practice* that they are developing to be effective in their domain (Wenger, McDermott, and Snyder, 2002). Etienne Wenger, who coined the term "community of practice" has recently presented a new model for creating virtual communities of practice and it is his work "Digital Habitats: Stewarding Technology for Communities" (Wenger, White, and Smith, 2009) that provides a useful framework for collaboration.

Wenger and colleagues propose that there are three inherent polarities that present challenges in creating and sustaining a virtual community. These three polarities are:

- Rhythms: togetherness and separateness
- Interactions: participation and reification
- Identities: individual and group

Figure 14.6 Representation of Tools Used by Virtual Communities

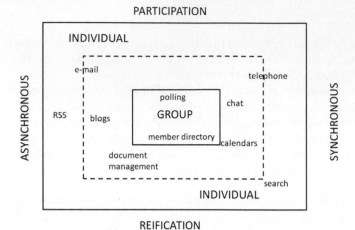

From Wenger, White, and Smith (2009), p. 60.

A simplified representation of these three polarities is shown in Figure 14.6, mapped into Wenger's three polarities.

David Radcliffe, whose voice has been present in earlier chapters, provided the diagram in Figure 14.7 in which he frames collaboration domains and technologies. This is a framing he uses with the students in Purdue's Multidisciplinary Engineering Program.

Curt McNamara has summarized his experience managing projects in the discussion in the following section, "There Is More to a Project than a Plan."

Figure 14.7 Collaboration Domains and Technologies

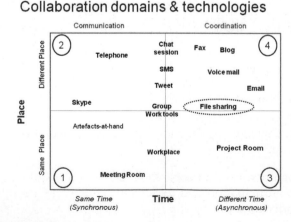

Collaboration domains & technologies

IDE 485 Multidisciplinary Engineering Design   1

There Is More to a Project than a Plan
(by Curt McNamara)

245

Chapter 14:
Project Management
Tools

Plans are useless, but planning is indispensable. (Eisenhower)

He who fails to plan is planning to fail. (Churchill)

Every project has a plan—whether it is explicit or implicit. The difference is that implicit plans are not shared between team members and this represents project risk.

A plan is a shared representation of the project, and is a means for a project team to bond around the work and commit to each other.

Creating the plan allows a team to explore the project before it unfolds, and to track the project as it progresses. This lets the team learn from their expectations and adjust their behavior.

Developing a plan and managing the project requires tools and techniques for:

- Breaking the overall project into modules or "chunks"
- Linking the chunks in time, and establishing dependencies between them
- Creating a detailed representation of those chunks (the project work)
- Getting team member commitments or buy-in on the work as expressed in the plan
- Tracking progress of the project

These tools can be used to create a public/reviewable representation of the work, ensuring that both sides (client/provider; worker/manager) agree on the work.

Once the project starts, various tools will be needed to manage the project elements:

- Issue tracking software
- Version control software
- Project communication software or portal
- Project management software for the overall project view
- Visual + voice meetings for periodic updates
- Word processing and spreadsheet software to keep track of details

Overview of the Process

Making a plan to achieve a goal requires several things:

-- A goal/vision/set of requirements
-- Knowledge of the subject area, or collaborators
-- Analytical thinking skills

For most projects a team is involved. This team ideally has knowledge of the subdisciplines required to complete the project. At a minimum the team needs a process to discover the required steps and tasks, and uses that process to fill in the missing pieces.

Project plans are an exercise in decomposition (or reduction) of a system to parts. These parts are the "modules" of the project, and each module will be assigned a minimum of four attributes:

-- Definition
-- Duration/work required to complete the module
-- Dependencies on other modules
-- Owner

There are a range of approaches to project decomposition. At one end of the spectrum, the output of the project may be well known, and there may be existing plans that can be modified to fit the requirements for this project. At the other end, the design or set of tasks hasn't been done before.

For projects that are similar to past work, it is important to identify best practice for previous projects, and apply the lessons learned.

If the design is new, the team may start from the final deliverable and create a set of phases, with a working prototype for each phase. The prototypes and phases proceed from simple to complete, with features and capability added in each phase. For each prototype, have the team brainstorm what elements will be required to make it work.

With new designs, gather a small set of stakeholders in a room. Have them prepare for the meeting beforehand by creating a mind-map or list of tasks. When the team gathers together, use a flexible medium like post-it notes or whiteboards or collaboration software to capture the team thinking.

At this first stage in planning, divide the output "spatially" into types of work and major components for each type. For an embedded computer design the hardware might be composed of printed circuit board, power supply, packaging, and interface. The mechanical portion might include an enclosure, thermal modeling, and environmental constraints. Software components could be user interface, processing, i/o, and data collection.

Next steps will be to subdivide those chunks into smaller chunks. Some of these chunks are independent of others, and can be worked on in parallel. Some chunks will be linked to other tasks that they depend on (predecessors) and will in turn be the predecessor of one or more subsequent tasks.

Linking tasks defines dependencies (or relations) between sections of the work. There is more than one type of dependency:

-- One task can't be started until the predecessor is done.
-- A task can't be finished until a parallel task is complete.

Besides these relations, tasks with dependencies have requirements that must be met before they can be started or before they can be completed. In effect each task is a module with several potential attributes:

-- Requirements to start the work
-- Requirements for the work to be considered complete
-- Duration of the work
-- Effort required
-- Resources required

In effect these attributes become additional requirements on the task: it can't start until the previous work is complete and the resources are available;

it can't complete until the effort has been expended and the requirements have been satisfied.

Once the work has been divided into chunks and dependencies assigned, the team needs to assign resources and have them critique the plan. They will be doing the work, and the team is looking for their commitment. The plan itself is a way for the team to establish group estimates and commit to one another: *Fred will have the user interface ready for review on Nov. 15.*

Once the plan is complete it needs to be reviewed weekly. This can be done in a simple stand-up meeting; by individual team members submitting their inputs to the leader; or in the weekly team meeting. Reviewing the plan is primarily for the purpose of seeing what didn't happen, and deciding if changes need to be made to accomplish the goal. It is inevitable that some parts of the plan won't work according to the estimate, and the earlier this is determined the better.

Many teams update their plans regularly with progress noted and revised estimates for future work. It is a best practice to keep a baseline plan available to track where the changes occurred for reference in future projects.

There are a variety of tools available and needed for project work. This chapter is about project planning and tracking, and there are numerous industry standard packages to capture the tasks, effort, and dependencies.

In addition to the plan, the following project management software will aid the team:

-- Issue tracking software. This allows the team and the client to enter issues, track progress towards their resolution, and acknowledge when the team has solved an issue.

-- Shared communications portals. It is easy to use e-mail for most communications: project updates, review minutes, and shared files. However, it quickly becomes a challenge to manage all these elements in e-mail software. A shared portal allows a team to have an archive available for the whole duration of the project. In addition to file sharing, many portals include to-do lists, messaging, and whiteboards for shared communications. The portal stores all the files, and e-mail notices can be sent to one or all team members, reducing the load on team member computer storage space.

-- Version control. This is useful for software, hardware, industrial design, mechanical design, and project management. Having a repository with the current design revision as well as all the past history can be incredibly useful.

A project can be managed to the plan, and/or to some observable in the design such as:

- Weight
- Battery life
- Reliability
- Product life
- Device cost
- Plan duration

- Plan costs
- Staff utilization

Managing to an observable gives early visibility on progress and challenges. It can allow the team to adjust course, add or subtract resources, or revise requirements if progress is not as expected.

Project management is about planning, scheduling, monitoring, and controlling projects, so there are enormous benefits to having a central project file located at a website rather than in a project notebook (or in the project manager's head). The challenge involves moving from our comfort zones of familiar practice and learning new tools and approaches.

Questions

1. Describe the advantages and disadvantages of different calendar/planner formats—pocket planner, three-ring binder, pocket electronic organizer (e.g., smartphone), and computer-based personal data assistant.
2. What are the major types of project management software? What are their common uses?
3. What are the advantages and disadvantages of the Gantt chart view and the precedence network (PERT) views available in commercial project management software?
4. How could you apply Lientz and Rea's suggestions for using project management software to a project you're currently involved in?
5. Check out project management websites on the World Wide Web. Keep a record of your findings in a journal.

References

Ashby, Andy. 2009. Technology changes construction industry, from PDAs to 3-D modeling. *Memphis Business Journal*, July 12, 2009. http://www.bizjournals.com/memphis/stories/2009/07/13/focus1.html?page=all (accessed 3-13-13).

Bryant, John A., and Jyoti Pitre. 2003a. Emerging technologies in the construction industry. http://archnt2.tamu.edu/contech/finalJ/home.html (accessed 1-4-03; not available 3-13-13).

———. 2003b. Web based project management. http://archnt2.tamu.edu/contech/finalJ/web_based.html (accessed 1-4-03; not available 3-13-13).

Cabanis, Jeannette. 1999. *Project management software survey.* New Square, PA: Project Management Institute.

Day, Peggy. 1995. *Microsoft Project 4.0: Setting project management standards.* New York: Van Nostrand Reinhold.

Doherty, Paul. 1999. Site seeing. *Civil Engineering* 69 (1), 38–41.

Feigenbaum, Leslie. 1998. *Construction scheduling with Primavera project planner.* Upper Saddle River, NJ: Prentice Hall.

Fox, Terry L., and J. Wayne Spence. 1998. Tools of the trade: A survey of project management tools. *Project Management* 29 (3), 20–27.

Lientz, Bennet, and Kathryn Rea. 1995. *Project management for the 21st century.* San Diego: Academic Press.

Lowery, Gwen. 1994. *Managing projects with Microsoft Project 4.0.* New York: Van Nostrand Reinhold.

Marchman, David A. 1998. *Construction scheduling with Primavera project planner.* Albany, NY: Delmar.

Pollock-Jackson, Bruce, and Matthew J. Liberatore. 1998. Project management software usage patterns and suggested research directions for future development. *Project Management* 29 (2), 19–28.

Project Management Institute. 2000. *A guide to the project management body of knowledge.* Project Management Institute.

Roe, Arthur G. 2001. Handhelds hold up well for variety of site uses. *ENR: Engineering News-Record,* November 5, pp. 31–32.

Roe, Arthur G., and Matthew Phair. 1999. Connection crescendo. *ENR: Engineering News-Record,* May 17, pp. 22–26.

Wenger, E., R. McDermott, and W. Snyder. 2002. *Cultivating communities of practice.* Cambridge, MA: Harvard Business School Press.

Wenger, E., N. White, and J. D. Smith. 2009. *Digital habitats: Stewarding technology for communities.* Portland, OR: CPSquare Press.

Wysocki, Robert K. 2012. *Effective project management: Traditional, agile, extreme,* 6th ed. New York: Wiley.

Teamwork for the Future*

I never predict. I just look out the window and see what's visible—but not yet seen.

PETER F. DRUCKER,
Forbes Magazine, March 10, 1997

Change happens. Sometimes it is gradual, at other times dramatic. Teams and projects exist in a changing environment, and some changes will have an impact on their performance. Changes that could impact teams and projects include these:

- Environment changes: regulatory, economic, organizational
- Requirements changes: revised needs, environmental changes
- Team changes: composition, staff availability
- Task changes: work complexity and size

There are many potential outcomes to a change: the team may be able to predict and prepare; the team can adapt; the team/project may change; or there may be a disruption.

This chapter looks at change and how it can impact teaming and project work. What is the nature and source of change? How will changes affect the team or project? What set of skills can give advantage today and in the future?

The Context for Teamwork

Teams and projects are ongoing interactions between people, tasks, and the organization that encompasses them.

A team or project is a web of relations with connections between each member and

- other team members;
- the work;
- the team as a whole;
- the organization; and
- family and friends.

---

*By Curt McNamara.

This web of relations is established when the team forms, and consists of interactions:

- member <> member
- work module <> work module
- member <> work module
- member <> team
- team <> organization

In a typical team or project there is a hierarchical structure—members and leadership. Work is often organized modularly with higher- and lower-level structures. In addition there are interconnections across the same level in both the team and the work. These connections can be viewed as a web or network to give insights into connections and behavior.

Once the relations among workers and the work are established, they tend to remain in that form as the project progresses. For example, the project plan might state that establishing requirements is an early task, and once they are accepted, they set the stage for all subsequent work. In a similar way the implementation work is often partitioned into modules and assigned to individuals or subteams early in the project. Both these examples illustrate a task structure that is sequential, based on dependencies in the work, and becomes a known and accepted set of relations (a network).

Changes in environment, work estimation or difficulty, or team composition can all affect this network. If the changes are small, most teams will make small adjustments and "carry on." If the changes are larger, then the team or project may be reexamined at a more fundamental level (see box "Coping with Change in Learning"). The emotional effect of a major change can be substantial, and can affect team performance for some time. It is best practice to acknowledge the change, have team members voice their frustrations and concerns, and allow time for the team to come back on track. It is also important to review the plan when a major change occurs. There are often unforeseen consequences of a change, and reviewing the plan can allow these to be adjusted.

Coping with Change in Learning

I teach my students (undergraduate chemical engineering students) using a highly student-centered technique called Cooperative Problem-Based Learning (CPBL), where they have to learn new concepts in the course syllabus through solving an unstructured realistic problem in a small cooperative group of three to four students. I choose the groups for my students, so they usually have to work with students they are not familiar with initially. I do not give them lectures, but instead, I facilitate and guide them through the CPBL cycle, where they first identify and analyze the problem, and learn the new concepts, which they synthesize with existing knowledge to solve the problem. Finally, they have to present the solution and reflect over their learning and problem solving process.

Since this is the first time my students learn using CPBL, it is quite normal for me to see them feeling very unhappy over the tasks that they have to do to learn in my class. I give my students an avenue to express their feelings and thoughts in the class e-learning forum so that they may express their frustrations, as well as motivate one another. I also encourage students to come and talk to me over difficulties that they face in learning. I do not get angry at those who dislike the method, but instead, I use this information to give better support and feedback to my students.

The reason I am not upset at students when they express their discontent over the learning approach in my class is because I understand that it is normal for all of us to be uncomfortable when we have to face change, or do things that are very different than what we are used to. Professor Donald Woods explained that it is quite normal for students facing change (such as problem-based learning) to undergo a grieving process identified by psychologists as similar to a person facing trauma. This is further supported by Professor Richard Felder, who also observed the same phenomenon among students who faced student-centered learning (such as cooperative learning) for the first time.

Every semester, I can identify the grieving process that my students go through. They will initially feel negative emotions, starting with shock, next going into denial, after which strong emotion, such as anger, sets in and then resistance. However, once students realize that they still need to face the change, they begin to accept, and struggle to adapt, which leads to better understanding, and finally reaching integration of the new method, which results in a higher level of performance.

As I explained, I encourage students to talk about what they feel and think because acknowledging what is happening will actually help them to move along and get over the grieving process faster. No doubt, some do not have any difficulties, or face varying pathways in going through it. But from my experience, most students do feel traumatized and helpless by the change. Being honest and expressing what is felt actually helps us to be aware of our feelings, why it happens, and how to best deal with it. This is important because how we feel affects how we think, and consequently how we perform. Being aware of ourselves is, in fact, an important domain of emotional intelligence. It will also help us to learn about ourselves as learners, and thus develop our meta-cognitive skills. In addition, it will assist others (i.e., teammates and instructors) in knowing how to best provide support.

So, what can we learn from all this when we have to face changes as learners or in our lives? In pushing on to face the challenge of something new, we need to realize that in order for us to grow and develop to a new level, we have to allow ourselves to take the opportunity to struggle beyond our comfort zone. Yes, it is troublesome; yes, it will make us uncomfortable initially; and yes, most of us feel it, so it is perfectly normal. It helps to express the hardship and frustrations, but remember not to overdo it, because worrying and complaining about a task is always worse than actually doing it. Most importantly, if we keep trying, we will ultimately succeed and become a better person from it.

Khairiyah Mohd Yusof

A team or project is established to achieve a goal. It has a purpose or destination, and is a living system with needs for energy and information. The team can connect to systems at all levels (across, up, and down). Depending on the team or project goal, it may have processes or structures to sense, decide, act, design, acquire, consume, test, and produce. These processes or structures are revised over time based on effectiveness, and can be seen as the operating instructions or "DNA" of the team or project.

Definition: A team or project is a web of relations between members, stakeholders, and the work. It is a living system with purpose and structures, designed to fulfill a goal or purpose.

 REFLECTION Think back to a team or project you were involved in. What was the larger environment? How did the team or project connect to, sense, or react in response to the larger systems?

It can be informative to consider that the members, team and project are separate yet interrelated systems with their own boundaries, internal components, processes, and lifecycles.

Chapter 15: Teamwork for the Future

The larger environment is the supersystem. For a team this can include the project, the larger organization, the economic system, and the physical environment. There are organizational supports, external forces, and the food or energy the team or project needs.

In Figure 15.1, below the team or project are the elements (subsystems) each is composed of. Possible subsystem elements are the members, the components of the work, forces in the environment, and available resources.

There are also teams, projects and organizations at the same level. The result is a set of elements that interact with the team and project that can exhibit complex behavior.

In other words, teams and people involved in projects are continually acting to accomplish their goals. They have internal models of the world (Senge, 2006) and anticipate that using previous actions or responses will give similar results. However, in some cases an action creates an unintended effect. If the environment and the external systems are stable, a system with many parts can show predictable reactions. If the environment or external systems are changing rapidly, then responses can be complex or less predictable.

It is worth noting the difference between complicated and complex systems. A *complicated* system is one with many parts connected in a known network that behave in a predictable way. For example, the U.S. Postal Service is a complicated system. There are tens of thousands of interacting pieces; however, the time for any one piece of mail to reach its destination is predictable. Interactions between elements of the postal system are well defined and produce consistent results.

In contrast, a *complex* system may have fewer parts yet its behavior is less predictable. Individual interactions in a complex system have a larger effect on the overall behavior than similar interactions in a complicated system. There can be many reasons for this: some system components are sensitive to small inputs; the overall system structure is balanced between structure and chaos; there are many components acting in parallel; and the network of connections may determine behavior more strongly than what any individual component does (Axelrod and Cohen, 2000).

How does complexity in the environment affect organizations and individuals? If the environment and external systems are predictable, standard responses can give effective and consistent results. In this case a simple or even a complicated system can perform well.

Figure 15.1 Team, Supersystem, and Subsystem

	Supersystem	
Time before	Team or project	Time after
	Subsystems	

Team and project performance can be impacted when any of the following are true: the environment is changing rapidly, other systems are exhibiting complex behavior, or complex behavior is arising from the interactions. In these cases, a standard response may not provide the expected result, and the team can fail to achieve its goal.

A standard organizational model is hierarchical, with well-defined interactions between the members (Anklam, 2007). This is the most effective structure for standard processes and stable environments. When the situation contains substantive environmental changes or complex actors, these well-defined interactions and structure may not produce the desired results.

Individual vs. Team

Individual members of the organization can and do learn to be effective in a complex environment. This learning is individual, and may be passed from one employee to the next. For an organization to learn, a team is required (Edmondson, 2012).

Projects can be the most effective part of an organization, and are the way team members commit to each other, determine dependencies, and share work (Berkun, 2008).

An individual will have a limited range of potential perceptions, scenarios, and reactions to the environment. A set of individuals that communicate together (a team) will have a larger set, and by sharing their individual views will also increase the set of possible perceptions and responses.

Teaming Tools

Teamwork is a joint activity, with the members' behavior driving the response and determining the team effectiveness.

What are the key teaming skills and activities that members should know? In particular, are there fundamental skills that can be used to guide individual and team behavior and response?

Compare the team or project to a sailing ship. Each has a destination, the need to track changes in the environment that affect the journey, navigation skills to set the course, resources, and a crew that may need to reconfigure itself in response to change.

Using this perspective we can list specific skills that will be required regardless of the environment: structuring and performing the work (analytical skills); interactions with other team members; and action skills.

- Analytical skills
  - Plan (Predict, Estimate, Forecast)
  - Reflect
- Interactive skills
  - Listening, Supporting, Sensing
  - Coordination, Dependencies
- Action skills
  - Complement, Lead, Offer

- Decision Making
- Response to Unpredicted Events
- Risk Management

This is a large list and good coverage would take more pages than this chapter has! Luckily, the behavior of systems in complex environments is driven by a small set of properties that can be covered.

Teaming skills will be the same today and tomorrow if they are based on the principles of systems. These principles have been the same for millennia in living systems, and the team is a living system.

There is a continuum of structure and behavior: from highly structured and constrained (to achieve high performance in stable environments) to adaptive and self organizing (to fit into a rapidly changing or complex environment).

What are the fundamentals of systems that these tools and techniques are based on? While there are many approaches and the literature is broad, this chapter focuses on the team and project as a system; on the team and project as a living system; and on the team and project as a Complex Adaptive System (CAS). Particular topics include modularity (also known as aggregation, chunking and tagging); decision making; knowledge mapping; self-organization; and exploration/learning.

The Background to Teaming and Projects

Organizations and teams are structured so that members can accomplish greater tasks than they could alone. They accomplish this by having members specialize on specific tasks, by dividing work between members, by creating modular processes and designs that can be reused (Garud, 2002), by building or scaffolding on the work of others, and by having diversity of viewpoint (Page, 2008).

Project work often follows the architecture of the team, and vice versa. In many organizations, workers are assigned to a specific role or a department with similar workers. In contrast, teams and projects can be created and staffed to span roles and departments, increasing diversity of approach and ability.

The result is that teams and projects are more flexible than other structures within organizations. They can adapt to changing conditions more quickly, and they can lead the organization into the future by responding more comprehensively to change. Edmondson puts teamwork on a continuum from execution (getting things done efficiently) to exploration (organizational learning). She notes that employees can increase their skills by individual work, however the *organization learns* when a team is involved.

This chapter will discuss the forces that teams and projects can utilize in the region of change between steady state (highly structured) and chaos (unstructured). This boundary is known as the sweet spot where organizations can gain value by extending their reach and abilities (Clippinger, 1999). A very highly structured organization cannot respond quickly to a changing environment, while an unstructured organization cannot respond effectively.

There are several perspectives in this text:

- Team member
- Team leader
- Nature of shared work
- Team/project as a system
    - as a living system
    - as a complex adaptive system

Teaming is a verb (Edmondson, 2012), that is, a set of skills that can *be used* for organizational learning.

"Creating a project consists of committing to one another, establishing dependencies, and exploring interdependencies in the work" (Berkun, 2008).

This chapter presents a high-level view of teaming and project management. It views the team and the project as an entity, a living system that lives within an ecosystem of other teams, projects, and systems of people.

Boundary Teams and projects are entities that are distinct from, yet connected to, their environment. The distinction is visible at their boundaries. Inside the boundary the elements are tightly bound to each other with strong links, while connections to the external world are weaker links (Hoagland and Dodson, 2001).

Communication Messaging occurs between members of a team, between the team and the organization, and between modules in the work. All messages occur at boundaries. The boundary allows a fixed set of messages to be transmitted <> received. Internally the system responds to the message. Limited messaging limits responses; however, it also protects a system (consider a computer virus). A larger set of messaging (or perception of signals) can be used to advantage in a changing situation.

Lifecycle Projects and teams have a lifecycle: they are born, consume energy and materials, serve a purpose, and come to end of life. In short, they are biological systems, and have the characteristics of biological systems.

Ecosystem Teams and projects live inside or between organizations, and organizations are changing along with the economy and environment. Below the team and project level, the members are also changing. The result is that teamwork and projects can improve their effectiveness in navigating the changes.

Structure In the past team and project structures have been mechanical or functional, and not open to change. Today organizations and teams are moving to more flexible structures inspired by complex adaptive systems and biology. This movement mirrors changes in the economy and society, and allows teams to respond quickly and adaptively to their environment.

Adaptation Teams are evolving from groups that carry out a predefined set of tasks to more freeform approaches in problem solving. In many ways teams are the most flexible part of the organization. By spanning departments, positions, locations, and organizations, a team brings a diverse view to the situation or opportunity. Team members view the situation or goal from different perspectives, and they view the ways to solve it differently as well.

Diversity Different viewpoints are advantageous.

- Wider and different views of the situation can help the organization expand from its current processes into the sweet spot between order and chaos.
- Team discussions can bring ideas from the edge of change back to the organization, and give a renewed view of the situation.
- New processes and strategies can be formed by the team acting at the boundary of the organization.

Viewing a Team or Project as a System

The high-level view of a team or project is a systems view. Systems are distinct from their environment, and "stick together" by having higher internal cohesion than attachment to the environment. Systems persist in the face of external changes.

Using the systems view can encourage other aspects of a situation to be considered (Armson, 2011). How do we find or describe systems? When characterizing systems, there are multiple aspects that can be used.

- Behavior – how does the system act?
  - An ant will carry decayed matter to the garbage dump in the anthill.
- Goals – does the system demonstrate goal seeking?
  - For example, a flower may track the sun as it moves across the sky.
- Structure – how is the system constructed?
  - A tree has a trunk, branches, and leaves.
- Flows – what are the inputs and outputs?
  - Plants take in water, CO_2 and nutrients. They give off oxygen.
- Ecosystem – how does the system fit into the larger context?
  - Bushes may be part of a forest. Birds can live in their branches, and small animals can dig burrows under them.
- Function – what are the properties that the system exhibits?
  - The tree shades, circulates water, makes oxygen and propagates itself.
- Control – does the system react to its environment to maintain desired conditions?
  - Leaves fold in high winds, plants grow toward the light, and flocks follow each other for protection.
- Self-organizing – a system creates its own internal order.
  - A beehive is highly structured yet arises from simple construction rules.

 REFLECTION Take a few minutes to think back on a project or team you worked on. Use two or more of the perspectives above and illustrate how they would apply to your team.

Each of the systems viewpoints can be used to see how teams and projects operate.

- How would you create a control function in a team?
- What does it mean for a team to be self-organizing?
- What elements need to be in place for that to occur?
- How can system perspectives be tied to teamwork skills?

At one time systems were viewed as mechanisms designed to achieve a particular function or goal. This can be advantageous in a fixed environment; however, there are advantages to more flexible viewpoints of team and projects, especially in a complex environment or if many other systems are involved (Sheard, 2005).

Organizations and teams can be described by their behavior, and that behavior is often driven by feedback. This is analogous to how a thermostat and furnace are coupled to maintain a constant temperature. There will be multiple feedback loops in any human activity system, and individual goals will differ even if the team goal is shared. Using this perspective on coupled loops as a driver of behavior has led to insights on system behaviors. There appear to be fundamental system behaviors or archetypes (Senge, 2006).

System archetypes identify constraints on performance (Figure 15.2), and Meadows (2008) and others have summarized strategies to combat each archetype. For example, Success to the Successful can result when the most effective performers or strategies are rewarded. This strategy works well at the level of individuals or particular designs, but suppresses overall team and organizational performance. The antidote is to diversify: measure and reward other behaviors as well.

The systems behavior and archetype views can also be used to "debug" organizational problems. Meadows describes 12 ways to intervene in a system. The more effective strategies are focused on exchange or flows rather than structure.

Figure 15.2 System Archetypes and Potential Solutions

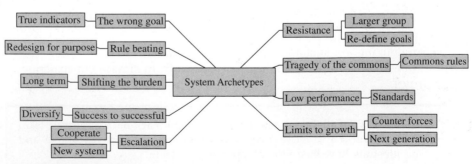

Adapted from Meadows (2008).

Applying Systems Ideas: Boundaries

Each team and project has multiple boundaries: physical, energy, material, and information.

The physical boundary might be the area where team members and the lab are located, or it might encompass the organization. In some cases a team is connected across different locations, and the physical boundary has separate parts.

Energetic boundaries can be observed by mapping the flows. These include the inputs that drive the design work (needs and requirements), the outputs from the design team, payments made to team members, and the limits of the workers.

Material boundaries can be seen by studying the flows: some are energetic while others are physical. For example a manufacturing operation takes materials, water, air and energy in. After the material is processed, products, water, air, energy and waste flow out of the boundary.

The information boundary includes the teams' internal messages, communications with the larger organization, and design documents.

The team or project boundary keeps the concentration of materials, energy and information high internally to increase the effectiveness of the work. At the boundary material/energy/information is allowed in or out, or is sensed to trigger activities inside the boundary.

Exchanges occur at the boundary: money for work products, sharing best practices, engaging in open source projects. The external environment signals direction, supplies funding, gives feedback, and accepts waste products (rejected designs and ineffective meetings). The boundary keeps the inside of the system at a constant level of temperature and pressure, concentrating the internal interactions while shielding the team (workers, work process, and work products) from the external environment. At the interface there are standards that allow recognition of "good" inputs and reject bad inputs.

The boundary interface is a point of contact between two systems.

Bob thought his team was busy enough—why have any meetings other than the one with the stakeholders (or clients)? After a few sessions where it became apparent the internal team processes were becoming meshed with the larger group, he instituted separate team meetings. This gave the team an internal boundary, and allowed them to process decisions internally, and provide a consistent and focused interface.

There is a tug and flow of teamwork: internal work which then expands outward into the organization. The internal team meeting keeps the boundary of the team secure, and provides a safe environment to explore alternatives.

Edmondson notes that there are two informational boundaries inside a team: one is based on status or rank of team members, and the other is based on domain knowledge. Team impact can be measured by their abilities to cross these boundaries effectively.

 REFLECTION Think back on a team or project you were involved with. What were the boundaries of the team, and how did you sense them? How did the team sort and classify input? What were the design outputs, and how were they checked?

Living Systems

If a team or project is a living system, what insights can be gained by studying other living systems?

Biological systems have created or evolved solutions to numerous problems including:

- Utilization of scarce resources
- Reliable passing of information (reproduction)
- Communication in noisy environments
- Adaptation to a changing environment
- Expansion into new territory
- Utilization of wastes
- Adaptation to challenging environments
- Challenges from other organisms

The range of living systems covers the micro (bacteria, protozoa, and amoebas) to higher levels (mammals, vertebrates, and managers) and then to systems of organisms.

Biology has inspired design and structure in many forms: a better swimsuit (Speedo), more efficient buildings (Pauli, 2010), improved software (Alexander, 1979; Gamma, 1994), and flexible business systems (Beer, 1972). There are many ways to connect biological thinking to teamwork and projects (Thompson, 2008; asknature.org).

 EXERCISE Take three of these approaches and apply them to your current work or problems that society faces.

Applying Living Systems Ideas: Modules

Biological systems are composed of building blocks that are used over and over again to create great variety. Examples are the bases in DNA or the letters of the alphabet. Teams, projects and designs can use modularity to great effect.

The key to modularity is that work can be partitioned with a boundary and defined interface. Work is performed within the module boundary, and that work does not affect other teams or project members: each side works to the defined modular interface. This partitioning can be done at the design level or at the team or project level. For example, there can be a power supply hardware module or a user interface software module. Each is defined at the interface, and each can be worked on by a single team member or a group of team members. In this way the work can be divided modularly just as the design is.

Modules can be tested incrementally, with test fixtures that fit the module interface. In this way work can proceed at different rates in the design, and modules can be tested early.

It is worth noting that we are surrounded by modular design, and living systems are constructed modularly. Many of the organizations we work in are designed modularly. Examples of modular structures in living systems are organs, limbs, and bones in mammals. In a product design the components of enclosure, power supply, and user interface are modules. For an organization, functions such as payroll, engineering, and sales are modules. Teams already use modularity, and there is value in studying it to make better use of the approach.

A team or project is also a module. It has internal composition and an interface to the external world. Most complexity of the team is "behind" the interface, and exchanges with the external world are mediated through the interface. Internally, the team divides work up into modules, with defined interfaces between these work products. Examples include interface specifications, work breakdown structures, project plans, project phases, requirements, and test specifications.

Modules can be rearranged quickly to form new designs and responses. If most of the design works well yet the user interface needs work, that module can be updated independently of the others. The modules represent "known good solutions" to elements of design situations or process steps.

Applying Living Systems Ideas: Metabolism and Pulse

Organisms need energy in the form of food, water, sunlight and air to survive. Their internal processes run in cycles, and have pulses that time their internal processes. Every team and project also needs a pulse of meetings and updates to time and drive its metabolism. This pulse may be in two parts: one for the internal team and a second for the larger environment. Information passing to others (communication or reporting) can be adjusted as the environment changes.

The study of individual systems can yield insights. There is also benefit in examining the interactions between systems to observe what behavior emerges at that level.

Complex Adaptive Systems

Teams, team members, projects and organizations can be seen as complex adaptive systems (CAS). CAS encompasses a set of ideas that focus on the interactions of living systems, and how these interactions produce complex and emergent behavior.

"Newtonian science assumes that simple systems produce simple behavior, that complex behavior necessitates complex rules, and that all systems tend towards stability. Complexity theory proves that all three of these assumptions can be wrong" (Sheard, 2005).

One breakdown of the most important ideas in CAS (Simon, 1996) includes the following items:

- Aggregation. Also known as emergence and synergy. Collections of objects exhibit high-level behavior that is not predicted by the behavior of the parts. Teams exhibit emergent behavior when they self-organize to adapt to changing conditions. Members respond to the changes in their own sphere, and the sum of these changes alters the overall team dynamics and response.

- Flows. These are the interactions and the exchanges within the system, and between the system and other system elements. Leaders can vary the flows of information and resources to encourage some behaviors and discourage others. The team lives in an environment of flows, and these can be used to aid and guide the work.
- Nonlinearity. Small triggers can produce large effects. Living systems have thresholds below which they do not react and above which they do react. Each team and project has a boundary with thresholds. A casual request for a change may not produce an effect, while a formal request will. Team members may ignore certain signals or information if they are low-level or infrequent, and respond after they increase in intensity or frequency.
- Diversity. Diversity can be measured many ways: in viewpoints, in potential responses, in relations, and in flows. System robustness and resilience can be characterized by the variety of ways that a new situation can be viewed or solved (Page, 2008).
- Tagging. Tags are labels that represent system behavior or characteristics in a shorthand form. Tags can be assigned to actions, to responses, to prices, or to work. Teams and leaders use tags to assign work, to map markets, and to encourage particular internal behaviors that have high utility in the external environment (Clippinger, 1999).
- Internal models. All living systems use internal models to predict the environment, and these models can drive behavior as strongly as perception (Senge, 2006). For example, human systems use internal models to determine the response to change. Responses are tested against the internal model first, and only those that pass testing are tried out in the external environment. The results of this testing are used to update the internal models.
- Building blocks or modules. Letters, words, DNA bases, design patterns, and components can be combined in new and varied ways to form solutions. These solutions can be tested against the environment, then recombined based on the response. Teams and projects are arranged modularly, with division of labor and work products used to increase flexibility and efficiency.
- Parallelism and interaction. In many cases it is the lower-level behavior of agents interacting that produces the complex behavior at the higher level. Consider a product development team working on designs that are aimed for a changing market, with multiple competitors headed for the same goal, and with multiple views of the design goal within the organization.

These properties of CAS and living systems are present and available to drive team and project responses and behaviors.

Applications of CAS to Teams and Projects

"Nowadays, most engineered systems are becoming complex, interconnected, software-intensive systems, so nearly all systems engineers are working with complex adaptive systems, whether or not they are aware of it" (Sheard, 2005).

What are some important team and project elements that relate to the ideas from CAS and living systems?

Clustering This is closely related to the ideas of modularity and aggregation— grouping work or combining tasks based on interest, ability, or demands. This idea includes contacts with outside groups: one team member can be the link between the group and other groups. Due to the boundary of the team or project, members are connected to each other with strong links and to outsiders with weak links. The strong links reinforce the boundary and team membership, while the weak links bring in information from outside sources (Thompson, 2008).

Self organization Teams are formed with leaders who report into the structure that formed the team. Team leadership consists of two parts: managerial and work content. To get the most from team members, each member can be part of the leadership. The forces inside teams allow self-organization and leadership to emerge in ways that traditional hierarchical structures do not allow. High performance teams and groups of organisms share leadership as the tasks and environment changes. This reorganization of the team happens organically and is due to the circumstances of changing environment or need (Thompson, 2008). To aid this, communications must be excellent.

Organisms that flock or show emergent behavior at the aggregate level have mechanisms for one-to-many messaging. There is no delay or intermediary. Similarly, high performing teams communicate instantaneously and effortlessly (Thompson, 2008). This allows quicker detection and response to external events. This can be done with e-mail, text messaging, and shared information systems that are available 24x7. There may be an internal team archive, and another that is shared with the larger organization. This allows exploration of alternatives before presenting them to a larger audience.

If the team senses a change in need or environment, they can respond. This is an example of self-organization—the team reacts to change and adjusts its structure.

Ways that teams self-organize include:

- Shared leadership and work breakdown structure. If new information or requirements arise, the team will distribute tasks and leadership to enable a quick and comprehensive response to the change.
- Exploration of issues. Individual team members will pick up signals from their weak links outside the team and start to explore issues before they come to the attention of the entire team.
- Finding resources. Team members can use their external networks to find resources in the environment that are not visible to the team management.
- Adjusting pulse and reporting. When changes are sensed in the environment or external systems, team members bring the information back, prompting quicker reviews than the normal process.
- Scaling and prototyping. Teams use scaling to break situations apart into components, and they use prototyping to test solutions. As the situation changes, team members automatically adjust how they decompose the work and test the pieces.

Team leaders and team members can aid the process of self-organization by coaching others. Examples would be to encourage conversation, respect the energy of team members, be an idea carrier, see criticism as building material and serve the higher purpose of the team.

Leadership is distributed and dynamic in a high performing team. Best practice is to have both a logistical leader and a technical or content leader (INCOSE). The logistical leader makes sure the team mechanics are functioning correctly and that all team elements are working well, while the technical or content leadership focuses on the work products to ensure they are high quality. Leadership may be spread across multiple disciplines and subdisciplines. At times of change there will be a need for a new way of working, whether that be structure, process, interface specification or decision matrix. In a high performance team members will feel free to speak up, claim the work, and thereby adjust team leadership dynamically.

Sheard notes that there are up to 12 Systems Engineering Roles in a project: Requirements Owner; System Designer; System Analyst; Verification and Validation Engineer; Logistics and Operations Engineer; Glue Among Subsystems; Customer Interface; Technical Manager; Information Manager; Process Engineer; Coordinator. There is also a 12th role: Other or unrecognized systems engineering tasks.

Consider that all these jobs have to happen in a project or team, and there are most likely not separate individuals assigned to each. Self-organization can be the most effective way to ensure the bases are all covered.

Knowledge Management *"Wealth consists of physical energy (as matter or radiation) combined with metaphysical know-what and know-how."* (Buckminster Fuller)

An organization creates advantage by its ability to take action/design/manage and so on. Its skills are a measure of its wealth. This wealth is carried in team members' heads, in organizational process, and in existing designs. Apple Computer's advantage is not one particular computer or music player; it is in their process and internal knowledge.

A team or project is a network of members, work, and the larger organization, and its effectiveness improves when knowledge is shared. This requires a set of practices known as KM.

Team Ecosystem Every team lives in an external environment. The environment provides energy, goals, sustenance, and feedback. An organization (and a team) can be seen as an organism since it is a collection of living systems. As the environment for the organization changes, the organization changes and adapts, altering the environment for the team. The team ecosystem includes external stakeholders, organizational chain of command, external forces from market or physical environment, and changes in the team members.

For example, Chuck managed the interface to the larger software community at his workplace. He let people know what the team was doing, brought new ideas to the team, and provided a permeable boundary.

Teams live on the edge between order of the organization and the chaos of the marketplace. They bring multiple viewpoints to complex situations, and structure responses to those situations. Team outputs often flow back into the operating instructions (the DNA) of the organization.

Figure 15.3 Team, Supersystem and Subsystem (After Mann)

	Supersystem	
Time before	**Team, Project, or Design**	Time after
	Subsystem	

Teams may be formed to explore new territory, to structure designs, or to investigate new opportunities. In each case they exist at the organization's edge or boundary for process, for work, and interface to the external world.

Teams and projects dwell in the middle of a matrix: organization above, team members below. The higher-level environment for teamwork is the organization or external world. We made this point in Figure 15.1 earlier, and we emphasize it again now in Figure 15.3. Below the teamwork in Figure 15.3 are the components that it is composed of (team members, solution components, resources) (Mann, 2002).

 REFLECTION Think about this material. What is the higher-level system that includes you, your work, and this knowledge? What are the lower-level elements that you, the team, project or design are composed of? How will those elements look in the future?

On the left side of the matrix is time before the present: what has led to this situation, what expectations existed in the past which are influencing us today? On the right side is the future: what will happen to the team, the work, and the larger environment in the future?

One way to use this larger view of the team is to simultaneously work both upwards and downwards. In one direction, produce system-level maps and architectures. In the other direction, develop/define/find components that can be combined into larger wholes (Maier, 2009).

Decision Support To decide on a course of action, teams need to work through issues, do investigations, and determine next steps for their work. Each task step is predicated on the previous, and decisions are needed to progress. Traditional decision-making processes can be updated to be more robust. Steps in a robust process include explicitly deciding on and sharing the goal for the decision, getting stakeholder inputs, ranking and weighting priorities, understanding the background of the stakeholders, and knowing what is more important: getting more information, revising priorities, or deciding (Ullman, 2006).

In other words, teams need a way to process information and make decisions. The decisions are two-fold: managerial and technical. Decisions are best made with multiple viewpoints heard, and full information available

(Page, 2008). For this to happen the team needs a process with the following characteristics:

- Accessible to all
- Anyone can comment and their contributions are acknowledged
- The decision process is clear and understandable
- Decision results are clearly communicated and acted upon

A potential issue with team decision making is that the most vocal members of a group can get extra influence in the process. To help mediate this, a written assessment created from individual contributions can work well. The priorities for the decision can be established, weighted, and ranked in order of importance. Each member provides input, and this is collated and summarized by the team leader.

There will be exceptions—decisions where input is taken, and team leadership makes the decision. This still works if all members or stakeholders are heard, are acknowledged, and the priorities are clear.

Team member inputs may need to be ranked according to their source of information.

Bill believed strongly that a distributed architecture would have significant challenges. Some team members felt differently, and when the team explored the source of his knowledge, it became clear it was secondhand (from a friend) and not based on his own experience. This allowed the team process to adjust Bill's input based on his knowledge of the alternative.

This adjustment of inputs can be seen as a Bayesian process (Ullman, 2006).

Diversity

Increased group diversity can lead to better decisions. Group members will have different experiences and viewpoints, giving a more comprehensive view of the situation if they are expressed. If the team ignores or leaves concerns unexpressed, these will surface in the quality of work products or conflict within the team.

Diversity is a hallmark of teams: they distribute work and encourage members to participate in the process of structuring, managing, and interfacing to the team environment. Page describes several advantages to diversity:

Multiple viewpoints: Give more options, thereby increasing responsiveness, robustness and resilience to change. This is similar to the idea of an immune system and its ability to respond to disturbances. This increase in ability improves core competencies in dealing with change.

Different work styles: Enable different ways to work on the work, giving comparative advantage to the team with diversity of approach.

Specialization: Some workers are better at one type of work, and distributing the work according to ability gives overall gain. Individual workers also learn to do their tasks better (increased productivity).

Competition: Productivity increases if there is more than one way to accomplish a task or approach.

Synergy (super-additivity or aggregation): When two or more parts combine, and the response is greater than the sum of the individual parts. Page (2008) compares two teams, each having the same number of members. The first team is more uniform, with average abilities that are greater than the second team. The second team has greater diversity and heuristics (ways to approach a problem), resulting in more potential ideas and increasing the chances for an optimal solution.

Diverse representations aid in exploring and exploiting the business landscape and in problem solving. With the correct representation, any problem can be solved.

Team Learning and Exploration

Edmondson talks about team execution (getting the work done efficiently) vs. team exploration (organizational learning). Figure 15.4 illustrates one perspective on how teams or projects work toward solutions in a complex environment.

A complicated environment is one with many pieces (for example, the U.S. Postal system). Even though there are many parts, the response to inputs is very predictable. Even in cases where a natural disaster damages some parts of the system, there is parallel redundancy to reroute traffic and achieve the system goals.

Complex environments are different in that a small change in inputs can give a large change in response. For example, one level of information may be rejected by a team (an informal request), while a slightly larger level

Figure 15.4 Organizing to Execute or Organizing to Learn? (After Edmondson, 2012)

Management Approach	Execute	Learn
Staff	Follow the rules	Solve the problem, experiment
Tools and techniques	Learn them first	Pick them up as you go
Performance	Individual	Team learning
Work assignments	Silos, experts	Group expertise
Ability to make decisions	Options provided	Learn through doing
Empowerment	Only in special cases	Team is in charge
Improvement goal	Understand and reduce variance	Use change to improve
Office talk	Current events, weather	Project challenges
Business goal	Now	Future
Works best	With clear trajectory	Fuzzy future

(a change in requirements) can alter the system dramatically. In a similar way, environmental signals will be ignored until they reach a certain level, beyond which a large change in system state can take place. In addition to this property, complex systems have many parts and their interactions depend on the state of these parts.

This difference has been explored in computing, where a search for solutions can be as simple as "hill climbing" or heading in the direction of maximum profits or market share. In a complex environment there are multiple hills (or maxima), and hill climbing in the local area can result in the enterprise failing to keep up with the competition.

There are search strategies in computing to move around and explore the solution space. In the world of teams, having diverse viewpoints to consider and using knowledge management is key to better solutions.

Summary

Teamwork and project work are here to stay. This chapter and this book have given you some insights into what works and how to make best use of your unique skills. Work environments continue to focus on collaboration and group work, and your success will improve with knowledge, awareness, and insights.

Recommendations:

- Practice your skills on
  - how people relate to each other,
  - how work can be distributed effectively, and
  - how a team can manage itself.
- Remember key ideas: boundary, structure, modularity, behavior, and team ecosystem.

What is your list?

References

Alexander, Christopher. 1979. *A timeless way of building.* Oxford.

Anklam, Patti. 2007. *Net Work.* Butterworth-Heinemann.

http://Asknature.org.

Armson, Rosalind. 2011. *Growing wings on the way.* Triarchy.

Axelrod, R., and M. Cohen. 2000. *Harnessing Complexity: Organizational Implications of a Scientific Frontier.* New York: Free Press.

Beer, Stafford. 1972. *Brain of the firm.* Allen Lane.

Berkun, Scott. 2008. *Making things happen.* O'Reilly Media.

Clippinger, John. 1999. *The biology of business.* Jossey-Bass.

Edmondson, Amy. 2012. *Teaming: How organizations learn, innovate, and compete in the knowledge economy.* Jossey-Bass.

Krausse, J., and C. Lichtenstein, eds. 1999. *Your private sky: R. Buckminster Fuller.* Lars Muller.

Gamma, Erich, et al. 1994. *Design patterns.* Addison-Wesley.

Garud, Raghu, et al. 2002. *Managing in the modular age.* Wiley.

Hoagland, M., and B. Dodson. 2001. *Exploring the way life works.* Jones and Bartlett.

INCOSE. *Systems engineering handbook,* http://www.incose.org.

Maier, Mark. 2009. *The art of systems architecting,* 3rd ed. CRC Press.

Mann, Darrell. 2002. *Hands-on systematic innovation.* Creax.

Meadows, Donella. 2008. *Thinking in systems.* Chelsea Green.

Page, Scott. 2008. *The difference.* Princeton University Press.

Pauli, Gunter. 2010. *The blue economy.* Paradigm Publications.

Senge, Peter. 2006. *The 5th Discipline.* Crown Business.

Sheard, Sarah. 2005. Practical applications of complexity theory for systems engineers.
    In *Proceedings of the Fifteenth Annual International Council on Systems Engineering.*
    (cd). International Council on Systems Engineering.

Simon, Herbert. 1996. *Sciences of the artificial,* 3rd ed. MIT Press.

Speedo. LZR Racer, http://en.wikipedia.org/wiki/LZR_Racer.

Thompson, Ken. 2008. *Bioteams.* Meghan Kiffer Press.

Ullman, David. 2006. *Making robust decisions.* Trafford Publishing.

CHAPTER 16

Where to Go from Here

The next step for many of you will be the completion of your undergraduate degree, which occurs after meeting the degree requirements and having the degree conferred.

One of the great joys of my serving as Director of Undergraduate Studies in the Department of Civil Engineering was participating in our annual Graduation and Awards Ceremony followed by the College of Science and Engineering Commencement. Congratulating the graduating seniors and celebrating with them and their parents and friends was extraordinarily satisfying. It reminded me why I spent so much time helping students complete their degree requirements.

I can't tell you much about most of the graduation speeches I heard, starting with my own at Michigan Technological University in 1969, but I started wondering about these speeches and so began paying more attention to them. I've selected excerpts from a few recent speakers for their messages to graduates. The speakers are John Seely Brown, Retired Vice President of Research at Xerox Corporation and former Director of the Xerox Palo Alto Research Lab (Xerox PARC); Steve Jobs, former CEO of Apple Computing; Thomas Friedman, *New York Times* Foreign Affairs columnist; and Sara Evans, Regents Professor of History at the University of Minnesota.

Sara Evans reminds graduates that graduation means "completion" and commencement means "beginning." She reminds graduates of the Albert Einstein quote, "Not everything that counts can be counted, and not everything that can be counted counts." Yes, you will be counted as a graduate, but Sara Evans argues that what matters most is the knowledge and skill that you gained. She states, "An educated citizenry is a public good, fundamental to a democratic society." I agree and remind you that by graduating from a college or university you have an enormous privilege bestowed on you and a responsibility to ensure that education is a public good.

Tom Friedman is a fascinating chronicler of the global landscape whose work I follow. I chose his 2005 commencement address at Williams College in which he spoke about his life as a journalist and told the story of his tenth-grade journalism teacher, who had a profound effect on his life. Overall his talk was organized around six lessons:

1. Do what you love.
2. Being a good listener is one of the great keys to life.
3. The most enduring skill you can bring to the workplace is the ability to learn how to learn.
4. Don't get carried away with gadgets.
5. There is a difference between skepticism and cynicism.
6. Call your parents.

One common story among his commencement addresses is the story about a CEO who, snidely mocking the salaries of teachers, asked a teacher, "What do you make?" The teacher responded, "I make kids work harder than they ever thought they could, I make kids wonder, I make them question, I make them criticize, I make them write, and I make them read and read and read. You know what I make? I make a difference. What about you?"

I hope you have had teachers who have made a difference in your life.

Steve Jobs' commencement advice to graduates of Stanford University is one of the most watched videos on YouTube and, if you haven't already seen it, I encourage you to watch it. Jobs dropped out of Reed College after six months and said in his opening statement, "This is the closest I've ever gotten to a college graduation." Jobs told three stories from his life. The first was about his passion for learning what he was interested in after dropping out of college and how it influenced the design of the Macintosh computer. The second was how he got fired from Apple, the company he started, and the profound effect it had on his learning. The third was about being diagnosed with cancer and being told to prepare to die. Yes, as you can imagine, this news had a profound effect. He said, "Death is very likely the single best invention of Life. It is Life's change agent." Jobs repeats the mantra of many commencement speakers: "You've got to find what you love." He closed with a quote from *The Whole Earth Catalog*: "Stay hungry. Stay foolish." He said that he always wished that for himself and he wishes it for the graduates. Stay hungry. Stay foolish.

John Seely Brown's articles and books on design, information technology, learning in the digital age, and many others are scholarly and insightful. His commencement address to the Claremont Graduate University on May 15, 2004, reminded the graduates "to think differently, to listen with humility, and to proceed with openness and thought." Seely Brown has great hope for social software tools and hopes we can "transform the Internet into the platform of life-long learning and social construction, so that we can understand story telling and knowledge sharing." One year later in a Commencement Speech at the University of Michigan (his alma mater) he emphasized the ability to *listen with humility*. He wrote that "This skill underlies the art of collaboration and is increasingly important as we interact with partners all over the globe. But it also underlies the art of innovation, listening not only to your customers but also to the world at large." He also highlighted the *ability to see*. He wrote, "If you want to excel in innovation, especially socially responsible innovation, then learn how to look around with unbiased eyes."

Graduation is one important step in your becoming an engineer, but as you can tell from the messages of these commencement speakers, commencement is just beginning.

Reflection on the State of the World—Global Interdependence

These commencement speakers provided their insights into the world you are entering. In this section, I offer my gaze into the crystal ball of the world you're entering. The world is changing and we are facing many global challenges involving poverty, education, health, innovation, climate change, human rights, resource availability and utilization, and others. These concerns are not new. They have been documented for decades by organizations such as the Worldwatch Institute, whose annual publication *State of the World* articulates our interdependence.

The term *global*, popularized by writers such as Thomas Friedman, shows up in many conversations about engineering and engineering education as well as in prospective outcomes for engineering graduates. The notion of "global" first became clear to me and many of my generation on December 24, 1968, when Apollo 8 circumnavigated the moon. As the image of the earthrise was transmitted and showed up on TV screens around the world, CBS News Commentator Walter Cronkite said:

> I think that picture of the earthrise over the moon's horizon, that blue disk out there in space, floating alone in the darkness, the utter black of space, had the effect of impressing on all of us our loneliness out here. The fact that we seem to be the only spot where anything like humans could be living. And it, the major impression I think it made on most of us was the fact, how ridiculous it is that we have this difficulty getting along on this little lifeboat of ours floating out there in space, and the necessity of our understanding each other and of the brotherhood of humankind on this floating island of ours, made a great impression, I think, on everybody.

This was an extremely poignant and defining moment for me although I didn't recognize and fully appreciate it at the time. You can see the Cronkite segment and read more about what was described as his "Call for Harmony on Lifeboat Earth" on the *American Experience* program on Apollo 8 (PBS American Experience, 2008).

Recently various world leaders have called for recognition of our global interdependence aimed at solving international problems such as terrorism, poverty, and climate change. During his talk at the John F. Kennedy Presidential Library and Museum in April 2008, former British Prime Minister Gordon Brown said, "We urgently need to step out of the mindset of competing interests and instead find our common interests, and we must summon up the best instincts and efforts of the humanist in cooperative effort to build new international rules and institutions for the new global era" (Lavoie, 2008). Tom Boyle of British Telecom describes our current era as the "age of interdependence" and he argues that individuals' Network Quotient (NQ) is more important than their IQ (Cohen and Prusak, 2001). Former U.S. President Bill Clinton asked the question, "Will interdependence be good or bad for humanity?" in his 2002 *Los Angeles Times* editorial, "Living in an Interdependent World" (Clinton, 2000). *The World Is Flat* author Tom Friedman (2007) argues that we have to move to a more horizontal—connect and collaborate—value-creation model. Friedman argues that Curiosity Quotient (CQ) plus Passion Quotient (PQ) is more important than Intelligence Quotient (IQ). John Seely Brown, former Chief Scientist of Xerox and Director of its Palo Alto Research Center (PARC), argues that social/emotional intelligence (EQ) and communication intelligence (CQ) are equally or more important than IQ (Brown and Adler, 2008; Brown, 2008). If, as these pundits claim, interdependence is the current coin of the realm, then what can we do to help you who are entering it prepare for this interdependent world? What are the skills and competencies that students need and how can we ensure that they gain these skills and competencies? In the preceeding chapters, I've tried to address the knowledge, skills and habit of mind for navigating our interdependent world.

Before proceeding too far down the collaboration path, let me reassure those who argue that competition is the "be all and end all" that I agree there is a role for competition and we have an obligation to help develop students' skills for competing. There are several occasions where competition is the norm; sports contests, of course, are the most common. But there are also proposals and hiring. My sense is that we've emphasized competition far more than cooperation and haven't helped students develop skills for cooperating. Buckminster Fuller argued that "cooperation is pragmatically necessary," and W. Edwards Deming (1993) made the following compelling case for the importance of cooperation and interdependence in his book *The New Economics for Industry, Government, Education* (pp. xi, 90):

> We have grown up in a climate of competition between people, teams, departments, divisions, pupils, schools, universities. We have been taught by economists that competition will solve our problems. Actually, competition, we see now, is destructive. It would be better if everyone would work together as a system, with the aim for everybody to win. What we need is cooperation and transformation to a new style of management. . . . Competition leads to loss. People pulling in opposite directions on a rope only exhaust themselves: they go nowhere. What we need is cooperation. Every example of cooperation is one of benefit and gains to them that cooperate.

The United States has been guided recently by calls for increasing competitive advantage and I argue for increasing emphasis on global collaborative advantage and developing the knowledge, skills, and habits of mind that support developing collaborative approaches to challenges and opportunities. The idea of global collaborative advantage was framed by Lynn and Salzman (2006, 2007) and they argue in a series of articles that we need to prepare graduates for developing global collaborative advantage. For example, Lynn and Salzman argued in their article "Collaborative Advantage" in *Issues in Science and Technology* in winter 2006: "The United States should move away from an almost certainly futile attempt to maintain dominance and toward an approach in which leadership comes from developing and brokering mutual gains among equal partners. Such 'collaborative advantage,' as we call it, comes not from self-sufficiency or maintaining a monopoly on advanced technology, but from being a valued collaborator at various levels in the international system of technology development" (p. 76). They argue that the United States "needs to develop a science and technology education system that teaches collaborative competencies rather than just technical knowledge and skills" (p. 81). Their research indicates that cross-boundary skills (working across disciplinary, organizations, cultural, and time/distance boundaries) are needed more than technical skills.

Another group of researchers providing strong support for the centrality of interdependence are those studying complexity and complex adaptive systems

(Axelrod and Cohen, 2001; Miller and Page, 2007). Page (2009) claims that a "system can be considered complex if its agents meet four qualifications: diversity, connection, interdependence, and adaptation" (p. 4) and "the attributes of interdependence, connectedness, diversity, and adaptation and learning generate complexity" (p. 10). Furthermore, Page (2009) notes that "interdependence refers to whether other entities influence actions, whereas connectedness refers to how many people a person is connected to" (p. 11). Preparing students with a deeper understanding of complex systems is essential, since complex systems (1) are often unpredictable and can produce large events as well as withstand trauma, (2) produce bottom-up emergent phenomena, and (3) produce amazing novelty (Page, 2009).

Your challenge (or opportunity, depending upon how you frame it) is to embrace interdependence and continue to adapt to making a difference in an interdependent world. Best wishes on your journey.

Projects and teams are going to be with you for the rest of your life, no matter what profession you eventually work in. They are already prevalent in engineering, medicine, law, and most areas of business and industry. Even if you become a college professor, you will be involved in projects and teams, especially on research projects and with your graduate students. Now, having studied this book, and in your course of study, you have made a start at learning how to effectively participate in projects and teamwork. I hope you've also developed skills for managing and leading a team. There are lots of additional resources available, and I hope you will continue to read about teamwork and project management. More important, I hope you will talk with colleagues (fellow students and faculty) about teamwork and project management. If you aspire to become a project manager, I encourage you to check out the Project Management Institute. They have a special student membership rate, and your membership in this organization will help connect you with project management professionals. Most professional organizations, such as ASCE, ASME, and IEEE, have a division that emphasizes engineering management. Check these out as you become a student member of the professional organization in your discipline.

Periodically reflecting on your experiences, writing down your reflections (as I have asked you to do throughout this book), processing them alone and with others, and reading and studying further will help ensure that your team and project experiences are most constructive. A sustained effort will ensure that you continue to learn and grow.

If you are in a team or project situation that is not working well, rather than just endure it and hope it will pass quickly, try some of the ideas in this book for improving the team or project. Suggest that the team members discuss how effectively they are working together. For example, suggest a quick individually written plus/delta processing exercise (discussed in Chapter 12) to survey the team. Successful project work and teamwork do not happen magically; it takes continual attention not only to the task but also to how well the group is working together. And this is *work*. The satisfaction and sense of accomplishment that come from effective team and project work are worth the effort. So many things can't be accomplished any other way. The more you learn during your college years, the easier it will be for you after graduation. Paying attention to these skills now will save you from what previous generations of engineering graduates have had to endure—learning project management and teamwork skills on the job in addition to all the other complex things they had to learn.

Jason Fried, co-founder of 37 Signals and author of *Rework* (Fried and Hansson, 2010), argues that "to be more productive, take time off," and at 37 Signals they change schedules with the seasons by working four days per week (32 hours) May through October (Fried, 2012). Also you may find it helpful and renewing to take a break periodically, that is, to step away from the work during the day or week. Mary Pilotte in the nearby box describes the power of taking a coffee break for providing new perspectives and enthusiasm.

As you work with this book and the ideas and strategies for effective teamwork and project management, think about what else you need to know. Develop a learning and teaching plan for yourself and your team and project

---

The Importance of Taking Breaks

As an engineer that "turned coat" and went to work in the Finance department, I found myself leading merger and acquisition projects that were not only controversial and complex, but also highly confidential. It was lonely work, which involved having chief executive's secretaries bring stacks of files to pore through, and being sent financial files to consolidate, verify, and analyze. I was even relocated to an old dingy office in an abandoned manufacturing facility the company owned, to keep what I worked on a secret.

After months of working alone, the announcement regarding the next impending acquisition was made; at the same time it was announced that I would be the first assigned member of the integration team. Team? Did I hear that right? That implies more than one person, right? It was music to my ears. I hadn't really thought much about working alone, but the day that noble Six Sigma Black Belt showed up to partner with me on the team, I couldn't have been happier.

The weeks ahead of us were difficult, wrought with decisions involving systems integration, optimizing operations and most importantly, retaining our loyal customers. Beyond the common bond of an engineering education, my teammate Murray and I also shared an unnatural addiction for poor-quality black coffee. We quickly located the only coffee pot in the building and paid to share it with the only other two people in the building. Unfortunately, the walk to the coffee pot was nearly six minutes away. Alas, our addictions had us—so on no less than three walks a day,

Murray and I would cross the facility to "hunt, kill, and bag" our extra-large portable cups of Joe.

We found that these brief six-minute walks away from our desks were not only supportive of our black gold addiction, but they allowed us time to shed some of the frustrations, fears and problems that were filling the corner of our little "army of two" world. The walk became known as the "walk of shame," partly in admission that we could not control our need for coffee, partially because on occasion an expletive or two may have slipped out as we parlayed our most perplexing situation at hand.

As I look back on the walks of shame, I see clearly that they offered many smiles as well as lasting life and work lessons:

1. With a tough enough constitution, one can probably tackle any problem alone, but it is far more fun with two.
2. Letting go of things that are bothering you will not only free your mind for more productive thoughts, but also allow you to rethink the problem as you speak it aloud.
3. Sometimes, a brisk walk down the hall is the best remedy to work off a tough day.
4. If one small cup of premium coffee can power the average person through a workday, imagine what you can accomplish with four large insulated Thermos cups of high-octane coffee! Every assignment is easier to swallow with hot, black coffee!

Mary Pilotte

members. A few resources are listed in the references below; these barely scratch the surface of all the resources that are available. Check out a few of them. The earlier you learn the skills and strategies for effective project work and teamwork, the more productive you will be and the easier life will be for you later. Start now!

Although the up-front goal of this book is to facilitate the development of teamwork and project management skills in engineering students, the deeper goals are to change the climate in engineering courses and programs from competitive or negative interdependence to cooperative or positive inter-dependence; from suspicion, mistrust, and minimal tolerance of others to acceptance, trust, and valuing others; from egocentric "What's in it for me?" to community "How are we doing?" and from a sense of individual isolation and alienation to a sense of belonging and acceptance. I recognize that these are lofty goals, but until we not only take responsibility for our own learning and development but also take more responsibility for the learning and development of others, we will not benefit from synergistic interaction.

If you find that teamwork and project management, and perhaps even leadership, are of great interest to you, then you may want to read some of the business magazines, such as *Bloomberg Businessweek,* the *Harvard Business Review*, or my favorite, *Fast Company.* Check out your local bookseller or a bookstore on the Internet for some spare-time reading on these topics. You'll find an enormous body of literature available.

If you're more interested in teamwork and project management specifically within engineering and technology, then I suggest that you look into some of the books and video documentaries on projects, such as Karl Sabbagh's *Skyscraper* (1991) and *21st Century Jet* (1996).

Closing Reflection on Reflection

Much of the material taught and concepts covered in college consist of *declarative knowledge*, which emphasizes knowing *that*; whereas the heart of project management consists of *procedural knowledge*, which emphasizes knowing *how*. This distinction between knowing that and knowing how was articulated by Ryle (1949). Furthermore, a lot of the essential procedural knowledge needed for success is implicit (or tacit, as Polanyi, 1958, 1966, described it) rather than explicit. This implicit, or "insider," knowledge is usually picked up on the job; however, I'm convinced that we can do a much better job of preparing people to "pick up" this knowledge. The opportunities for reflection I've encouraged you to engage in, as well as my own reflections, are designed to help you more quickly pick up the tacit dimension.

Best wishes to you in your project endeavors.

References

Axelrod, R., and M. D. Cohen. 2001. *Harnessing complexity: Organizational implications of a scientific frontier*. New York: Simon & Schuster.

Brown, John Seely. 2004. Comencement Speech. Claremont Graduate University, May 15, 2004. http://www.johnseelybrown.com/CGU.pdf (accessed 3-13-13).

Brown, John Seely. 2005. Comencement Speech. University of Michigan, May 30, 2005. http://www.johnseelybrown.com/UM05.pdf (accessed 3-13-13).

Brown, John Seely, and Richard P. Adler. 2008. Minds on fire: Open education, the long tail, and learning 2.0. *Educause Review* 43 (1), 17–32.

Clinton, William J. 2000. Living in an interdependent world. *Los Angeles Times*, January 13, 2000.

Cohen, Don, and Laurence Prusak. 2001. *In good company: How social capital makes organizations work*. Cambridge, MA: Harvard Business School Press.

Deming, W. Edwards. 1993. *The new economics for industry, government, education.* Cambridge, MA: MIT Center for Advanced Engineering Study.

Evans, Sara M. 2005. *A beacon bright and clear: The university and the common good.* University of Minnesota Graduate School Commencement Address. http://www.grad.umn.edu/current_students/degree_completion/commencement/addresses/address_spring_05.html (accessed 8-22-05; not available 3-13-13). Excerpts at http://conservancy.umn.edu/bitstream/60834/1/Discovery05.pdf

Fried, Jason. 2012. Be more productive. Take time off. *New York Times*, August 18, 2012.

Fried, Jason, and David Heinemeier Hansson. 2010. *Rework*. Crown Business.

Friedman, Thomas. 2004. Commencement Address. Washington University–St. Louis. http://news-info.wustl.edu/news/page/normal/887.html (accessed 8-22-05).

Friedman, Thomas. 2005. *Journalism as life*. Commencement Address. Williams College. http://www.williams.edu/home/commencement/friedman.php (accessed 8-22-05).

Jobs, Steve. 2005. Commencement Address. Stanford University. http://news-service.stanford.edu/news/2005/june15/jobs-061505 (accessed 3-13-13).

Lavoie, Denise. 2008. British prime minister calls for global "interdependence." *USA Today*, April 18.

Lynn, L., and H. Salzman. 2006. Collaborative advantage: New horizons for a flat world. *Issues in Science and Technology*, Winter 22 (2), 74–82. www.nsf.gov/attachments/105652/public/Collaborative-Advantage-1205.pdf (accessed 3-13-13).

Lynn, L., and H. Salzman. 2007. The real global technology challenge. *Change: The Magazine of Higher Learning* 39 (4), 8–13.

Miller, J., and S. E. Page. 2007. *Complex adaptive systems: An introduction to computational models of social life*. Princeton, NJ: Princeton University Press.

Page, S. E. 2007. *The difference: How the power of diversity creates better groups, teams, schools, and societies*. Princeton, NJ: Princeton University Press.

———. 2009. *Understanding complexity*. The Great Courses. Chantilly, VA: The Teaching Company.

PBS *American Experience*. 2008. Apollo 8. http://www.pbs.org/wgbh/amex/moon/peopleevents/e_earthrise.html (accessed 3-13-13).

Polanyi, Michael. 1958. *Personal knowledge: Towards a post-critical philosophy*. New York: Harper & Row.

———. 1966. *The tacit dimension*. New York: Doubleday.

Ryle, Gilbert. 1949. *The concept of mind*. London: Hutchinson.

Sabbagh, Karl. 1991. *Skyscraper: The making of a building*. New York: Penguin.

———. 1996. *Twenty-first century jet: The making and marketing of the Boeing 777*. New York: Scribner's.

Index

Note: Pages followed by "n." indicate material in footnotes or source notes.